THE BEST WINE LAST

An autobiography through the years
1932–1969

ALEC WAUGH
has written over fifty books. They include

NOVELS
The Loom of Youth (1917)
Kept (1925)
So Lovers Dream (1931)
The Balliols (1934)
Jill Somerset (1936)
No Truce With Time (1941)
Unclouded Summer (1948)
Guy Renton (1953)
Island in the Sun (1956)
Fuel for the Flame (1960)
The Mule on the Minaret (1965)
A Spy in the Family (1970)
The Fatal Gift (1973)

SHORT STORIES
My Place in the Bazaar (1961)

TRAVEL
Hot Countries (1930)
The Sugar Islands (1958)

AUTOBIOGRAPHIES
My Brother Evelyn and Other Portraits (1961)
The Early Years of Alec Waugh (1962)
A Year to Remember: A Reminiscence of 1931 (1975)

MISCELLANEOUS
In Praise of Wine (1959)
A Family of Islands (1964)
Wines and Spirits (Time-Life Books) (1968)
Bangkok: The Story of a City (1970)

THE
BEST WINE LAST

An autobiography through the years
1932–1969

Alec Waugh

W. H. ALLEN · LONDON
A Howard & Wyndham Company
1978

Printed and bound in Great Britain by
Butler & Tanner Ltd, Frome and London,
for the Publishers, W. H. Allen & Co. Ltd,
44 Hill Street, London W1X 8LB

ISBN 0 491 02374 X

Contents

Foreword

Books have their destinies. *Habent sua fata libelli.* So do their authors; studies of their lives showing more often than not how relentlessly fate has twisted circumstance so that they are accorded the kinds of experience that their work requires, experience that bears no relation to the practical ordering of their lives, to their own happiness or that of those whose fortunes are involved with theirs.

> What was he doing the great god Pan
> Down in the reeds by the river?

He was, Elizabeth Barrett Browning tells us, tearing out the reed from which he proposed to make a pipe, hacking and hewing at it with his hard bleak steel, then drawing 'the pith like the heart of a man, steadily from the outside ring', and notching 'the poor dry empty thing'.

> 'This is the way,' laughed the great god Pan
>   (Laughed while he sat by the river),
> 'The only way, since gods began
> To make sweet music, they could succeed.'

The music is sweet, blinding sweet.

> Yet half a beast is the great god Pan,
>   To laugh as he sits by the river,
> Making a poet out of a man:
> The true gods sigh for the cost and pain,
> For the reed which grows nevermore again
>   As a reed with the reeds in the river.

Elizabeth Barrett Browning does not, however, complete

I

the picture. She does not show how the poet welcomes his fate and profits by it. She leaves it to her husband to present the other side in 'Andrea del Sarto'.

> ... some good sun
> Paint my two hundred pictures; let him try.

The biographies and autobiographies of writers do not offer too many edifying examples of family obligations proudly accepted and faithfully fulfilled, of civic worthiness, of dutiful service to the state. That is not the way in which books get written.

To that general rule, the following pages provide no exception.

I have written two autobiographies. *The Early Years of Alec Waugh* tells my story up to June 1930. I was the elder son of Arthur Waugh, the literary critic and managing director of the venerable publishing house of Chapman and Hall, the firm that published Dickens. My father had a home on the edge of Hampstead Heath. I went to school at Sherborne as my father had. I was born in 1898. In September 1915 I joined the army. I went to Sandhurst and was gazetted to the Dorset Regiment. During the months in training, I wrote a novel about public school life called *The Loom of Youth*. In the month of July 1917 my novel was published, I sailed for France as a Second Lieutenant attached to the Machine Gun Corps, and I became engaged to be married.

My novel was a *succès de scandale*. It was the first novel to refer to the prevalence of homosexual practices in English public schools. It was a best-seller and not only was my name removed from the Old Shirburnian Society but my father's too. I was at the battles of Passchendaele and Cambrai. I was taken prisoner at Arras in March 1918.

After the war I transferred to the Regular Army Reserve of Officers and embarked on *la vie littéraire*. I was found a post as editor with Chapman and Hall. I married in July 1919. Within a year I had elected to relegate my post with

Chapman and Hall to one of part-time employment, going to my office only two days a week. My marriage lasted thirty months.

In April 1925 I published a novel called *Kept*, a story of post-war London, which without being a best-seller did well enough on both sides of the Atlantic to make me feel I could support myself by my pen. I resigned from Chapman and Hall and started a trip round the world. I spent six weeks in Tahiti. On the way back, on a liner between Tahiti and San Francisco, I became involved with Ruth, an American married woman, seven years older than myself. We arranged to meet in Tahiti five months later. It was a star-crossed romance. It lasted three and a half years. During those years I made a five months' tour of the West Indies. That trip and my other earlier ones provided me with the material for a travel book, *Hot Countries*, that was a Literary Guild choice in America. I went to New York to be fêted, and fell in love with the city and the life there. I went on to San Francisco and there my star-crossed romance ended.

That was the story told in my *Early Years*. Later on I wrote a second much shorter autobiography, *A Year to Remember: A Reminiscence of 1931*. I married for the second time in October 1932, and 1931 was for me a watershed. It was also a watershed for England, the dividing line between the post-war and the pre-war worlds. In September 1931 the Bank of England abandoned the gold standard. A national government was formed and the country set out upon the road to Munich.

A book of literary memoirs, *My Brother Evelyn and Other Portraits*, contains four personal chapters: an account of my three years in Baghdad in counter-espionage; a picture of the Macdowell colony in Peterborough, New Hampshire, where I have done most of my more solid writing since the war; a sketch of myself 'on the edge of sixty', and a final chapter about my novel *Island in the Sun*. I have also described, in the third person in *His Second War*, some of my experiences in the army.

I have covered, that is to say, a good deal of ground. But I am far from having covered it all. I have said nothing about my seven married years in England between 1932 and 1939, a marriage that produced three children. I have said little about my life in New York before and after the second war. I have not written of my love affair with Virginia Sorensen. I am now in my eightieth year. If I am going to round off the record, it is time that I got on with it.

CHAPTER I

Trial Honeymoon

I married in October 1932 an Australian whose father, Andrew Chirnside, had a large estate near Melbourne. He was a racing man, a great sportsman, with many business interests.

I met her in May 1928. Lord Hastings, now the Earl of Huntingdon, on his return to England after a four-year trip round the world, gave a dinner at the Green Park Hotel for some of the friends whom he had made during it. I had met him in Tahiti; he had met Joan in Australia.

There were some thirty guests. I sat across the table from her. She was in her middle twenties. She was not pretty, but she was striking. She was dark, pale skinned, with a healthy out-of-doors look. She had a good figure. 'She looks fun,' I thought. I had a long talk with her after dinner and found that indeed she was. I hoped that I would be seeing her again. As she was a close friend of the Hastings, I presumed I should be, but that summer we missed each other.

Eighteen months later, however, Hastings' sister, Lady Marian Cameron, asked me if I would join her and Joan in sending off a gramophone record as a Christmas card to the Hastings who had returned to Tahiti. We made the record in Selfridge's. Peter Rodd, the Basil Seal of Evelyn's novels, was the fourth. We were not going to give our names. The Hastings must guess who we were. 'We must have an indecent limerick,' Peter said.

We selected one that retailed the unfortunate experience of a young lady of Devon who was brutally ill-used 'by seven degenerate beasts of Catholic priests, of such were the kingdom of heaven'. We were to take alternate lines and drew lots as to who would get the unprintable one. Joan drew it. At that time four-letter words were not in general use. Joan delivered her line without embarrassment, but not gloatingly. 'I must try to see more of her,' I thought. But she was going back to Australia at the end of the week.

In May 1932, a singularly wet month, a cricket match in which I was to have played was cancelled, and I was sitting in my flat in Chelsea in the early afternoon. The telephone went. A feminine voice that I did not recognise asked me a question. I did not get what it was about. 'Now could you please start all that over again,' I said.

She laughed. 'A couple of years ago we sent off a gramophone record to the Hastings. I've just come back to England. Do you know where they are?'

'They are in Mexico.'

'What about the Keith Camerons?'

'They are in Davos.'

'Davos?'

I hesitated. Owing to the cancelled cricket match I had an empty evening ahead of me. 'Why don't you come round and have a drink and I'll tell you all I know.'

'When?'

'As soon as you can manage.'

She was round within half an hour.

I started at the sight of her. I had forgotten that she was so attractive. She was one of those women who look better in the late than in the early twenties. I told her about the Camerons. He had TB and had been sent to Davos. Two summers ago I had gone out to see them. I was thinking of going out again in June. I told her of my other plans. That winter, MCC was sending a cricket side to Australia. I was hoping to be commissioned by the *Evening Standard* to report the Test Matches. 'Will you give me some letters of introduction there?' I asked.

'I can do better than that. I'll be back myself by then. I'll throw a party for you.'

I asked her about her immediate plans. In July she was going to Berlin. An Australian couple, the Arthur Yenckens were at the Embassy. He was first secretary. 'Why not stop at Davos on the way?' I said.

'Rather a roundabout way, isn't it?'

'The night we went to Bannockburn by way of Brighton Pier.'

Our talk went fast. Half-past five became quarter to seven.

'I suppose you aren't by any lucky chance not doing anything tonight?' I asked.

'I'm afraid not.'

'Then I must ring you up and see if we can't fix something later on.'

I have still the address book in which I entered her address and telephone number. She is entered as Joan Fernside. I had forgotten or never known her name. I knew as little as that about her when I started my campaign.

'Boy meets girl, Boy loses girl, Boy finds girl.' That was the editorial formula for a magazine short story at that time. But it is doubtful whether that formula satisfied the actual condition of most adult marriages. Marriages in mature life are more often than not attended by complications, on one side or the other. It is not so very common for two people in the early thirties who are attracted by one another to find themselves without obligations of some kind somewhere. When they do, there is no reason why they should not get married right away.

Joan and I were the right ages for one another. I was thirty-four, she was thirty. I was reasonably established in my career, making about fifteen hundred pounds a year.

We did not, however, go to Davos. We went to the Côte d'Azur, to the Welcome Hotel at Villefranche. We had a fine time, and it went very well in what used to be and probably still is called 'that way'. I considered myself extremely lucky.

'Oughtn't I to write to your father about this?' I said, which was the equivalent of a proposal in 1932.

She shook her head. 'Wait till I come back from Germany.' She was perhaps feeling a lack of the 'Boy meets girl' formula in my courtship. It had all gone too smoothly, there had been no equivalent for the 'Boy loses girl' interval. I had not been tested. She had doubts, perhaps, of how I should behave under pressure. She knew as little about me as I knew about her. She did not want to commit herself too far, too soon.

Her hesitation put me on my guard. I tried to discover on what points she might have doubts of me. At Villefranche we met a certain number of my friends. Eddie Sackville West and Raymond Mortimer were staying at the Welcome. Eldred Curwen, who had toured the West Indies with me, was at Antibes in his villa. We lunched with him a couple of times. With Raymond and Eddie we rowed across to the Passable beach to bathe and picnic. They were lively occasions. I was glad that Joan got on well with them. They were the kinds of people whom we would be meeting if we married.

'I'm glad you like them,' I said.

'I do. They are amusing. All the same . . .'

'All the same what?'

'They don't seem quite real.'

'You find them affected?'

'No, not that. But they are so different from the people I know at home.'

'Are those people more amusing?'

'No, but they are more real.'

I think I saw her point.

There were also one or two Americans about. Katherine Brush, whose *Young Man of Manhattan* had stood high on the best-seller list two years before, with her husband Bob Wynans, and Bostonian Lorna Lindsay, with her fifteen-year-old daughter. We had some good times with them. 'I usually feel at home with Americans,' I said.

'I've noticed that,' Joan said.

I asked her about her friends in Melbourne. I had only once been to Australia, for a ten-day stop at Sydney, between ships. I had by now abandoned or rather the *Evening Standard* had abandoned my plan to report the Test Matches. 'I wonder how I'd have got on with them,' I said.

'They'd have got used to you.'

'Is there a lot they'd have needed to get used to?'

'You're not very definite, you know.'

'Not very definite?'

'Not very self-assertive.'

I didn't suppose I was. I do not enjoy arguments. I want to know what the other man thinks, not to inflict my opinions on him. I do my arguing on paper.

Not very definite, not very self-assertive. Did she want me to be more self-assertive, to impress other people with my point of view, to take the lead more in conversation? I pondered this on my way back to London.

CHAPTER 2

Skirmish with Wyndham Lewis

Joan and I had started in the same train from Villefranche, but she had changed in Marseilles to a train for Berlin, where she was to stay a month.

I was planning after a couple of nights in my father's house , to go down to Chagford, to the Easton Court Hotel of which I have written in *A Year to Remember* to start a novel. But this plan had to be modified in view of the news that awaited me in London.

'Peters has been on the telephone,' my father told me. Peters was my agent. 'There's some trouble about a book attacking you by Wyndham Lewis. Godfrey Winn is bringing a libel action. He wants to know if you'll join in with him.'

It was the first I had heard about any book by Wyndham Lewis.

'That looks as though I may have to stay on an extra day or two,' I said.

Next morning I called on Peters. On his desk was a copy of a book by Lewis called *Doom of Youth*. It was a general attack on what Lewis called 'youth politics'. Among a number of contemporary writers, I was pilloried, in my case on account of a novel called *Three Score and Ten* that had been published two years earlier. Lewis finished his attack by writing,

If I had to say what I thought of the strange case of Mr. Alec Waugh I should say that all the feminine maternal elements were excessively developed in him and of course being a man were thwarted. They relieve themselves by means of these incessant literary compositions about small boys with sooty faces and bulging pockets. One feels that this outlet was critically necessary. If Mr. Alec Waugh does not play marbles at home, it can only be, one feels, with the exercise of the greatest self control. I do not wish to be offensive to Mr. Waugh but I think it is fair to say that there is something of an obsessional nature at work and I do think that psychoanalysis would reveal the fact that motherhood in its most opulent form was what Mr. Waugh was destined for by nature and that a cruel fate had in some way interfered and so unhappily he became a man.

I do not know what the name Percy Wyndham Lewis will convey today to someone who had no adult life before World War II. One of the first Vorticist painters, he burst upon the London scene about 1910. He was a very fine portrait painter; several of his paintings are in the Tate Gallery. His portraits of T. S. Eliot, Rebecca West, and Father D'Arcy are often reproduced. In a contemporary sketch he would not need to be introduced as a painter, but I question if anybody under forty knows very much about his writing. Most of his books are out of print, and none of them had a large sale. In 1914 he issued a magazine called *Blast*, bulky in size, set in heavy black type. General invective was the general style. One page labelled 'Blast' consisted of a list by name of the chief objectives of his irritation. He included 'Clan Meynell' as a single complete entry. The opposite page called 'Bless' included J. W. Hearne. Belligerent high spirits.

He also wrote short stories, the first of which was accepted by Ford Maddox Hueffer for the *English Review*, and a novel called *Tarr*. After the war, during which he became an official war artist, he became prominent as a publicist.

He wrote several novels, *The Apes of God*, *The Childermass*, *Snooty Baronet*. He was vociferously anti-Bloomsbury. He was forceful. He had humour. He used words effectively.

But he never received or in my opinion deserved any real critical acclaim.

Doom of Youth is typical of his manifesto-type of outburst. He had a theory about 'youth politics' that I did not understand when I read his book in 1932 and still did not understand when I re-read it the other day. He elaborated his theme with a series of exhibits. He had read in the *New Statesman* a long review of my novel *Three Score and Ten* (September 1929) that complained of my 'manifest inability' to drag myself for long away from 'the life of the public school and by always seeming more at home there than in any other life'. Lewis based his attack on me on this article.

I naturally resented it. 'But is it libellous?' I asked Peters. 'I think it is. Why don't you ask Harold Rubinstein?'

Harold Rubinstein was an old friend of mine. He specialised in authors' cases. Yes, he said, an action should lie there.

I debated with myself. I am a pacific person. I avoid squabbles. But was it not for that very reason that Joan had called me indefinite, unassertive? Was not this a chance to prove that my gentle manner concealed a bellicose refusal to take insults lying down? 'Fire ahead,' I said to Rubinstein, and I agreed that he should demand from Chatto and Windus the publishers, an immediate withdrawal. In issuing his writ however, Rubinstein acted, I think, injudiciously. He asserted in it that Lewis had accused me of homosexual tendencies. But that he had not actually done and when the summons was heard in the High Court, the Judge could not accept this contention. 'There are no facts set out in this affidavit,' he said, 'to give rise to the innuendo alleged and I do not think that the words would be held *prima facie* to mean what is alleged.'

This put me in a difficult position. I could withdraw from the case, paying Lewis some recompense for the inconvenience I had caused him and for the loss he had suffered from the book being temporarily withdrawn from circulation, but if I did that I should justify Joan's doubts about me. She would think me pusillanimous. Better to go down fighting. I went with Harold Rubinstein to take the advice of counsel, of Mr Cartwright Sharpe. This advice was reassuring.

Sharpe felt that although the first steps had been taken without proper forethought, I had a strong case if I attacked from a different angle, namely that I had been falsely and maliciously abused in respect to my livelihood as an author and a novelist. He asked me about the kinds of book that I had written. I had by then published some fifteen books, on a variety of subjects. Most of my novels dealt with adult London life. My most successful novel after *The Loom of Youth* had been *Kept*, which was subtitled 'A Story of Post-War London'. I had travelled extensively and my book *Hot Countries* had been a best-seller in America. 'Lewis has therefore,' Sharpe said, 'labelled you inaccurately. You have not indulged in incessant literary compositions about small boys with sooty faces and bulging pockets.' Lewis had not, that is to say, said anything personally damaging, but he had on false grounds attacked me professionally.

'Carry on,' I said.

Next day I went down to Chagford to get started on that novel.

I took with me a bag of golf clubs – this was a new addition to my luggage. Joan had brought her clubs with her to Villefranche. She was expecting to play in Germany. They were hickory-shafted clubs and the blades were not of stainless steel. She would sit on her balcony polishing them. 'It's a pity you don't play,' she said.

I made a quick resolve. I would take lessons on my return to London. When she came back from Germany, I would have a surprise for her. During the five days I had to spend in London, I went to a golf school in the Strand. Those five days were enough to implant a fever in my veins. P. G. Wodehouse has claimed that it is as dangerous to take up golf in the middle thirties as it is to be subjected at that age to an attack of measles. In *The Heart of a Goof* he made high sport over the thrills and ardours of the tyro.

The danger about golf is that it appears so very easy. A man who has never ridden a horse cannot mount a steed and impel it towards a hedge. He will be in the ditch. A man who has never handled a cricket bat cannot walk to a wicket and drive an Australian fast bowler through the covers. But the novice on a golf course will three or four times in every round hit what seems to him a perfect shot. The ball will sail straight from the tee, high and white against the pale blue of the sky; it will climb high, higher – then it will begin to drop; but as it drops it will appear to gain extra length, it will go on, on, on. At last it drops, to run straight on for another thirty yards towards the green. Bobbie Jones could not have improved on it. Why could he not do that every time? He tries to remember what he has done and what he has avoided doing. It is only a question of getting the knack. He walks to the next tee with cosy confidence. He looks down the course. A par 4 hole, three hundred and fifty yards. He will aim his drive to land to the right of that narrow bunker. That will open the green nicely, a number 4 iron will see him home. He takes his stance. His club goes back. Once again he feels the ball in the centre of his club. But this time it curves into the rough. That was how it was with 'the Goof'; that was how it was with me.

The fever was in my veins. It had to run its course. Two years is the standard period of incubation. In my case it was a little longer. I never got any good at golf. I had taken it up too late. I was impeded by my cricket. I bent over the ball, my instinct was to hit it along the ground. But I got an immense amount of fun out of golf for twenty years.

CHAPTER 3

First Months of Marriage

Joan returned from Germany in mid-August. On August the 24th, my father's birthday, our engagement was announced. We fixed our wedding date for October the 25th, at the Old Church, Chelsea. Everything went very smoothly. We had a clear idea of what we should be needing. My Chelsea flat would serve as a base for our London visits. It had a large sitting room, a bedroom, a minute dining room that could seat eight, and a very small study. We would rent a house sixty or so miles from London. This we were to find quickly. Oswalds, the dower house of the Bourne Estate, within four miles of Canterbury, in the village of Bishopsbourne; a pleasant Georgian house which had literary associations in that Joseph Conrad had spent his last years and died there. We took it over as a running concern, with a staff consisting of a chauffeur-gardener and gardener's boy, a cook, a parlour maid, a housemaid, and a kitchen maid. We arranged to divide expenses. I was responsible for the rent, the heating and the gardener's wages. Joan took care of the household expenses and the wages of the indoor staff. The annual rent of the house, furnished, was four hundred pounds. In 1932 a couple could manage comfortably on three thousand pounds a year.

The arrangements for the wedding itself were very simple. Joan was to be 'given away' by her cousin Captain Poss Chirnside. The mother of an old friend of Joan's – Pat Buckley the author of several travel books – lent us her house in Egerton Gardens for the reception. Poss and his wife made all the catering arrangements. 'A sound non-vintage champagne, don't you think?' he said to me.

'Fine,' I said. 'Fine.'

But Joan's father sent Poss so generous a cheque that he changed his order to Möet and Chandon 1926. Evelyn was impressed. 'At smart weddings the champagne's rarely drinkable,' he said.

We spent our honeymoon in Eldred Curwen's villa in Antibes. He and I did a 'swop', he taking on my flat in Chelsea.

Eldred's villa was in the Chemin de L'Ermitage, with a garden running down to the Garoupe beach. Maupassant has described the view from that beach as one of the loveliest in the world. First there is a stretch of water, then the old town of Antibes with its twin square towers, beyond that the sea again; the long blue *Baie des Anges* with the *Promenade des Anglais* stretched along it; the town of Nice climbing back into the hills and on the far side of Nice the humped outline of Cap Ferrat; beyond are the snow-capped summits of the Alps. I never wearied of that view.

In terms of weather December is usually the worst and wettest Riviera month. November is problematic. We were lucky. We stayed there for four weeks and were able to play golf every day. We played at Biot, Nice and Montagel. We set out in a taxi about eleven. We played nine holes, then ate our sandwiches, finishing our round just as the sun was lowering and we felt across the eighteenth fairway the first warning of that chill half-hour that has proved fatal to so many elderly northerners, who have fled south to avoid the rigours of their own frost-bound climate.

There were hardly any other players on the course. The coast was deserted. The smart shops on the Croisette were closed. The big hotels were shuttered, the cafés empty. Once we went into Villefranche and found Ethel Mannin and James Stern lunching at the Welcome. 'I'm finishing a novel,' Ethel told us. 'I'm getting ready to begin one,' Stern informed us. Comments that were typical of each. Ethel was prolific. James had a real talent but wrote very little. We asked them over to dinner at the Villa. They were our only guests there.

I looked up one or two names in the telephone book. Maugham was in London, but Michael Arlen was in his villa at Cannes and invited us to lunch. He had a novel, *Man's Mortality*, in the press. He had just bought Morrison's book on golf and was convinced that he had got the secret of low scores. 'Point your chin behind the ball.' That was the Morrison formula. In the summer of 1932 high handicap golfers all over the world were persuading themselves that they only had to 'keep that chin pointed' to shoot in the low eighties.

Among the olive trees, on the Nice golf course, which now has been supplanted by the race course, we met Phillips Oppenheim. He had a villa, just beside the seventeenth hole. He liked to win two up and one to play so that he could walk straight from the green to his first dry martini. We played one round with him. He had a disconcerting habit of conceding himself putts. His ball would be two yards from the hole. You were putting for the half that might win the hole. Your ball would quiver on the edge. 'Bad luck, that puts me two up,' he'd say. One did not challenge him. He was the host. Moreover one knew that if one did, he would sink his putt.

We lunched with him our last day. We were catching the Blue Train that evening. 'You'll be in London tomorrow night; how I envy you,' he said. He was one of the first English authors who chose to live abroad to avoid income tax. There were times when he wondered if he had done wisely. There was so much about London that he missed. He talked nostalgically about the Savage Club and its Saturday night dinners. 'Is that scamp old Odell around still? You've got a flat in London, and you've rented a house near Canterbury. I suppose that you'll work there quietly for a week, ten days or so, then come to London for a show or two and a party. Ringing the changes.' There was envy in his voice. He did not want to subject himself to English income tax but he wished he could have it both ways. He gave Joan one of his books to read upon the journey, inscribed 'from Cannes to Calais'.

Those weeks should have been the happiest of my life. And they were happy, very happy. But all the time I had a niggling anxiety about the Wyndham Lewis case. I did not look forward to facing the cross-examination of an astute and hostile counsel, whose business it would be to present me in a ridiculous light. No doubt he would reveal the fact, as I have told in my *Early Years*, that I left Sherborne under a cloud.

'I think, M'lord,' I could hear him saying, 'in view of the fact that much of the case turns on the plaintiff's writing about public school life that we should examine in some detail Mr Waugh's own experiences at Sherborne. I have a list of the members of the Old Shirburnian Society. His name does not appear upon that list. Mr Waugh, will you tell us why.'

Though I might win the case I might emerge from the courts with a tarnished reputation. It would embarrass Joan. Her father would have doubts about my suitability as a son-in-law. I did not relish the prospect. Ten days before my marriage, I received from Harold Rubinstein a request for twenty-five pounds to meet preliminary expenses. How much would the final score be? If I lost I should have to meet Lewis's costs as well. I asked Rubinstein when the case was likely to be heard. 'In the early summer,' I was told. The early summer. Seven months away. I remembered at haymaking watching the harvesters driving in long curves round and round the fields. There would be a number of rabbits in the centre. They were safe at the moment; but the area of that protected haven kept diminishing. Every so often a rabbit would dash out into the open where boys would be waiting with sticks and stones and yapping dogs.

* * *

Phillips Oppenheim's anticipation of my routine was very much as I had myself foreseen it. I was used to working in country inns and beach hotels and I did not see why Oswalds should not prove the equivalent of those settings. It was a quite large house. On the ground floor it had a dining room, a large sitting room, a small library that was called the Conrad Room because Conrad had used it for his study. There was a gun room between the drawing room and the Conrad Room. That could be my study. I should be as quiet there as in any hotel. I did not anticipate that marriage would in that direction present any special problem and I did not foresee as a complication the discovery that I could expect to be a father in July. I did recognise, however, that living in the country was likely to prove as big a change as any that I had ever known. I had never lived in the country. I had been a week-end guest. I had been on cricket tours. For Joan on the other hand it was a familiar atmosphere. Her parents had taken houses in England for the summer. She had paid long visits with friends. Her life in Australia had been a country one. She was in her natural element.

The owners of the house had made things simple for us. They had told people we were coming. One or two of them I already knew, since in 1928 I had stayed for a week-end cricket match at Bourne, as Sir John Prestige's guest. The house nearest to ours was owned by the former Kent cricket captain, L. W. H. Troughton, who had been a prisoner of war with me at Karlsruhe. The rector Canon Burnside had only just retired from the headmastership of St Edmund's, Canterbury. He had three very attractive daughters, two of whom were married to officers in the Buffs. The other was married to a neighbouring farmer who had been an oarsman at Oxford. We could not have had a better introduction into East Kent life.

I fancy that Kent is unlike any other English county. It is a county where you belong or don't. According to which side of the Medway you are born, you are a man of Kent or a Kentish Man. Kent is a great cricketing county. Its 'family' side is called 'The Band of Brothers', but you cannot become a member just through owning a house in Kent. You have to have been born there. That did not worry me. A traveller like myself has always known himself to be a sojourner. Within a week I had made myself at home. I joined the Canterbury Golf Club. Joan had decided not to run the risk of playing golf while she was pregnant, but through the secretary of the Club I found two or three other members whose standard of play roughly matched my own. We had parties most week-ends and one or two of our guests were golfers. My enthusiasm for the game increased. I would practise in the fields round the house, driving into the paddock off the lawn. I was weak in bunkers, so I had one dug in the garden which I had filled with sand by a local builder. From the London Library I ordered a constant flow of books on the subject, memoirs and manuals of instruction. I kept buying new clubs.

The golf course was about three miles away, so I learnt to drive a car. It may seem strange that I had not learnt already. But in the early twenties very few of my London contemporaries had cars. Cars were expensive. There was a dearth of garages. Nor was there any need for me to have one. I could get anywhere by bus or tube. When I had played Rugby football, the team travelled down by train. The weekly card had said, 1.35 from Liverpool Street, tickets taken. The captain would be waiting at the barrier. In the cricket season one would be unlikely to find more than one member of the side who had a car. If that member was a friend one tried to cadge a lift back to town. I remember Ralph Straus buying a car in 1925 as the result of the film sale of a novel. He was very proud of it. It was a proof that he was doing well. 'I suppose you'll be getting one soon, won't you, Alec?' he remarked not unpatronisingly. I supposed I would, but by the time I could have afforded one I had begun to travel. I never had an opportunity to learn to drive. Now, clearly, I had to. I would be a prisoner without one. I could not rely on Joan exclusively or the gardener-chauffeur.

I bought for twenty-five pounds an open two-seater. The gardener gave me lessons. In those days you did not have to pass a driving test. Within a couple of weeks I felt competent enough to drive to the golf course, and within two months to drive into Canterbury station to meet a guest. But I never felt comfortable at the wheel. I am unmechanical. I could not concentrate upon the road. I thought of something else.

Before we married, I had pictured us as going up to London for a week or so every month. But it did not work out that way. On the 15th of December a dinner was given for J. C. Squire, and we decided to go up for it. It was a curious occasion. It had no *raison d'être*. It had nothing to celebrate. It was apparently Squire's own idea. He felt that it was time that he was honoured with a dinner. I cannot recall whose name appeared on the invitation card. But we were informed that 'orders would be worn'. It was a very large gathering with the chief speech delivered by Duff Cooper. Shortly afterwards Squire received a knighthood. Was there any connection between the dinner and the title? I have no idea.

Joan and I made it the occasion for a ten-day visit to London. It gave Joan a chance to introduce me to some of her friends and for us to have a party or two at Cheyne Place. But the weather was bad. Londoners are busy with their own affairs during the two weeks before Christmas and anyhow London is a place where plans are made quite a way in advance. It is difficult to organise a London life from the country. We also spent rather more money than was convenient. I suggested that we did not come up to London again till the weather mended. 'Why don't we let the flat till March?' I could get some solid work done and concentrate on golf.

The novel which I had begun at Chagford was now with the printers. It was announced for early May, with the title *Wheels Within Wheels*. I was now working on short stories. They were not very satisfactory ones. I found it hard to concentrate. I kept thinking about golf, playing over my last round hole by hole, vowing to make amends that afternoon. I was also worrying about Wyndham Lewis. The date of the trial was growing nearer.

A few years ago I received a letter from a young American student, Victor N. Cassidy, who is writing a life of Wyndham Lewis. He had a question or two to ask me about my case with Lewis. He gave me a great deal of very interesting information about Lewis. At the time when I issued my writ, Lewis had several other cases on his hands. He had contracted to write a book for Constable entitled *The Life Story of a Tyro*. He never wrote it and Constable sued successfully to get its money back. A titled lady had commissioned a series of pictures and paid an advance on them, but died before the work was finished; her estate sued successfully for a partial return of her advance. An English citizen resident in Agadir claimed that Lewis had libelled him in a travel book, *Filibusters in Barbary*. The book was withdrawn, an apology was made, and damages were paid. Chatto and Windus had published in 1928 Part I of the *Childermass*. Lewis did not deliver the manuscript of Part II and Chatto in this same year sued for a refund of their advance. HM Inland Revenue was suing for back taxes. His plate was pretty full and Lewis was a belligerent man. He had his back to the wall. He had over-extended himself, taking advances on books he had not written and pictures he had not painted. He had lost friends and he had made enemies. He was ready to fight back wherever he saw an opening, and my case had seemed to present that opportunity. That had been the situation as far as Lewis was concerned when I first issued my writ. Now eight months later Lewis's mental turmoil had substantially increased, deepening an already virulently active persecution mania. He believed that a 'dirty little gang' with myself at its head was combining against him. He felt that Chatto and Windus had let him down. He quarrelled with his own solicitors who demanded partial payment of their fees before proceeding further on his account. They agreed reluctantly to withdraw as his solicitors, but insisted that they must receive a payment before handing over the pertinent papers. Finally his new solicitors told him that they were expecting a bill from Chatto's solicitors as they had lost the breach of contract suit.

How I wish I had known all this at the time. Today the sums involved seem very small, but a hundred pounds was a lot of money then. Finally Lewis was persuaded to settle my claim to avoid additional expenses. He continued to rant that he would not be 'blackmailed by that gang' but he finally agreed to a compromise. He would withdraw *Doom of Youth* from publication provided that I agreed categorically to withdraw the homosexual charge, which of course I was perfectly happy to do; all I wanted was to have the book withdrawn.

Lewis's counsel in these closing stages was F. G. Mitchison, Naomi Mitchison's husband. I was surprised at first at Mitchison accepting the brief. We were quite good friends. I had often been his guest and he had dined at my house. I had always thought that it was one of the traditions of the bar that a barrister did not accept a brief that would involve the hostile cross-examination of a man he knew socially. I never met him after the case, but it is very possible that through his wife he was a friend of Lewis, and that he was performing an act of friendship in taking on a case that he could manage to keep out of court, a case that could have done no one any good. If so, I am grateful to him.

I have seldom felt more relieved than I did when I opened the envelope that contained news of the final settlement. I vowed never to bring another libel suit. My honeymoon and my first months of marriage would have been so much more enjoyable without the shadow of Wyndham Lewis hanging over them.

CHAPTER 4

A Tranquil Summer

1933, a great vintage year for claret, was a memorable summer. Day after day the sun shone on the county that has been called the garden of England. Joan sat under a copper beech, contentedly awaiting her confinement, while I worked on a family chronicle that was to be called *The Balliols*, about five children who had grown up in Hampstead during the early years of the twentieth century; it began with the suffragettes. As a small boy I had been taken for walks on Sunday mornings by the Whitestone Pond and listened to the speakers advocating 'Votes for women'. I had been so affected by their oratory that I joined the Drummers' Union, a club of young militants. I wore a white medallion with the word 'Drummer' inscribed on it in black. I was prepared to distribute leaflets at meetings, though as it happened my services were never requisitioned. The new novel grew longer than I had expected. It would run to a quarter of a million words, it would not be finished until close on Christmas. There are few more satisfactory feelings than the settling down to a long solid stretch of work.

I had now joined Prince's Golf Club, one of the world's great courses, a difficult but an exciting one. It was a delight to walk along the sea with the line of the coast curving towards Ramsgate.

I played cricket for the village and also for the Canterbury side, St Lawrence. I rarely went up to London. I got rid of my Chelsea flat and moved my library and pictures down to Oswalds.

I am told that Canterbury has lost much of its charm. The Fountain Inn was hit by a bomb during the war. Multiple stores have taken the place of personal shops such as Jackman's. But the Cathedral mercifully survived the air raid. Its tower still dominates the neighbourhood. I am sure that the town must be very special still. When in 1935 Reading became my county town, I could not resist unfavourable comparisons. How different was the river that ran through Canterbury. Going there as a boy I had for the first time seen weaving, and the St Lawrence cricket ground with its vast tree that trespasses on the playing area. No cricket week can compare with Canterbury's; it is not only the ground itself with its tents and banners. There is the Old Stagers' performance of a play. The standard of acting is very high, a London actress is imported for the key role. *The Times* and the *Daily Telegraph* send down their dramatic critics. In my two years there they were Charles Morgan and W. A. Darlington. One evening they dined with us and next day we watched the cricket. Darlington was an old friend of mine. We had played cricket together for Hampstead; I had met Morgan several times without getting to know him, but our acquaintanceship became a friendship in the relaxed atmosphere of the Canterbury Festival. During the Festival Old Stagers are allowed to wear IZ ties.

We had guests most week-ends. They usually came down for lunch on Saturdays, though sometimes they came on the Friday night. There was an exciting atmosphere of preparation for their arrival. There would usually be a dinner party on the Saturday night to which we would invite neighbours. Thanks to the letters of introduction which the owners of the house had given us, and the Burnside family, we had acquired quite a group of friends. These week-ends gave Joan and myself an opportunity of getting to know each other's friends.

We had come from very different worlds, and the fact that she had spent so much of her time in Australia meant that I had a much larger English acquaintance than she had. At the same time she came from an important Australian family, and in England she had been meeting her opposite numbers, so that her friends were considerably grander than the majority of mine. This was, I felt, something that needed watching. I remembered how she had found unreal some of my friends in Villefranche. I had a suspicion that she would be puzzled by some of my other friends and that she could not be sure how her own friends would like them. I also felt that she was not sure how some of her friends would take to me. I imagine something like this happens in most marriages, and each partner is on guard against transporting figures from the past into their new life; there is a tendency to play for safety, which can mean that each avoids their more dramatic acquaintances; there is thus a loss of liveliness.

Perhaps I was too self-conscious on this point, but my feeling that Joan was not quite sure of me, the feeling that had made me bring the action against Wyndham Lewis, was influential still. I was especially careful in regard to Americans. There was at that time, as a result of the war, a strong anti-American feeling in Europe generally and particularly in England. The war had made America rich and powerful while it had impoverished England and the English.

This feeling was particularly marked in Joan. She had a virulent dislike of them, a dislike that was exacerbated by my own high regard for them. In the autumn of 1931 I had published a novel that was obviously autobiographical called *So Lovers Dream*; in New York it was called *That American Woman*, but Cassell had urged me to change the title. 'Over here they don't want to read about Americans,' Newman Flower assured me. 'Particularly they don't want American heroines. They say "What's wrong with the English?"'

My novel described a love affair between an English novelist and an American married woman. Joan had bought it in Australia and read it on the trip across. 'How much of this is based on fact?' she asked me; I told her quite a lot. 'Did you go with her to Villefranche?' she asked.

I shook my head. 'I altered the settings. I didn't want her friends to recognise her.'

'That's something to be thankful for. I wouldn't have gone with you if you had.'

'Oh come now, surely –'

'No, of course not. To have to go to the same places that you'd been with her two years before. It's bad enough to have had you taking me to places that you've been thinking about taking her.'

I could see her point. I think being Australian increased her dislike of Americans. 'They are so pleased with themselves,' she'd say. 'They are so rich and smart and they've been everywhere. It's maddening that somebody like you should write a whole novel telling them how wonderful they are.'

Yes, yes, I could see her point. In earlier days I had annoyed my English friends by talking too much about America. 'If you think it so wonderful, why don't you go and live there?' they would say. I soon learnt not to talk about America when I came back home. Instead I would ask them about things in England. And indeed nobody who has been staying at home ever wants to hear travelling stories. I wished now that I had been more careful during my first weeks with Joan. I must be on my guard in future. I must certainly not ask any of my New York friends to Oswalds.

In a year's time, I thought, Joan and I would go to New York together. She had never been to America. She had only seen Americans as tourists. You cannot judge a country by its tourists. She would feel differently about the country when she had once seen it. It was important professionally for me to maintain my links there. It was not important for me to have American characters in my books, but it was important for me to see enough of America, to have an American audience in mind when I was writing about England. Yes, that was what we would do, go over there in the spring of 1934. In the meantime I must concentrate on Oswalds.

So through that hot summer I played golf and cricket; and worked upon *The Balliols*.

Wheels Within Wheels was published in early May. Books then came out within three months of the manuscript being delivered. I saw no point in going up to London for its publication. There was no promotion, no publisher's parties in London as there were in New York; at any rate, Cassell did not believe in spending money that way. The novel did quite well. It was a routine book. Nothing special was expected of it. It would keep my name before the public, and maintain the librarians' interest in me; as was expected of an author at that time; a novel a year then was the pattern.

Publishers talked about 'the break through'. An author would go on publishing his books with steady slowly mounting sales. Then suddenly there would be 'the break through', his sales would be quadrupled and the process would increase with each new novel. No one had expected that to happen with *Wheels Within Wheels*. Perhaps it might come with the long family chronicle. There was nothing to worry about. I had to wait, just as Joan had to wait till her nine months had passed.

Sometimes as I sat at my desk, as I strolled round the village, as I followed my ball at Prince's, I would compare my present life with what it had been a year earlier, eighteen months, two years, three years earlier. Eighteen months ago I was in New Orleans. I had at very short notice gone over to New York. I needed a change, I planned a six-weeks visit, but on arrival I changed my mind. New York in the third winter of the Depression was inert and grim. Why not go to the West Indies? Why not catch a boat from New Orleans? I had always wanted to see New Orleans. I had there two good friends whom I had met in Villefranche, whom I had been seeing every day that summer. There must be regular sailings to the West Indies. I would catch a ship that sailed in ten days or so. I could take a first view of

New Orleans; then if I really liked it, I could pause on the way back. Eighteen months ago I could change my plans at a moment's notice.

I arrived on a Sunday morning. My friends were there to meet me. 'We've fixed up a Sunday breakfast for you,' they said. They had asked half-a-dozen of their friends. I felt at home with all of them at once. It was absurd, they said, for me to leave so soon. I couldn't come to New Orleans and miss the carnival; that was only six weeks away. They would find me a flat. That would be easy nowadays.

It proved to be. They found me one in Jackson Square, a studio flat in the Pont/Alba Building. The PA of the iron work shone up on the sloping ceilings. And then I found that Barbara Starke – who had made my heart beat faster a year earlier in New York, of whom I was to write in *A Year to Remember* – was in town. In New York we had hardly time for one another. Now we had. It was a halcyon interlude. Was that only eighteen months ago? I looked twenty-four months farther back. I had been at Villefranche then, working quietly on *So Lovers Dream*. My father and mother had come down to join me. My brother Evelyn had come down too. And a little later Patrick Balfour and Keith Winter had come. We had all been working upon manuscripts. There was a day-to-day eventlessness about our routine. Yet each day something amusing seemed to happen. I was getting to know Somerset Maugham. Later Paul Morand had come to his villa, the Orangerie. Only two years ago.

A year further back I had been in New York, celebrating the publication of *Hot Countries*, with a whole new world opening for me. How full life had been. How varied. It was the kind of life that could only be lived by a novelist, who carried his office with him. What full use I had made of my opportunities. What had happened to that Alec Waugh?

CHAPTER 5

Enter Carol Hill

It was, I will not say a lack of satisfaction with the placidity of my life at Oswalds, but it was surely a certain restlessness that made me during this summer reorganise the background of my writing pattern. I had a need for something new to happen. I changed my New York agent.

When I arrived unexpectedly in New York in February 1927, I had known no one there except my publisher, George Doran. I was sailing that night. I went straight round to see him. He arranged for his editor, John Farrar, to take me out to lunch. 'Do you know who my agent is?' I asked him. 'Oughtn't I to see him?'

'You certainly should. He's probably Paul Reynolds or Carl Brandt.'

He was Carl Brandt.

Brandt's office was only a few blocks away on the corner of Park and 40th. It was on the seventeenth floor. It looked out on the East River. It was my first view of the stupendous panorama of Manhattan. I couldn't help looking over Carl Brandt's shoulder as I talked to him.

'It's terrific, isn't it?' he said. 'You'll never quite get used to it. That's why I sit with my back to it.'

I had come out from San Francisco by the Union Pacific. My first evening in the club room, as I was turning the pages of *Harper's Bazaar*, I had seen at the head of a column the line 'Alec Waugh's short story'. It was a very pleasant surprise. Not only had I not known that I had sold that story, but it was the first story that I had sold in the United States. For me, as for every other English novelist, the prospect of selling short stories in America was a dream flickering on the horizon. 'How much did I get for it?' I asked Carl Brandt.

'I'll ask my secretary. I think it was three seventy-five.'

Three seventy-five dollars. Seventy-five pounds. That was as much as a great many English writers got for an entire novel.

'I mailed a couple more stories from Tahiti six weeks ago,' I said.

'We'll try to get you a bit more this time.'

Carl Brandt was one of the greatest agents, particularly in the magazine field. John Marquand portrayed him in *Wickford Point*, a character study that has more useful advice on how to write for magazines than any of the 'how to do it' manuals. He was also a most delightful person. But he had one very great weakness – drink. He would without warning 'go on a bender', be lost for three days and have to be sent to a sanatorium. One of these collapses coincided a few years later with one of Peters' New York visits. Peters felt that he could not trust his clients' interests to so unstable an operator and closed down his connection with Brandt. He decided to have his own representatives in New York, and eventually founded his own firm, Hill and Peters.

Stephen Birmingham in his biography of John Marquand gives a full-length portrait of Carol Hill, who was to become in 1940 the chief woman in Marquand's life. When I crossed to New York in April 1930, Peters asked me to take a brooch to her. I assumed that he was in love with her. I think he was, but it was soon apparent that she was an emotional concern of Brandt. They married in the summer of 1931. This rather altered my own position in regard to the Brandt office. I had remained Carl's client when he and Peters ended their association, but I did not find it easy to work through his office under these changed conditions. Carl did not, naturally, particularly like Peters; his staff quite definitely disliked him. Carl dealt only with the magazine side of my work. Most of my income came from my books. I was at this time having some difficulty with my publishers, Farrar and Rinehart, and it was not easy for me to resolve these difficulties when the various issues were being argued out by two offices that were at odds with one another. I wondered whether I would not be wise to transfer my custom to Hill and Peters. I asked Peters if he thought Carl would mind. 'I don't see why he should,' Peters said. 'The money will still be in the family.'

To my surprise and to Peters', Carl did mind very much. Money did not matter to him. What did matter was his personal relations with his clients, and he had a more personal regard for me than I had suspected. Had I known he would be so offended, I would not have made the move. At the same time I have no doubt that the move was, at that time, very greatly in my own interest.

Carol was a handsome Amazonian creature, elegant and bejewelled. On some men, on quite a number of men, she exerted a very powerful attraction. She never did on me, but I fancy that with many women sex appeal is a current that they turn on at will, a characteristic that they only exercise when they are in the mood. But I was soon to realise that Carol possessed a magnetism of a very different kind.

In the autumn of 1933 she crossed to London. My first son, Andrew, had been born in July. Joan was still nursing him. I was within sight of the finish of my long novel. I was not coming up to London. Carol suggested that Peters should motor her down to lunch one Sunday. It was a wet day, I remember. After lunch Carol said to Joan, 'I want to take your husband away and have a long, long talk with him.'

We went into what was called the Gold Room. It was an evening, rather than a winter room. The sun was hardly ever on it. A large fire was highly stoked. I can still see her lying back in the corner of a sofa, one foot raised upon a footstool.

'Peters tells me that you are finishing a novel,' she began.

I told her about *The Balliols*. 'I'll have finished it in a month,' I said.

'After that, what are you planning?'

'My mind's a blank.'

'Then may I suggest that you concentrate upon short stories.'

That was vaguely what I had in mind. I usually wrote short stories in the interval between novels. I wrote five or six a year. Peters sold them for forty to fifty pounds apiece. *Nash's* was my best market. I occasionally sold one in America. *Harper's Bazaar* was still my best market there. Five years before *College Humor* had bought me, but I had had no luck there for some time. *Harper's Bazaar* had been used to pay $375 but they were down to $150 now. Three months back *Pictorial Review* had bought one. It was my first appearance in an established 'glossy'. I had been very pleased about the sale. It brought me £400.

'That story in *Pictorial*,' Carol said, 'I was really annoyed with you over that. It was so very nearly right. I wished it could have gone to *Colliers*.'

I had not expected that. What was wrong with it? I thought she would tell me, but she did not. She began to talk about writing for the big magazines, about the excitement of it, of its rewards, its drama. Carl had tried to interest me in magazines. He was an expert at fixing stories. He talked about suspense, about rewards, of how the reader always rooted for the first character about whom he read. I had listened carefully. 'Next time I write a story,' I had thought, 'I must remember this.' But he had never got me excited about the idea of writing for magazines.

Stephen Birmingham examined at length the extent and nature of Carol's hold over John Marquand. She wanted him to need her, he explained. She made herself necessary to him. And that in Marquand's case was no doubt true, but the need to be needed was only a part of her attack on life. She was extremely ambitious. She had always been attracted by the world of books and writers. As a very young woman she had written a novel that had been by no means unsuccessful. But she did not feel that she could realise as a writer her ambitions for herself. The solitary dedicated nature of a writer's life did not appeal to her. She did not want money for itself, but she wanted the aura of success. She felt that she could achieve this through her clients. She wanted success for them, so that their success would reflect on her. Her belief in their success was contagious. Because she believed in them so much, they believed in themselves. They wrote better because of her. She identified herself with them to such an extent that she felt aggrieved when they did not write as well as she believed they could. Carl was not like that. Once when I presented him with a rather weak set of stories, he shook his head sadly. 'I feel like an executioner, but it's no good, I can't sell these over here.' He was distressed on my account, because I had been disappointed. But Carol was indignant if I delivered a weak story because she herself had been let down. She had been enthusiastic about me to editors – and that was one of her very strong points, she got editors to share her enthusiasm – and I had not delivered the goods.

An agent occupies a very humble position in the literary hierarchy, but Carol always behaved like a prima donna. In very early days, Burton, the editor of *Cosmopolitan*, complained at 'Mrs Hill giving herself such airs. She is only an agent after all.' In the same way, Edith Wharton's friends complained that she insisted on being treated as royalty. But because she insisted she was treated so, and in the same way Carol Hill was treated as a prima donna. She set a high standard for herself. She would never travel anything but first class in a plane. She entertained elegantly in her own apartment or in a gourmet restaurant. She only accepted invitations to gourmet restaurants. In the early sixties, John Farrar invited her to lunch at the Yale Club with his wife, myself, and Lynn Caine, Farrar-Straus' publicity girl, who was later to write the best-selling *Widow*. She neither accepted nor refused the invitation. But I did not expect her to turn up. She didn't.

In 1935 Katherine Brush made her the heroine of a short

story called 'Free Women' in which she was presented as a cold calculating careerist. She was a careerist, right enough, but she was not cold. She had a heart. I was dining at her house many years later with Marcia Davenport on the evening that the news of Blanche Knopf's death came through. It upset her so much that she went to bed directly after dinner.

Her personal devotion to her clients was unlimited. Vincent Sheean was one of her special concerns. In July 1936 I arrived in New York for a three-week visit. It had been planned that I was to go down to the Brandt house in the country for the week-end. I was met on my arrival at the Algonquin with a message that Mrs Hill had had to alter her week-end plans. She had had to leave for England at a moment's notice. Next morning I went round to her office. Her secretary pointed down to the East River. 'You'll see her ship out there in twenty minutes.'

'What's happened?'

'Jimmy Sheean. Another of his breakdowns.'

Vincent Sheean had a drinking problem, and Carol had not felt that his young bride was capable of coping with this particular manifestation of it. That was typical of Carol. There was no trouble too great for a special client.

After that long talk at Oswalds on that wet Sunday afternoon, I felt quite differently about working for magazines. She gave me no advice, but she inspired me with resolve. As soon as I had finished my novel, I would concentrate on short stories. I would take more trouble over them. I was a quick worker. I averaged two thousand words a day. That meant three days to a short story. That was not enough. It meant that I did not get inside my characters. I only knew them superficially. I knew nothing except the plot. In future I would take two weeks over a story, I would make them longer, seven to eight thousand words; I could always cut, and they would have the difference between a story that sold to *Pictorial* and one that sold to *Colliers*.

Indeed, that was how it turned out. During the next eighteen months I broke into the big magazines.

CHAPTER 6

New York Revisited

In retrospect, most of us feel that our lives have gone according to plan; perhaps they have in terms of the broad pattern. After a certain point there is only a certain number of courses open to us, and we can only do things that are in character. On New Year's Eve, 1933, I thought I foresaw exactly what would be happening during the spring. Joan had become pregnant again, the second child was due at the end of July. I pictured us spending a quiet winter at Oswalds. Joan would be happy with her baby. I would put my good resolution about magazine stories to the test. But then, one morning shortly before lunch, the telephone rang. Joan said, 'I'll answer, it's probably for me.' It was. I could hear her talking though I could not hear what she said. Then came what sounded like an explosion and she was back in the Conrad Room convulsed with sobs. 'I've got to go to Australia. My mother's very ill. My father needs me at once. It's too much.' To have to leave her baby.

'But must you? With the new baby due, won't they understand?'

She would not let me argue. 'No, no,' she said. 'I've got to go, my father needs me.'

'Who was on the telephone?'

'Dalgety of course. Who else?' She laughed as she said that. Dalgety's was the firm, largely her father's own creation, that fixed everything. 'Ring up Dalgety's' was a family joke phrase. No matter what went wrong – Australia in trouble with a Test Match – 'Ring up Dalgety's' was the answer.

Dalgety fixed everything now. Within five days Joan was on her way. Oswalds was closed: Nannie and the baby had been moved to a hotel outside London. I was in my parents' flat at Highgate. Our neighbours the Burnsides had offered to put up Nannie and the baby, but Joan was not sure that their house would be warm enough. It was not centrally heated. The cost of things was not discussed. It was the first time I had seen how indifferent to money really well-off people are, with the equivalent of Dalgety's at their beck and call.

I offered to go with her.

'No, no,' she said. 'It would be very grim for you. It'll be a trying time. I want to concentrate on my father.'

As we drove away to the station, the baby was held up at the nursery window to wave goodbye. My heart bled for Joan.

It had all happened so quickly that I did not realise what was happening. Here I was back in London on my own, with three months stretching ahead of me.

I lunched at the Savile. I had hardly been there during the last eighteen months. I was joined by A. D. Peters. 'I suppose we'll be seeing you here a lot during the next few weeks,' he said.

'I suppose so.'

I had hardly begun to think what I was going to do during the next three months; there was so much to do. For eighteen months I had been living within the radius of marriage.

'Don't you feel rather lost?' Peters asked.

I shook my head. On the contrary I felt I had become myself again. I was able to make my own arrangements for myself without having to consider anybody else. Only one thing puzzled me: to be living in my parents' house.

On my way up from Canterbury I had noticed outside Victoria Station on a big new building, an announcement of 'Miniature Luxury Flats from £95'.

I wondered what they were like. I went round to see. Fountain Court was a large barrack-type building with ten or twelve stories of narrow oblong windows. London is now peppered with such buildings. But they were the newest thing in January 1934. They had a model flat on view. It was very small, but it had a bathroom, a kitchenette and a frigidaire. It could be made quite attractive with a picture or two and a few bookshelves. The very thing I needed. I could not bury myself permanently in the country. I was a writer. I had to be in touch with what was going on. I had to have some place where I could take a couple of people back for a drink and chat after a party. The block had a restaurant attached. Probably it would not be very good but it would be adequate for the sort of casual entertaining for which I could use this kind of flat. It was all very well during the first year of a marriage to live within its radius, but that could not go on for ever. I had to keep in touch. That was what I kept repeating to myself.

'We've bigger flats of course,' the owner of the block was telling me. 'We've two-room flats.'

I shook my head. I did not want a flat that would be a home. I wanted a place to myself. 'We've flats like this in other parts of London, in Kensington and St John's Wood,' I was told.

St John's Wood. That would be near Lord's. That would be convenient and St John's Wood was well served with tubes and buses. It was central. There was nothing the other side of Victoria. I had realised that when I had a flat in Chelsea. 'The Wood' had traditions. There were quiet tree-shaded streets where fashionable Victorians had maintained discreet establishments. There was a new block at 20 Abbey Road. I could get a slightly larger flat for £110 a year on the eighth floor. £110, two pounds a week, I could afford that, and I could always let it. A 53 bus ran past the door. Abbey Road was convenient for the Savile, a fifty minutes' walk or ten minutes in the bus.

*   *   *

41

Within three weeks I had moved into a flat in Abbey Road. That kind of thing could be done quickly then. My cousin Betty Holmes was running a decorating business and she took charge of it. A flat of that size does not need much furniture. When I had given up my flat in Chelsea, I had moved the furniture down to Oswalds. I now moved some of it back. I did not need to buy very much from Heal's. I gave a very small house-warming party. But already I had other plans in mind.

My American publisher, Stanley Rinehart, and his recently acquired English wife were over. They were sailing back in a few days on the *Washington*, a popular eight-day boat. Why did I not come over with them?

I was tempted. It was nearly two years since I had been to New York, it was high time I went again. The manuscript of *The Balliols* had just arrived. They were enthusiastic. They could arrange press interviews. I was tempted but I had spent quite a little money on my flat. A trip with the Rineharts would be great fun, but their presence on board would double the cost of the trip. I would be wise to travel by one of the American Transport ten-day ships that went straight from London to New York at the cost of a hundred pounds. Moreover on one of those boats I would have peace of mind for work. I had an idea for a short story. I wanted to put Carol's exhortation to the test.

I arrived with the story finished. The temptation to send it straight to the typist was very strong. But I wanted to make sure this time. I would put it away for the length of my stay in New York and come fresh to it for revision on the journey back.

The next three weeks were as exciting as any I have known. If I had found London changed, I found New York transformed. In 1932 in the third year of the Depression, it had been grim and sad, helpless and hopeless. Every week things got worse. But now the whole atmosphere was changed. F.D.R. was in the White House. Every window was placarded with the blue eagle of the NRA. 'We do our part.' Prohibition was over. There were notices outside the bars 'Bock beer is here'. Restaurants were no longer half empty. They were bright and crowded. There had been drama, it must be admitted, about 'speakeasies', about the tapping on a basement door, of seeing a slot shot back, of showing one's card of membership and being admitted into a brightly-lit interior; but how much more gracious it was to be conducted by a head waiter to a corner table in a res-taurant filled with elegant, well-dressed men and women with bottles standing upon the tables.

I had asked Stanley Rinehart to see if he could rent me a flat, but instead he had booked me into a suite at the Algonquin. During my long stay in New York in 1930–1 I had only been there once. Although the Round Table still flourished there, public restaurants had no appeal for me during Prohibition. Now I found it as much a home as any club. I cannot believe that any hotel has such a personal atmosphere. The restaurant was congenial and I learned to appreciate the intimacy of having meals served upstairs in a suite.

I had made a number of friends on my earlier visits and my diary was quickly filled with dates. I gave a welcome home party for myself and the Alan Rineharts gave a party for me. Two ex-loves of mine happened to be in town and what was more important I was introduced into the world of the *New Yorker* magazine. In 1930–1 one of my chief friends had been Elinor Sherwin, a very pretty young socialite for whom I had entertained what were then called 'honourable inten-tions'. She was, however, unsatisfactorily entangled with a married man. I did not reach second base, but we became excellent friends.

She was now married to Wolcott Gibbs and through her I met James Thurber, John O'Hara, St Clare McKelway. The *New Yorker* group was very exclusive then. At parties they kept among themselves. A young woman who mar-ried one complained that it was impossible to introduce her old friends to them. She might ask them to the same party but her husband's friends would stay huddled in a corner.

With me for some lucky reason it was different. I was never one of them on paper, but I was socially. Elinor's friendship was a visa on my passport. Love pays unexpected dividends. In March 1931 I might have seen my falling in love with Elinor in terms of complete frustration, but by February 1939 when I paid my last visit to New York before the war I was recognising that half of my good times there had come to me through her.

That spring of 1934 was a period of opening horizons. Carolyn Cobb who ran the Easton Court Hotel in Devonshire had given me a letter of introduction to The Seaboard Society. Carolyn Cobb was a great friend of Zaidie Bliss to whom the Museum of Modern Art is so indebted. After the second war her daughter Eliza Parkinson was to become one of my closest friends. At Henry Cobb's party I met the enchanting Lily Cushing, the artist whose daughter was to marry Anthony West. Everywhere I was conscious of expansion, of mounting enthusiasm. There was a new note of excitement in the theatre; *Sailor Beware, Wilderness, As Thousands Cheer.* Farrar and Rinehart were optimistic about the *Balliols,* so was Carol Hill. I lunched twice at her house, and she gave a dinner for me. 'And now,' I told her, 'I'm going to work on those short stories.'

'You do just that,' she said.

Much as I had loved New York four years earlier I could not have believed it would be such a revelation. I felt that I belonged here. I felt a little guilty at having such a good time there without Joan. But would she have enjoyed herself I wondered? She had this unreasoning anti-American prejudice. She kept making snide remarks about Americans. Her dislike of them had increased since our marriage. I myself never now referred to America or Americans. Usually the anti-American English change their attitude once they have seen the country. But I doubted if she would, her dislike went so deep. I wondered too if I should have enjoyed myself so much had she been with me. Could I have been quite natural? I should have had to be on my guard. Americans liked me, I believed, because I was more expansive than most Englishmen, because I was so obviously having a good time. 'You're bilingual as regards America,' Carol Hill once said. New York was important to me not only professionally but personally. This presented, I was beginning to recognise, a serious problem to my marriage.

Joan was due back from Melbourne at the end of April. I planned to meet her in Marseilles. The *Aquitania* was the most convenient ship for a return. I had originally booked myself to travel second class. I had spent quite a little money in New York but my morale had been raised so high by my welcome in New York that I thought I could indulge in an extra extravagance and I transferred to a minimum rate first-class cabin. I was glad I did. One is always wise to travel first class in one of one's own country's ships. There is always a chance that one will meet someone whom one would be unlikely to meet on equal terms in the ordinary run of one's routine. On this particular trip I was more than ordinarily lucky.

E. V. Lucas was aboard. Until this visit to New York I had only met him once, when we had sat at opposite ends of the table at a dinner party given by the Editor of the *Sunday Times*. He was an old friend of my father. In distant days they had considered collaborating on a book of letters of which E.V.L. had eventually taken the idea for his own *Listeners Lure*. His daughter Audrey had been a close friend of the family. In 1930 and 1931 she had had an affair with Evelyn. This was generally well known in London and I was not sure whether E.V. knew about it. E.V. and his wife were separated but not divorced. When I had met him at a small dinner party that Stanley Rinehart gave for him at the Harvard Club before a public debate between Carl Van Doren and Henry Seidel Canby he had told me he was returning to England in the *Aquitania*.

'I shall be too,' I said, 'but I'll probably be travelling second class.'

'I shouldn't do that if I were you,' he said.

E.V.'s presence on the ship was one of the reasons that made me decide to travel first class.

My first morning on board a letter was delivered to my cabin. It was signed E.V.L. The script ran at an angle across the page in a style to which I had been familiarised by E.V.'s letters to my father. It invited me to take tea with him one day in his suite. The letter was addressed to Monsieur Jourdain.

'Why Monsieur Jourdain?' I asked.

'I'm afraid you don't know your Molière,' he said. 'Monsieur Jourdain was a character who if he were living today would have moved from second class to first and then felt himself ill-at-ease in his new surroundings.'

I had two very pleasant teas in E.V.'s cabin. He was a great charmer. He could also be very rude. I wonder what his name conveys today to anybody under forty? He was a great personality. He was a man of influence, with his position on the board of Methuen's and his seat at *Punch*'s table. I wonder if any of his books are still in print. Audrey wrote a very good short book about him.

I thoroughly enjoyed the trip. I remember a crossing on the *De Grasse* in 1950 with S. J. Perelman, Irving Shaw and Robert Standish, each with his wife aboard. That was the best crossing I have ever made. But of the rest, and I have made some fifty crossings, this one on the *Aquitania* was the best.

S. N. Behrman was aboard. I had met him in January 1928. *The Second Man*, his first big success, was about to be produced, with Noel Coward in the lead. Carl Brandt had a minute house in Chester Street and Behrman had rented it. He was as good company as anyone that I have known. In 1931 he had become involved with Elinor Sherwin, and there had been some talk of a marriage. It was very good to have a chance of seeing him for several days on end. He told me that he did a great deal of his writing in country inns. Had England any equivalent for Woodstock? I recommended him the Easton Court Hotel and 'those stout tables' were soon supporting the manuscripts of another writer

Gilbert Miller was on board; because he was a good friend of Sam's I saw quite a little of him. That is a typical example of how in the days of ocean travel you could meet people whom in the routine of your life you would be unlikely to come across. Francine Larrimore was on board. She was very pretty and agreeable. I had never seen her act. I did not know anything about her. I had the feeling that she was worried about herself: that she was hoping to make use of Behrman and Miller. Sam seemed anxious to avoid being alone with her. I felt sorry for her; I do not know how things turned out for her. One lost touch during the war with so many people and failed to pick up their tracks afterwards.

Also aboard were A. D. Peters' brother-in-law Edward Mayne who was in 1941 to serve with me in Lebanon in the Spears Mission, and a lively whisky salesman, R. G. Cuming, whose name appeared some years ago in the Honours List among the Knight Bachelors. I returned to London feeling that all my batteries had been recharged. I felt that I had, as a writer, reached a dramatic point to which in ten years' time I should find myself looking back. 'That's where the parabola began to climb,' I could hear myself saying.

I had good reason for thinking that. My new novel was a long way my best since *The Loom of Youth*. My publishers both in New York and London were enthusiastic. Carol Hill was assuring me that my next batch of short stories would take me out of 'the little magazines'. I foresaw a quiet summer in the country awaiting the birth of my second child. Three solid months at my desk. Three short stories at the least.

* * *

We docked early in the afternoon. I planned to drop my luggage at 20 Abbey Road then go out to have dinner with my parents. The hall porter at Abbey Road said, 'I'm afraid, sir, I've bad news for you. A telegram came through three days ago. Your father-in-law has died.'

That was on a Thursday. Joan was due in Marseilles the following Wednesday. I had planned to go straight down to Villefranche. Four days there by myself would be very pleasant: playing a round of golf with 'Opps', catching the autobus into Nice, strolling along the *Promenade des Anglais*, taking Cecile, my old friend from the Garden Bar, to a coffee and ice cream, gossiping with Germaine. I had foreseen those four days in terms of a cosy nostalgia; I had not imagined that I should have a situation such as this to work into focus. The death of my father-in-law would reorientate my whole existence. As I strolled along the waterfront at Villefranche I realised that I was shortly to be presented with an entirely new set of problems. What was their exact nature to be, I wondered.

I had not to wait long for that answer. Within ten days Joan's lawyers had informed her that her father's entire estate was to be divided between her and her children with her having the use of the children's income, during her lifetime. The income of a certain sum of money had been left to Joan's mother during her lifetime but on her death the capital was to go to Joan.

The details of the will did not surprise Joan. 'I told my father how hard you worked.' Joan said to me. 'He said "He won't have to do that much longer."'

'Did he know that he was ill?' I asked.

Joan shook her head. 'I knew that I should never see him again,' she said.

That was a surprise to me. It was on her mother's account that she had gone out to Melbourne. She had gone with her father every day to see her in hospital. Her mother was indeed very ill. At the end of May a cable warned us that the end was near; the final cable coming three days later. It was then that we got an approximate statement of her father's finances. It was a quarter of a million pounds estate. With what Joan had already that amounted to three hundred thousand. Australian death duties at that time were not confiscatory. In 1934 that was a substantial sum of money.

Joan handed me the letter that contained the news. 'You've fallen on your feet,' she said. I did not like the tone of voice in which she said it. I am a very independent person. I did not intend to cease to be. I *had* fallen on my feet. I recognised that, but I was determined to remain on them on my own terms.

And indeed, on my own terms, things were going very satisfactorily. *The Balliols* was published at the end of May. It was a minor best-seller. It had a large and very complimentary press. It transferred me into a higher category of writer. It did well, too, in America and figured for five weeks in the best-seller list. Later in the summer I had another piece of good news from America. A. D. Peters and I saw each other so frequently, at the Savile, at Lord's and at cricket matches, that he did not need to write to me very often. One morning on a cricket tour in Bath, as we were changing our boots before a game he said, 'Oh, by the way, do you remember that last short story of yours? I can't remember what it was called. Carol tells me that Balmer's bought it. I don't know who Balmer is. I think he's *Red Book*.'

This was my first sale to one of the glossy magazines. I enjoyed the casual undramatic way in which Peters made these announcements. I cannot remember if I told Joan about this. She was pleased for my sake that *The Balliols* was doing well. Her friends wrote to her about it, but the sale of a magazine short story on the other side of the Atlantic could not be expected to interest her very much. To the English generally magazines had little standing: they were considered rather cheap. They were not read in England in the way they were in the USA when the new number of

Cosmopolitan or the *Saturday Evening Post* was an event. To Joan the amount of dollars that *Red Book* paid me can only have seemed chicken feed. She was glad for my sake that my stories were selling well, but it made no difference to her.

I did not indeed talk to her much about my writing. The temptation to talk about one's work at the end of the day to one's companion is very great. When I was travelling with Eldred Curwen through the West Indies, at work on *Hot Countries*, he used to read every evening what I had written during the morning. He was intimately interested in the narrative of our experiences together. It was a great help to me. While I was writing I would often think 'this will make Eldred chuckle'. When I was a boy, my father on Saturday mornings would write his daily article at home. When he had finished he would read it out loud to my mother, and when he was writing his autobiography *One Man's Road* at home he used to read his manuscript to her every evening. 'Do you remember the skipper saying that?' he would say. She regarded it as her job to listen appreciatively. But it bored her. 'I've lived with this book for nine months,' she said as she might have spoken of a long and arduous journey. 'It's what this house is supported by, I would think.' But Joan would not have that source of consolation. It did not matter to her whether I wrote or not. My writing did not add to the family's comfort. It was, as far as my family was concerned, a private hobby.

When I was writing *The Balliols* I was often greatly tempted to read Joan a passage that I liked, but I resisted the temptation. If I once read one passage I should read every passage and I could not run the risk of seeing that she was bored with something that was so important, so supremely important to me. I must keep my writing to myself, as I always had, except *Hot Countries* and my first novel *The Loom of Youth* which I had posted to my father every morning on my way to the parade ground.

I never discussed with Joan how much I was making from my books, articles and short stories. We had had at the start no difficulty in working out a system by which we divided joint expenses. Joan would now take over the rent of Oswalds and the chauffeur's wages, I would be responsible for the cellar. I also made a contribution to the cost of my own upkeep. It was not very much, four pounds a week, I fancy.

'Isn't that rather ridiculous?' Joan said.

'I must be self-supporting, I must keep my self-respect,' I said.

When the chauffeur drove me to the station or the golf course I would buy the petrol. We agreed to postpone the question of London expenses. I felt that London was my province, that parties there would be for my friends and that I should pay for them. If we decided to take a flat in London that would be Joan's responsibility. I saw myself in the position of Joan's manager. 'The great thing,' I said, 'is to plan a budget twenty-five per cent above what we expect to spend, then we shall have spare cash for any extras.' I advised her to place her capital in trustee stock. The warning of the Wall Street crash was acute to me. No dabbling with the Stock Market. 'Let's arrange money so that we don't have to think about it.'

I had fallen upon my feet all right, but I was resolved to maintain my independence and rely on my pen for my own support. I had, in fact, become Alec Waugh again.

CHAPTER 7

The Thirties

It is fashionable nowadays to denigrate the thirties, to speak of them as a period of cowardly appeasement, when sops were flung to the dictators, when the miners were out of work and the more fortunate classes calmed their consciences with the dole. But in point of fact, that is not actually how it was. 'The Thirties' were not one period, they were several periods. There had been two years of depression culminating in the creation of the National Government. There had been a period of recovery when the rise of Hitler had been something that was happening somewhere else. In July 1936 there was the outbreak of the Civil War in Spain with England desperately trying to maintain neutrality. Then there came the definite pre-war period when war had begun to seem unavoidable.

The thirties were four separate periods, and the years 1933-6 were on the whole pleasant ones. Moreover the weather in 1933 and 1934 was wonderful. The sun was so hot that by the end of August the grass round the greens at the Canterbury Golf Club was scorched. Roadhouses round London with swimming pools, like the Ace of Spades, were crowded after dances. It was an agreeable time for me. My second child was expected at the end of July. Joan never came up to London. We had guests down most week-ends. Now that Joan had the company of her baby I did not feel guilty about leaving her alone occasionally.

As on the last two years I went on the MCC Sussex College tour that was based on Brighton. The captain who was retiring at the end of the year asked me if I would take on the management and captaincy of the side in 1935. I said I would be delighted. An Australian XI was in the country. The controversy about body-line bowling had been concluded with a compromise that satisfied the Australians and left England with a greatly weakened side. Jardine was no longer captain and the two Nottingham fast bowlers Voce and Larwood were excluded from the side. Hammond was out of form. There was little doubt that the Ashes would return to Australia at the end of the tour; but there was one great day at Lord's where on a rain-ruined wicket Verity bowled out the Australians twice in a single day.

Myself I played regularly for the Bishopbourne XI with a reasonable measure of success. I played more golf at Princes than I did at Canterbury. But towards the end of the summer I was nearly involved in a car smash that made me decide to give up driving. Coming out of a narrow lane into the main Dover Road I failed to notice a policeman's signal. I was thinking of something else. 'It's no good,' I told myself, 'I'm not safe to drive, sooner or later I'm bound to have a crash.' The chauffeur-gardener would have to do less gardening. Joan shrugged.

'And I was going,' she said, 'to get you such an elegant small car for Christmas.'

One of the most pleasant incidents of the summer was the return of the Hastings. They had been away three years. It was through them that Joan and I had met, and we had not so many friends in common. We were delighted to have them back. They were in high spirits. They had spent a year in Mexico with Diego Riviera. Hastings had studied painting under him. Their political views had been coloured by Riviera's Communism. Hastings had originally been a Liberal. He had moved much further to the left. Cristina had moved even further. The effects of the Depression in America had made them feel that there was something basically wrong with the contemporary structure of capitalist society. While people were starving, fish were being flung back into the sea because they could not be marketed at a profit and in Brazil coffee was being burnt. They had read John Strachey's *Struggle for World Power*. They wanted to know what people in England were feeling about it all. Cristina's eye would blaze as she discussed the situation.

Her mother, the Marchesa Casati, had been one of the most striking women of her generation. Cristina herself was a wild creature of the jungle with dark skin and prominent white teeth. Her excitement was infectious. Hastings was the complete opposite. He was tall, apparently mild in manner but forceful in argument. They were excellent foils to one another. They had expected to find many of their friends in agreement with them. They were disconcerted by the general atmosphere of 'laissez-faire', the readiness to believe that England, as always, would manage to 'muddle through'.

Their ideas were new to me. I have never been political. In the spring when I had read Auden's poetry I had recognised that there was a new spirit in the air. Here there was another aspect of that spirit. I must get in touch with it. The characters in my novels would be susceptible to these currents.

Our new baby, a girl, was born at the end of July. My father wrote to me 'I always longed for a daughter. She will make a great difference to you when you are fifty.' We christened her Veronica.

The fine summer weather continued into the autumn and Joan and I set ourselves to the task of looking for a house. She would have liked to live in Somerset or Devon but I persuaded her that a writer needs to be near enough to London to come up for lunch and get back for dinner. Oxford was as far away as we could go.

In the early autumn Joan bought a car. She wanted a Rolls, but I argued that it would be bad publicity for a novelist to own one. She settled for a 20 Speed Alvis. It was a handsome beast; but unfortunately it developed a wheel wobble at between forty-eight and fifty miles an hour. Within two years we exchanged her for a serviceable Ford V8. In the meantime it was pleasant touring the countryside in a fast low car.

Finally we found a Queen Anne house on the Hampshire–Berkshire borders at Silchester, the site of the Roman city Calleva Attrebatum. It was a two-storied red-brick house. It had been built as a rectory. It had a fine avenue of trees leading up to the front door. Its appearance had not been improved by a late Victorian bow window, but facing south, the new window lightened the library and the main bedroom over it. A one-storey wing had been added to accommodate the dining room, which opened onto an unsightly but very useful concrete loggia that was protected against the wind and made a very good spot for daytime reading. It was the most occupied room in the house and was littered with deck-chairs and children's toys. It was also a useful background for practising tennis shots.

Downstairs in addition to the dining room there were two large sitting rooms. There was a kitchen across a narrow covered passage. There were three big bedrooms and one small. There was a smallish bedroom suite above the loggia. 'This will do as a nursery for the time being,' Joan said. We agreed that we would have to build a larger nursery over the loggia in a couple of years. There were three good sized servants' bedrooms. There were also over what would be the nursery, two very small adjoining bedrooms that the previous occupiers had allocated to two men servants. They had employed a larger staff than we expected to need. They were a wealthy couple, Firth's Stainless Steel, and they had no children.

There were three cottages, one for the gardener, one for the chauffeur, one for the under-gardener.

It was a warm comfortable house that was given a charming irregularity by having been built out of curved beams, the timber of a ship presumably. The landing was not level and the bottoms of the doors had had to be planed so that they could fit. The main drawing room was panelled and the main staircase oaken. Joan had, of course, no furniture in England and I had very little. We looked forward to the furnishing. Joan had very good taste and I knew that she would build up a delightful home for the children and ourselves.

We put ourselves, up to a point, in the hands of Lady Colefax. That was Evelyn's idea. 'It won't cost you very much more, if anything; and you'll be saved the kind of mistakes that are made by decorators who are not used to dealing with persons of quality, and she's very businesslike.'

I do not know what practical experience Evelyn had had of her. I presume she had worked for several of his friends and that he had been down to their houses when she was at work for them. But businesslike she certainly was not. A skilful and indefatigable hostess, she was always taking on a little bit too much. Our house – we proposed to call it Edrington after Joan's home in Australia – was forty or so miles from London, a very convenient distance for Lady Colefax. She could read her morning post, make two or three telephone calls, drive down to Edrington, supervise her workmen there and get back to London quarter of an hour late for luncheon. She had a chauffeur driven Rolls but roads were crowded. There was only one stretch of road near Slough where you could let a car out; it was the only stretch where our Alvis touched over eighty. She always arrived late at Edrington, with no time to deal with all the details that she found there. 'It's no good,' she would say, 'there's too much left over. I'll have to come down tomorrow. No, I can't tomorrow. I have to go to Cambridge. The day after, that'll be what I must do. As it is I'm going to be late for luncheon.'

As a designer she had no central plan. She filled the house with pieces of furniture that she thought might fit in somewhere. Half of them did not and had to be sent back. There were constant slips. The chair covers in the library did not match the curtains because we discovered the curtains, which were lined, had been hung inside out. The drawing room was long, narrow and panelled. Two rooms had been knocked into one. It ran the whole width of the house. Once the front door had been at its far end. The furnishing of this room presented a problem that she was never to solve. In the end we put at its far end a grand piano that we seldom used. We sat at one end of it. In later years we did not use it very much. When we relied on the radio we used to sit there after dinner but we had the television in the library. A creative decorator would have found some solution for the problem presented by the room's narrowness and length. One day I mean to go down and see what the present owners have done.

When we first planned the house I wondered where I was going to do my writing. Had Evelyn been making his home there, his study would have been his first consideration. Both at Stinchcombe and Combe Florey he furnished the best ground floor room with bookshelves that had some handsome bays. He had a fine writing desk. The room was sacrosanct. The children were not allowed to enter it. My mother asked two of them whether they had been inside it. 'No,' they said, 'but we've peeped through the window.'

It was appropriate that it should be so. It was Evelyn's house. It was supported by his pen. It was proper that the pen should be set in the fashion that he preferred. The library has now been dismantled and transported in its entirety to the university library in Austin, Texas. But I was not in that position. It was Joan's house not mine. My pen did not support it.

Eventually we converted into a study the two very small rooms in the roof that had been used by the butler and the footman. The result was low, narrow, on two levels. There were a few bookshelves, there was a wooden shelf running under the window which served as a desk. There was a wicker armchair. It was not a room in which I ever sat when

I was not writing. Once in later years when Joan came and saw me at my desk in a new study in what had been a servant's bedroom, she looked round her thoughtfully. 'You've made yourself very comfortable here,' she said. 'If I'd known you'd have liked a real study I'd have arranged one for you.'

But I had not wanted a real study then, I did not feel deprived. I did not want to impose my presence on the household, to have the children saying, 'Don't make a noise, Pa's working.' Had I at the back of my mind a reluctance to commit myself to Edrington, to become dependent on it? Indeed I was by no means certain that I should find it easy to work at Edrington. I had never worked in any of my flats; I had already had to go away in the October after Veronica's birth. I had wanted to write a long short story and I had left Oswalds for a week and gone to the Grand Hotel at Margate. A year later when I had wanted to start a new novel I had gone to St Malo for a week. In more than one interview, I have said a 'writer has a three-pronged problem. He has to find the material for his books, he has to find the leisure in which to write them and he has somehow to accommodate within that pattern the human beings with whom he is personally involved.'

I am not a domestic person. I have an instinct to remain a sojourner. And in the case of my study in Edrington, I had that one-room flat in Abbey Road.

Joan and I had a number of problems to work out that autumn. We would need some base in London and we decided to take a flat in one of the many blocks that were, on the same pattern as 20 Abbey Road, springing up all over London. We chose the one at 39 Hill Street. We took a three-room flat, knocked two of the rooms into one and got a very modern architect to fit it up with concealed lighting, built-in settees and table. It was a convenient address, it had adjacent to it a small, quite smart club – now destroyed – called Punch's, that made it simple to give small dinner parties. We could have cocktails at the flat, go across to Punch's for dinner, then go back to the flat afterwards for a final drink. There was a restaurant attached to the flat but the meals served upstairs were not satisfactory. They arrived late and often cold. Punch's was much more convenient.

1935 is the only year for which I have kept a day-to-day diary. It fills sixty typewritten pages. It is a factual not personal record. It reads now as a succession of parties. Joan had been in retirement for two years. She needed some fun and so did I. She had also met very few of my friends. In January we gave an evening party at the Savoy. We had 140 guests, with Douglas Byng giving an entertainment. We were not able to move down to Edrington until the middle of May so we took a flat at 39 for the children and our nanny wheeled them in the park. Most days we seemed to have a party of some kind. We had joined the Wentworth Golf Club. It was half-way between Edrington and London and I had imagined that we would play golf together two or three times a week, but it did not work out that way. My enthusiasm for the game was unabated though there was no corresponding improvement in my performances. But Joan never was very keen again. I think during the time when she could not play I had bored her with my talk about it. I had kept silent about my writing because I had not wanted to bore her but I had been less reticent about my golf. Day after day I had described my rounds, hole by hole, stroke by stroke. She was so bored that she had very little impulse to play herself. When we had week-end guests, as often as not she would stay at home; she had, she would say, so many things to do about the house.

I was sorry. I had enjoyed our games together. But I had no difficulty in finding friends at the Savile Club whom I could play with. I spent a good deal of time now at the Savile; I had belonged to the club for twelve years and was beginning to be a fairly senior member. My status had risen as a result of *The Balliols*. Evelyn was a member. He had published *A Handful of Dust* in the preceding year. Its success had sent my own stock up. I was invited to sit on the wine committee.

Wine had now become a hobby.

At Edrington I had a cellar and there is all the difference in the world between keeping a few bottles in a cupboard and surveying a succession of well-stocked bins. I had always taken wine with my meals. I had had preferences. I had maintained that the first duty of a wine was to be red, the second to be Burgundy. I drank vintage port at the Savile. But I had not read much about wine.

It was at this time that the Wine and Food Society was founded under the chairmanship of André Simon. Members were issued with small ivory cards that gave a list of the years in which wines were marked according to their quality from 7 to 0. Vyvyan Holland was one of the members of the committee; A. J. A. Symons, the secretary of the Society, was a member of the Savile Club, and the Savile Club was very much a centre of the Society. A certain amount of mockery was directed at the incessant production of those little ivory cards, there was talk of wine snobs, but through learning about wine our powers of appreciating wine increase. Wine is a friendly hobby; my studies of it greatly added to my enjoyment of the pleasures of the table and twenty years later were to increase my income: I was to write three books on wine.

The sales of *The Balliols* had enabled me to lay down the basis of a cellar. When Edrington was dismantled in 1969, I had still left a few bottles of the Cockburn's 1927 that I ordered then. I had originally ordered my wines from Francis Downman, but its proprietor Ernest Oldmeadow wrote in *The Tablet* of which he was the Editor a violent attack on Catholic grounds of *A Handful of Dust*. I closed my account and moved to Hankey Bannister, who has been my wine merchant ever since.

I had been elected in 1920 to the Sette of Odde Volumes, an eccentric dining club of which Evelyn made fun in *Brideshead Revisited*. I had resigned after a few years. I had found the members rather elderly for my taste, but I now rejoined. In October, Ralph Straus invited me to dinner at the Saintsbury Club which had recently been founded in honour of George Saintsbury. The dinner was held in Bath where Saintsbury lived. It was hoped that he would attend but he declined. In fact there is no reason to believe that he ever took the slightest interest in the club. Straus and Vyvyan Holland stayed the night at Edrington and we motored there. Horace Annesley Vachell was in the chair. It was an impressive occasion. I asked Straus if I could become a member. He expressed doubt. Membership was limited to fifty because that was the maximum number that could sit down to a jeroboam of claret. There were two meetings a year. At the April meeting no guests were allowed. And in October when they were, the gathering was limited to fifty, guests being allotted by ballot. Membership was confined to men of letters and men whose reputation stood high in the wine trade. The original committee consisted of J. C. Squire, André Simon and Ian Campbell. The list of members included Warner Allen, Hilaire Belloc, E. F. Benson, Lord Dawson of Penn, C. B. Cochran, the Duke of Devonshire, P. G. H. Fender, Sir Stephen Gaselee, Maurice Healey, David Low, Compton Mackenzie, Francis Meynell, David Tennant, C. M. Wells, Richard Wyndhams.

Of these only P. G. H. Fender is still alive.

Ralph Straus did not feel I stood much chance of getting in but Vyvyan Holland said, 'What nonsense. I can fix that.' A. J. A. Symons was the secretary and Vyvyan could fix anything where A. J. was concerned. In the following year I was admitted.

In October Lord Moynihan, the surgeon, became President at the Odde Volumes. He asked me if I would be his secretary. The President gave a dinner party for his officers at the Café Royal. My membership of the Savile Club Wine Committee resulted in my joining a number of pleasant dinners after the meetings. The brothers Barlow, Sir Alan and Sir Thomas were constant attendants at these gatherings. I had started travelling in the summer of 1926, and this was the first year since then that I had spent the greater part of my time in London. I greatly appreciated it. London is or was a city for Londoners. Through living in London, your life gets interwoven with innumerable other lives. You are part of a large family.

During 1935 I only made one substantial trip. In February Lord Hastings and I went to Moscow. We arranged a seventeen-day trip through the Intourist Agency. It was a strenuous trip. We provided ourselves with letters of introduction to people like Ivy Litvinoff. We had made contact with VOKS, the Society for Cultural Relations with the USSR. I had called on Ivan Maisky, the Soviet Ambassador. We both acquired a tweed suit of a nondescript grey-brown colour. We travelled second class. It was a long journey. We left Liverpool Street on a Tuesday evening. All Wednesday we were in a train to Berlin which arrived shortly after six, and where we had a five hour wait. We sought a mildly noisy beer-drinking bar. Not finding one we had recourse to a panelled Weinstube which announced itself with a cluster of green glass grapes.

We dined at the Waterland which we had been told not to miss. It was not very appetising. It was rather empty, only the Rheinesalle was crowded. The petting corners were unoccupied. There were no smart men, no pretty girls; the food was adequate, the cabaret was poor. The men who kept moving up and down the stairways looked like the members of an American Trade Convention before the first 'get together'. There was a sprinkling of brown shirts with swastika armlets. No one seemed to be enjoying himself. At the cloakroom they gave us each a card. We wrote our names on it. They tore the card in half across the signature. We were given the odd half.

After nine hours' sleep we woke to the sight of Warsaw through the window of a French Wagon-lit compartment.

For eight hours we crossed a bleak snow-covered land-
scape, reaching the frontier at six o'clock. There we changed
more than trains, we entered a new universe. One end
of the long bare customs' shed was emblazoned with a
fresco of the USSR showing the localities of the new cities;
the other with a mural of peasants harvesting and mine
digging. Round the walls in gold lettering and four tongues
the proletariat of the world was bidden to unite. The
soldiers looked very smart in khaki-grey tunics, Sam
Browne belts, red piping to their collars, red stars in the
centre of their caps. Customs examinations were lengthy
but no interest was taken in alcohol, tobacco, silk, only in
books and foreign currency. To get a porter I had to go
to the Intourist Bureau, ask for an order for a porter,
carry that order to the cashier to whom I paid 2s 7d (about
12½p). I took the receipt to the Bureau which handed a
duplicate copy of the receipt to the porter who was at last
entitled to put his hand upon my suitcase. Tipping is not
allowed in Russia.

On the other side of the customs' shed the Soviet Train
was waiting. It was like a scene out of *Anna Karenina*, the
high train, the snow-caked platform, the station lights
blurred by snowflakes, five or six furred figures stamping
to keep their feet warm, and indeed it must have been for a
very similar train that Vronsky waited on that village
platform; broad-gauged, the compartment heated by a
vast hand-filled stove, red-curtained windows, Victorian
lampshades. Four of us travelled in one compartment.
The couchettes were so narrow that I kept waking with
sore knees. One of the lights did not work and it required
patience and ingenuity to discover the switch of the one
that did.

We fulfilled during our seventeen days the programme
that VOKS prepared for all its clients. We saw a mother and
child exhibition that contrasted the condition of the Soviet
woman with that of her sister in capitalist and feudal
countries, and presented plans for a model nursery. It was

clearly the state's plan to break the influence of the home at the earliest moment. We saw Lenin's tomb, without having a lengthy wait. We were led straight to the head of the queue. The beauty of the Kremlin particularly at night with the red flag floodlit is unmatched. We saw an anti-religious museum, an automobile factory, a youthful prisoners' camp; we saw tennis racquets for export being strung at the rate of two an hour. We saw a park of rest and culture – culture and cleanliness were synonymous. We saw a museum of children's books. We visited the head of the State Publishing Company. He published 200 novels a year of which thirty-nine were best-sellers. The best critics were publishers' readers. We saw a couple of plays and were struck by the way in which the stages were sloped so as to give a sense of depth. The bottoms of the bottles were sliced so that they could stand upon the tables. We went to the ballet, to a couple of cinemas, to the law courts, and the magnificent Petriakov collection of pictures. We saw what the system was and how it was meant to work.

VOKS gave a large reception for us. We had tea with Ivy Litvinoff. The correspondent of the *Daily Telegraph* who had a Russian wife was very helpful. The British Embassy entertained us. Muriel Draper, whom I had met in New York four years before, was there; she seemed to be partially resident, in some semi-official capacity. In 1945 she was in New York employed by VOKS.

At the VOKS reception I sat next to D. S. Mirsky, whom I had not met during his stay in London. He was still confident about 'the great experiment': though it seemed there was a note of nostalgia in his voice when he asked how things were in Bloomsbury. I asked him if Turgenev was read much in Russia now. He shook his head. 'His problems are not our problems; literature has no eternal themes. Russia has evolved a new man who demands new themes.'

I had a similar conversation with Tetriakov, the author of *Roar China*. The family, he said, no longer existed, so no one wrote family novels. Proletarians see through a red glass. They see man as a part of many processes; the straightforward statement of how people feel has ceased to be their problem.

I was struck by how little they knew about Europe and America and about conditions there. Rubenstein of the Kammeny Theatre told me that *Journey's End* could not be acted in Moscow as it was all about officers, and 'of course the private soldier was the hero and victim of the war'.

I had a short talk with Leonov but his French was not fluent. Pilniak, on the other hand, spoke good English. He was the one Russian writer with whom I felt in tune. He asked me to come back to his flat after the VOKS reception, but the VOKS representative proved obstructive.

It was very difficult to see anyone alone. Transport was a problem. We could hire a car from VOKS but then VOKS would know where we were going. 'It would be much easier,' VOKS would say, 'for us to arrange for you to meet them here.'

There were taxis, of course, but we would have to pay them in Russian roubles; we had no Russian currency and the exchange rate at which we could have bought it was prohibitive. We had very little chance of seeing how the Russians themselves lived.

Through the *Daily Telegraph* correspondent we met one bourgeois couple who held no official post. They lived in a small one-room flat that had the use of a communal kitchen and no private bathroom. It was a neatly furnished flat but it was very cramped. It looked as though every article of furniture had to serve two purposes. I noticed that beside a desk there was a rack for toothbrushes. I presume that a basin was put upon the desk when they did their washing. I returned to London with no wish to see a Soviet system established in England.

Ten years later I was to find myself in Russian company again, in very different circumstances. I was serving in Military Intelligence on the Persian–Iraqi border. British and Russian forces divided the command and a Russian detachment was shortly to be relieved at Khanakin. They gave a goodbye party to which they invited three British officers. There were some twenty present including two young sturdy but not very attractive females. I never learnt who they were. The tables were spread with a miscellaneous variety of meats, fishes, salads, cakes, cheeses. There was an equal variety of bottles. No vodka, which I had hoped for, but a good deal of Palestinian wine, the white wine uncooled. There was plenty of beer and brandy.

My glass was constantly refilled. I remembered it was a Russian custom to make guests drunk. There were constant toasts. We toasted Roosevelt and Churchill, Stalin, De Gaulle and a number of Russian generals whose names I never got. There was no avoiding these toasts. I decided to switch to beer, but across the table I noticed that one of my brother officers was having his beer laced with brandy when he looked the other way. I presumed that mine was too. There was nothing to be done but accept the inevitable. It was not a fate worse than death. At the end of the evening when I stepped into the cold air my legs gave way. I fell on my face and was violently sick. I remained there half asleep for what must have been quite a while but at last I got back to my hut.

As a result of having been sick I felt quite well next morning – much better than my companions who had got back to bed on unsteady but obedient legs. Early next morning our hosts came round to see how we were feeling. I think they were not too pleased to find me in such sound shape. That seemed to me a real Russian evening in the tradition of Dostoyevsky. I had no such feeling during my seventeen days in Moscow.

My diary of 1935 is studded with a succession of names that already had been familiar to me in 1934. I did not seem to be breaking new ground. It was a year of consolidation. In retrospect it seems the last good year of the old régime, when one could meet the future with impunity, when one was getting to know old friends better.

I only made one new friend or rather two new friends, for my friendship for Arthur Calder Marshall's wife, Ara, was as warm as it was for him, and it was a delightful friendship. He had been born in 1908. He had been at St Paul's and Hertford College, Oxford. He had already published a number of novels – *Two of a Kind*, *At Sea*, *About Levy* which had been very well reviewed. His last one was a story of school life. He was referred to in most of the articles about the younger school of writing. He was very left-wing; I think he was already a member of the Communist Party. He was very much in the movement. He was not at all aggressive. He was sturdy, clean-shaven with rugged good looks. He had a very beautiful speaking voice. His wife was a year or two younger. She was thin and blonde with hair that fell loose about her ears. She was enchantingly pretty.

I had met him first in the spring of 1934 at a minute cocktail party. He had had very much too much to drink. He did not show it, his behaviour was strictly correct but he grew paler and paler. Eventually he got up, left the room, vomited, returned and continued the conversation as though nothing had happened. I was very impressed by his control of the situation.

When I met him again in the early summer of 1935 with his wife, our feelings of friendship, all three of us, were instantaneous. It was unusual for me to meet a couple so much younger than myself. The success of my first book had moved me into the company of men older than myself. None of my opposite numbers were contemporaries. As I had not gone to a university I had no opportunity of meeting the men of my own generation. My only friends of my own age, with the exception of a few old school friends, were those with whom I played Rugby football. I only saw them on Saturdays and I had given up football in 1927.

For me this friendship with the Calder Marshalls was most stimulating. Through them I began to appreciate how the younger generation were feeling about the political and social events of the day. In the late autumn, they went to stay in Cornwall at Mevagissey. I wanted to get away from Edrington to get some quiet in which to work and our friendship had progressed so far that I went down to stay with them. Our friendship remained very close until in 1950 I made my base in New York. When they came out by chance to Tangier in 1976 we picked up the threads most easily.

Anyone reading my diary with its catalogue of parties, at many of which I record myself as having drunk too much, might well wonder when I managed to do any work. I was, in addition to going to parties, playing a great deal of cricket. I captained the MCC Sussex College tour. Every August I went to Bath for ten days with Clifford Bax's cricket side which was now, after Bax's retirement, captained by A. D. Peters. I joined the Berkshire Gentlemen. J. C. Squire ran his side, the Invalids, and I played for him five or six times a year. I also played regularly for Silchester. But in spite of this I got through a substantial amount of work. I concentrated on short stories and as Carol Hill had prophesied, with considerable success. I devoted a fortnight to each story, and I sold practically every one either to *Red Book* or to *This Week* – the weekly supplement in the *Herald Tribune*.

I was thrilled by it all. There is or was a drama about writing for magazines in the USA that there was not about writing for English magazines. It was not just that one was paid so very much more money – I was getting $750 a story at this time – but the whole atmosphere was dramatic. There were the discussions with editors, either personally or in my case by letter. There was the uncertainty of never knowing whether or not the story would be accepted. A commission to write a story for an American magazine was no more than an encouragement 'to have a shot'. There were suggestions sometimes for a rewriting, though at this time in my case that rarely happened. The very fact of breaking into this foreign market was exciting; not so very many English writers did. Publishers' blurbs would read 'both here and in America' as though they were saying 'both in this world and the next'. I felt like a buccaneer plundering the Spanish Main. It was a proud moment when my name was for the first time printed on a *Red Book* cover. Then in the middle of the summer came the suggestion that I should write a novelette for the Christmas number. A novelette was around 15,000 words and I should be paid £1,500 for it. I devised a plot which would involve a New Year's party at the Savoy. *Red Book* wanted me to choose English and European backgrounds, with which fashionable and would-be-fashionable Americans would be familiar.

Most of the stories I wrote in 1935 appeared in a volume published by Cassells entitled *Eight Short Stories*. In addition to these stories I began a novel that was published the following autumn, called *Jill Somerset*. Every writer is warned not to attempt to follow up a success with a similar kind of book. I have made this mistake three times. In 1926 I followed a novel about post-war fashionable London called *Kept*, with a book *Love in These Days* which was a pale echo of it. In 1960 I followed *Island in the Sun* with a long story *Fuel for the Flame* set in the Far East. I now tried to follow up *The Balliols* with another family chronicle.

The Balliols had told the story of a family from the years 1907 to 1922. I planned that *Jill Somerset* should tell the story of 1913 to 1932. I made the central male character a conscientious objector. I tried to show how a man who was anxious to enlist in 1914 but was refused on medical grounds became by 1916 a pacifist believing that the war was being carried on longer than was necessary, for imperial reasons. When he is called up, with lower standards of fitness then required, he refuses to serve on conscientious grounds and is sent to prison.

It was a story of three sisters. The first part of the book, the part that dealt with the war, was pretty good, but in the end it petered out. It did not do badly, though not as well as *The Balliols*. I began it in early summer and to start it I went away for a week to St Malo. I could not concentrate when I was surrounded by the bustle of home. Later in the year when I wanted to have a second try at it, I went down to Cornwall to stay with the Calder Marshalls. I have always gone away to write. I had to be in an atmosphere which imposed no personal strain on me. I wonder if this was partly the result of the English boarding school system under which a boy is trained to work away from home.

In spite of this succession of short stories and the beginning of a novel, I wondered whether writing was a full-time occupation. At first, after the war I had had a half-time job with Chapman and Hall and then I had been travelling which had been in itself an occupation, involving me in a good deal of work studying the history and the customs of the places and people I was visiting. I spent most mornings in the local library. I had no such secondary occupation now. I wondered if I should not take on some alternative activity, some unpaid social work. I asked the advice of Sir Arthur Willert. He suggested that I should enroll at Chatham House, an organisation housed in St James's Square, that had no party connections and devoted itself to examination of various aspects of the contemporary scene. It had a number of study groups. I was put in charge of a group that examined the types of history textbooks that were sold in various countries. There were several students and members of Chatham House attached to the group, who did a great deal of research and provided the material out of which I prepared a paper which I delivered to an evening meeting of the House and my paper was printed in the organisation's monthly periodical. It was all quite enjoyable and served, I suppose, some purpose. At any rate it calmed my conscience.

CHAPTER 8

Donita

During this year I was kept busy with the day-to-day chores of moving into Edrington but all the time I was planning a return to New York. I had asked Colston Leigh to arrange a lecture tour in January and February. In October he wrote to say that he had made very few bookings for me, and that if I did not think it worth while to come across, he would release me from my contract. But I said, 'No, I would like to come.' The tour was an alibi, a commitment; if some domestic reason arose for my staying on in England, I could say, 'Alas I've got this lecture tour. I can't get out of that.'

I left on the 30th December by the *Washington*, an eight-day ship which along with its sister ship the *Manhattan* was very popular with those who did not want to hurry. There was always an amusing crowd on board. This time there was Lois Tredegar, Webb Miller the American correspondent, Eddie Tatham of Justerini and Brooks, and Norman Webb of the Easton Court Hotel. Mrs Cobb had given me strict instructions to keep an eye on Norman and see that he did not drink too much. We sat at the same table with Lois Tredegar and I saw to it that he drank wine at meals, rather than spirits.

West-bound journeys seem longer always because the clock is going back. I am an early riser. I had planned to get a good deal of writing done, and by lunchtime my daily stint was finished. I wanted to have my novel at least half finished by the time we docked. I was anxious to have something tangible to show the editors of *Red Book*.

I lunched with them on arrival. They were a curious couple; the Editor, Edwin Balmer, was tall, in late middle age, he was a little inarticulate and his lips had a curious ill adjustment that forced one to listen very carefully. He was one of the great editors of his day. His father had been an Englishman and he was very pro-English. He had written a good deal under his own signature for magazines. He had never, I think, had a hard-cover best-seller; not many of his books had indeed been published in hard covers, but he was a trusted serial writer.

The sub-Editor, Voldemar Vetlugin, could not have been more different. He was a Russian, short, slightly stout with a European accent. He was a man of great unconventional charm. He was completely foreign, by which I mean that he would have seemed equally foreign in England, France, Germany and even in his native Russia. He seemed highly intelligent. He had written a number of articles under the pseudonym of Frederick van Ryan.

They were an incongruous couple like conspirators in a Restoration comedy. Balmer used to tease Vetlugin. 'This Russian here,' he would say. They clearly liked Carol Hill, a lot. I felt myself in congenial company. The only difficulty was that Balmer was exceedingly abstemious. He was a one-drink man, usually a rather unusual drink, Madeira or sweet sherry. 'I suppose you'd like something like a Martini?' he said to me.

'I'd like an Old Fashioned if I could,' I said.

'You could,' he answered.

They were very flattering about my work. 'You can give us something that no one else can,' Vetlugin said. 'You write dramatic, romantic stories; a number of writers can give us that – Phil Wylie, Katherine Brush and Nancy Hale – but not against European backgrounds. Now tell us about this novel of yours.'

I told them about my novel. I told them that the hero was a first-war conscientious objector. I had not expected that that would interest them, but to my surprise Vetlugin looked across the table to Balmer with an enquiring glance. 'Isn't that what we were talking about the other day, about whether young people would refuse to fight if there was another war?'

Balmer nodded. 'We'd like to see as much of that manuscript as you've got,' he said.

I had once again that sense of having all my batteries recharged.

It was one of the best months of my life. It was two years since I had been in New York and a number of parties were given for me. I gave several myself. I had a substantial bank balance. I enjoyed entertaining and it was a relief to be able to ask exactly whom I liked to my own parties. In England I had to consider how they would go down with Joan. American hospitality is lavish and openhearted, but I was resolved to make my own contribution to the conviviality. English visitors during the twenties had got themselves a bad reputation with their readiness not only to accept hospitality but the frequency with which they ran up bills and left them for their hosts to settle. On my first trip across the Continent I had read in *Harpers' Bazaar* a story by Charles Hanson Towne called 'Much Adieu About Nothing', which made fun of the bad behaviour of a visiting English lecturer. I took the moral of that story to heart. No one was going to say that I was slow about picking up a check. I felt that I owed it to my country's reputation to be as ready as any American to throw a party. Party followed upon party. I was relieved that Colston Leigh had been able to arrange only six lectures for me. I did not want to be taken away from New York.

One of my lectures was in Montreal. When I got into the train the newspapers were headlined with the bulletin of George V's final illness. 'The King's life was moving peacefully towards its close.' When I arrived at Montreal next morning I learnt that he had died. I wondered if they would cancel the lecture. I presumed they would not. I should have to open my lecture with a tribute to what he had stood for. It was very cold, too cold to walk in the streets even with earflaps to my hat. I spent the morning in a hotel reading John O'Hara's *Butterfield 8*, of which I had found a copy at the bookstall.

In the audience I was surprised to find my cousin Claud Cockburn's sister Louise, who had been one of the brides-maids at my first marriage. I had not seen her for fourteen years. I had no idea that she had married a Canadian and settled in Montreal. I went back to her flat after the lecture for drinks and a sandwich before I caught my train. We had been good friends in my army days when I had been stationed with the Inns of Court OTC at Berkhamsted. We had a very cosy family gossip. It is sad that one sees so seldom some of the people one is closest to. I was only to see her once again, twenty-four years later, when by a coincidence I was lecturing in Chicago and she was in the audience. Her daughter Elizabeth married Ezra Pound's son Omar. He came to Tangier in the 1960s to run the American School. It pleases me that I have a blood relationship with Ezra Pound's grandchildren.

I had another cousin, Sir Edmund Gosse's granddaughter Helen, on the western side of the Atlantic. She rang me up on my second morning. 'I'm in trouble, I need your help,' she said. I had an idea as to the nature of the trouble. She was a tall, handsome and dynamic creature in her middle twenties. An early marriage had gone wrong, and she was in love with the Editor of the *News Chronicle*, Aylmer Vallance. Through his influence, she had become fiction editor of that paper, her chief job being to find and edit the five-day serial in which it specialised. Aylmer was married to one of Helen's best friends, an ex-girlfriend of Clifford Bax's. The affair had been active for a year, and most of their mutual friends believed that it would soon end. That, however, was not Helen's idea. She wanted to marry Vallance and when the *News Chronicle* sent him to New York on a tour of duty, she decided to follow him. This caused a considerable scandal in London. The *News Chronicle* was a left-wing paper of a rather sanctimonious nature. Its funds came from cocoa and it expected the senior members of its staff to set a decorous example. I was not surprised that she was feeling herself in trouble in New York. She was a dramatic person, very self-absorbed. She assumed that everyone was as interested in her concerns as she was. She talked a great deal, mostly about herself, but she had many devoted friends, of whom I was one.

Her voice on the telephone was vibrant with agitation. 'I've got to see you, I've got to explain everything. When can I see you?'

As was to be expected, I on my second morning in New York was extremely busy, but I glimpsed a loophole. 'I'm going to a very small cocktail party this evening. They are people I think you'd like. If you come round here at half-past five you could tell me what's on your mind, then we could go to it together.'

'That's fine, that's very fine. I've so much to tell you, the trouble, you see, is this . . .'

'Do you think you could let that wait until this evening? I've got to go out now.'

'You have? Well I suppose in that case you can't wait. The chief point's this . . .'

'This evening, Helen, please, this evening.'

At half-past five I learnt what her problem was. The management of her hotel would not let Aylmer visit her in her room.

'That's easily solved,' I said; 'take a suite. If you do that you are forgiven anything. You can say you are discussing literature until dawn.'

'You can, oh well, that's fine.'

She was a little deflated at having been given so simple a solution for her problem, but that was only one of her problems. She was feeling lost here. This was her first visit to New York. She hardly knew anyone as yet. Aylmer was very busy. He had *News Chronicle* obligations. He had to go here and there. He had to meet this and that person. He could not always take her with him. 'He's often engaged in the evenings, and the paper isn't happy about it all, about him and me I mean. They sent him over here to get him away from me. They are not pleased at all at my coming out. I'll probably find myself sacked when I get back. In the meantime I just sit and brood.'

'Perhaps the party tonight will be a help.'

The party to which I was taking her was being given by Donna Ferguson, a divorced socialite on the edge of fifty whom I had met in 1930. We had become good friends, and I always saw her when I was over. We usually went to a show together. She had a daughter called Donita who was at Vassar and was very pretty.

'I think you'll like her,' I told Helen.

Donita was not there when we arrived. 'She'll be here in a few minutes,' her mother said. 'She doesn't live here any more. She's got a flat of her own, you know.'

I didn't know.

'Oh yes, she's left Vassar,' her mother said; 'she's a freelance copy writer.'

Left Vassar. But of course she would, it was two years since I had seen her. She had been only nineteen when I had met her first, but that was five years ago.

When she did arrive she made quite an entrance; she was laden with magazines and had a bulging brief-case.

'I never thought I'd make it, the things that kept coming in at the last moment.' But she did not start a recital of the various things that had kept coming in. She sat next to Helen and began asking questions. What she was doing, how long she was over for, how she was liking it? Within two minutes we were being regaled with a continuation of the saga to which I had been listening at the Algonquin.

'Alec tells me I should get myself a suite,' she said, 'but that would cost the earth. How could I afford a suite?'

'Why not come down and stay with me? You can pay me five dollars a day; I could use them.'

Donita had changed a lot in these two years; she had

seemed years younger than me then, a member of a different generation, now we seemed contemporaries. 'Why don't you both have lunch with me tomorrow?' I suggested. 'Then you could talk it over.' That would be a fine idea, they said. 'The Algonquin then at twelve forty-five.'

But at half-past eleven Helen rang up to say there were complications. There were always complications where Helen was concerned. She could not manage lunch, no not possibly, but she could join us afterwards. 'I could get to you by two.'

'That would be all right,' I said.

'So you've got me all to yourself for an hour,' I told Donita. 'I hope you don't mind that.'

'I don't.'

She was wearing an extra elegant side-tilted hat. I was astonished at how at ease with her I felt.

'I'm beginning to feel glad that Helen couldn't make it,' I was saying half an hour later.

'I was hoping you'd be thinking that,' she said. 'I was wondering if you would. Will it be any different this time, I thought. You never noticed me before.'

'Come now.'

'No, it's true, I was a school-girl when you met me first. You went on thinking of me as being that. I wondered if you would realise that I was grown up.' Now she was twenty-four. That was grown up all right.

'Wasn't there a young man around two years ago?' I asked.

'There was.'

'Is he still around?'

'He is and isn't.'

'What am I to take that to mean?'

'Oh, you know. If one doesn't get married right away, or nearly right away, the gilt gets off the gingerbread. One day last fall he asked me to dinner at his flat. He'd cook me steak, he said. It was a hot night. He took off his coat to cook it. He sat down to dinner with his coat still off.'

She'd had an affair with him, I presumed. This was forty

years ago. I still hadn't quite got used to the idea of girls like that having affairs; though they did in my novels.

She told me about her work as a freelance copy writer. 'I'm a jack of all trades. I've an office of my own. I get around. Everything is booming now. It's not like three years ago. It's easy to pick up this and that. There's a new paper going to start, the *New York Woman*. I'm hoping to find something there. By the way your friend Alan Rinehart's on the board.'

'Do you know him?' I asked.

'No.'

'He's coming round for a cocktail tomorrow evening; why don't you join us?'

'That's an idea.'

By the time Helen arrived I was feeling that I had known Donita a long time. I was entranced by her.

On the following evening I introduced her to Alan Rinehart. It was a great success. Alan was younger than myself. He was very good-looking, his marriage was reported to be on the rocks; at any rate he was going out to parties without his wife. Why didn't we both lunch with him next day, he asked.

That was how it started. In a city like New York and probably it is true of Paris though I would not know – it is not true of London – if you once start going around with a person you find yourself going around with her all the time. The fact that Helen was now living with her increased the tempo. Helen had, naturally, found that she had friends of her own in New York. These friends gave parties for Helen and her hostess. I was included.

When and how the question of Miami arose I cannot remember now. Something to do with Philip Wylie, probably. On my previous visit I had made good friends with him and his wife Sally. I had been disappointed at not finding them in New York. 'I'm toying with the idea of going down to see them,' I may have said.

'I envy you. I've always wanted to see Miami.'

'Why not come along then?'

That's how it may well have been. At any rate we soon found ourselves talking of a trip there as a possibility. Helen had already gone down there with Aylmer. They had gone by train, by the orange blossom honeymoon express.

'But you can get there by plane inside a day,' Donita told me.

Lengthy travel by air was just coming into fashion. I had hardly been by air at all. In May 1930 I had flown to California. In those days you only flew by day, travelling by train during the night. I had boarded an afternoon train in New York at four o'clock on a Sunday afternoon. I was due to leave it at Columbus, next morning at six. But weather conditions there were bad. We went on by train all day till we reached St Louis, where we were to catch a plane next morning. I eventually reached Los Angeles on the Thursday evening. It was not an experiment I was anxious to repeat. This would be quite different. It would be exciting to wake up in icebound New York – 1936 was a desperately hard winter – and have dinner out of doors, under the stars. 'Moon over Miami.'

We began to talk of it as a settled thing. Where should we stay?

I asked Carol's advice. 'The Roney Plaza is the place for you. Garish but opulent. You'd better book right away, it's very crowded now. Two rooms and a sitting room I suppose.' Carol was adroit at fixing things. Within two hours we were booked. 'Our address will be the Roney Plaza,' I told Donita.

'But I'll tell Mother that we're house guests of the Wylies.' She still had to maintain appearances at home.

And so suddenly there it was, and I was calling for her at eight-thirty on a Saturday morning.

This is the most astonishing performance of my life, I told myself. We had not discussed the situation, we had not made love, we had not even kissed, but we assumed we were starting on a honeymoon.

I can remember few details of the trip. The aircraft seemed quite large to me then, but I do not suppose there could have been as many as twenty passengers aboard. There was no steward in uniform, only one official in a civilian suit. I cannot remember if he served us sandwiches. We made four or five halts. There was no bar on board. I had brought a hip flask with me. The official, who was very cordial and polite, warned me to be careful in my use of it. 'I should hate to have to put you off the plane,' he said.

We arrived around six o'clock. Miami from the air presented itself as a discordant blending of incongruous colours. A large dome changed from green to blue to red to yellow in a succession of thirty-second spasms. The Roney Plaza would have seemed strident in Piccadilly but here it seemed an example of conservative good taste. Our suite in red and gold looked as though it had been redecorated the week before, but all the same it managed to be cosy.

The Wylies were coming for dinner at eight o'clock. I had warned them that we were supposed to be staying in their villa, and that they might expect mail and cables. I presented Donita as 'your house guest'; 'We'll do our best to make her comfortable,' Sally said.

Wylie's reputation as a novelist was at the moment high and rising. His biggest success *Generations of Vipers* with its attack on Mormonism was to come eight years later. He was a prolific writer for the magazines: he frequently appeared in *Red Book* and had collaborated with Edwin Balmer in several stories. He was tall, slim, good-looking. He was a keen fisherman and was producing a series of fishing stories for the *Saturday Evening Post*. His wife Sally was tall and blonde and beautiful. They were excellent company. Their marriage was to break within two years but they were on good terms with one another. It was to be an unacrimonious divorce. There was no taking of sides among their friends.

We dined on a terrace in the open. It was hard to believe that that morning we had been shivering in New York.

It was after one before the Wylies left us. 'We'll call for you at eleven tomorrow morning,' Sally said. 'We've got a cabana at the pool; we usually lunch there.'

We waved them off. 'Do you feel like another drink?' I asked.

'Not really, unless you do.'

We looked at one another. I remembered Balzac's dictum in the *Psychology of Marriage*. Everything depends on the first night.

I tapped on her door. 'Come in.'

She was sitting up in bed, wearing a pink-striped silk dressing gown. 'You look adorable,' I said.

'I'm afraid that I've a disappointment for you.'

'You have?'

'You've read *Appointment in Samarra*, haven't you?'

'Of course.'

'Do you remember that bit about the days when the heroine was taken off the swimming list at college?'

'I do.'

'That's the disappointment.'

It was a disappointment but also it was a reprieve. It gave us three days to get to know one another. By the Tuesday night I was in love.

The next week was as perfect as anything I have known. The sun shone steadily. There was no wind. Most mornings we idled at the pool. I did all my swimming in the pool. The sea beyond the sand looked turbulent. I suspected it might be cold. One morning Phil said, 'Do you see that particularly blue strip of sea out there?'

'Yes.'

'Do you know what it is?'

'No.'

'It's the Gulf Stream. Just think how easy it would be if we went to war with Britain to cut off that stream with an electric current. You'd all freeze to death in your thin unheated houses. Tell your compatriots that when you get back. Advise them to be cautious.'

It was hard to know when he was being serious. He was an early experimenter with science fiction. In 1940 he collaborated with Edwin Balmer in a story about an atomic bomb. The publication was delayed until 1944. The Pentagon was worried. They thought there was a dangerous leakage. High-powered officers called on *Red Book*. It was difficult for Phil and Balmer to convince them of their innocence. 'Somebody must have told you something,' they insisted. Balmer and Wylie shook their heads. They had assumed that sooner or later someone would tumble on that idea.

Several of Wylie's friends would join us at the pool. There was Hervey Allen, benign scholarly type of man, bearing with modesty the mantle of 'Anthony Adverse'. Du Bose Heyward was also there. He is known today exclusively on account of *Porgy* but he wrote a number of sensitive and poetic books that were just not robust enough to survive the stream of change.

One day we went sail fishing. At least Wylie and Donita did. I get seasick in small boats. I preferred to drive down to Key Largo later with Sally and her daughter Karen. I was glad I had. Donita had been seasick quite a lot and had also got uncomfortably sunburnt. 'It'll be something to talk about,' she said, 'but I shan't want to go out again.'

That evening we went pronging. The very first spear I threw pierced a substantial fish. I was surprised by the shout of acclaim that greeted my achievement. I thought it was the kind of thing you brought off once in four. I did not realise that for a first-timer it was equivalent to doing a hole in one. In his book *The Big Ones Got Away* Wylie had a story about an untutored Englishman who performed with unexpected success at one of the Keys.

Most days the Wylies or the Wylie-friends devised some form of entertainment. Donita with her prettiness, smartness and enthusiasm added considerably to the enjoyment of the parties. I was very proud of her. And then as a final gift of providence I received from Carol Hill one of the most dramatic cables of my career. *Red Book*, it said, had bought my new novel as a 50,000 word one-shot. It had also commissioned the synopsis for a new novelette and two short stories. Hilaire Belloc wrote of that dream of all of us, 'the return of lost loves and great wads of unexpected wealth'. This was a modification of that formula. I had spent on this trip nearly all the money that I had saved during the preceding year, but this cable ensured that if I worked hard during the next few months I should be able to get back to America in the summer.

On the voyage back to England, I wrote the first of the two short stories. I was to find that a trip on an eight-day boat provided the right length of time for a short story. I had no distractions; the day-to-day eventlessness of shipboard life provides the ideal condition for concentrated creative work.

I now needed a suitable, not exactly excuse, but reason for a return within six months. The equivalent of a lecture tour or the publication of a book. A little thought provided one. Why not go over on the *Hindenburg*? Vetlugin had advised me to find romantic and unusual European settings for my stories, a setting that would illustrate well, a background in which American readers would be interested. Ascot for example, the Oxford and Cambridge boat race, the Eton and Harrow cricket match. 'Give us something that our own writers can't.'

The *Hindenburg* was just the thing. I devised a plot in which a husband and wife quarrelled, on a trip in London. She caught the *Normandie* for New York. He would take the *Hindenburg* and be there waiting on the docks to greet her.

I made enquiries in London and found that there was a flight in late July. That would meet my purpose. No one would ordinarily choose to be in New York in the summer, but it would be easy to find convincing reasons for crossing on the *Hindenburg*. I needed to get authentic details of life aboard an airship.

I once told an interviewer that the best condition for a writer was to be in love, separated from his loved one, knowing that he had to finish a novel before he was in a financial position to rejoin her.

That was how it was for me during the next five months. I cannot remember anything that happened. I kept no diary that year, only made entries in a pocket diary. There are very few entries during that five months. I must have been going to a certain number of parties but there is no record of them.

Only one occasion I remember vividly, for melancholy and nostalgic reasons. An old school friend, Malcolm Somerset, gave a dinner party for me at the Savile Club to wish me good luck on my trip to America. A week before I left I had a cable from Sally Wylie telling me that Philip and his brother Ted would be in London on the day for which Somerset's party had been fixed. They were leaving the next day for Russia. I had to do something for them. 'Could I bring them to the party?' I asked Somerset.

'Of course, of course, my dear boy, of course.'

I spent nearly the whole day with them. A touring Indian cricket eleven was playing the minor counties at Lord's. I took them to it. They were suitably impressed but they did not want to stay very long. 'What about the Zoo? What about Madame Tussaud's?' they said. They had heard so much about the Chamber of Horrors.

Somerset's dinner party was a great success. The Savile did that kind of thing very well. I say I remember it with melancholy nostalgia because it was for the Wylies the prelude to a tragic trip from which Phil never completely recovered. Somehow I have never found out exactly how they got in wrong with the Russians. Ted fell out of his bedroom window and Phil was certain that he was pushed. Then on the way back Phil's railway carriage got disconnected into a siding. For twenty-four hours he was abandoned there, in heavy heat with only tainted water. He returned to Europe in a state of near collapse. Sally had to come across to Paris to nurse him back to health. The experience left him with a profound distrust of the Soviet Union that coloured a great deal of his writing.

The *Hindenburg* provided me with the material for quite a sound magazine short story. Luckily *Red Book* in New York and *Strand* in London published it during March so that it managed to be topical. When I included it in a collection of short stories which I published in England in the autumn of 1937, I gave it the title 'It Happened in 1936', as one might twenty-three years earlier have entitled a story 'It Happened in May 1914'.

The passage in which I described the voyage makes curious reading today.

'Late on the Friday afternoon,' the story goes, 'the *Hindenburg* rose slowly from its moorings. His fingers clenched and unclenched nervously as he gazed down through the slanted windows of the lounge at the pine forests that encircled Frankfurt.' (I had had to fly to Frankfurt to catch the airship.) 'He was not nervous for any of the obvious reasons. He had no fear that this vast airship would be destroyed by gale or tempest. He had never felt safer in his life. There was no noise, no vibration, no movement of any kind. The ground seemed only a few feet below him. He could pick out landmark after landmark. He could see cars moving along a road, faces looking up from gardens. As they passed over a chicken farm, the fowl in a frenzy of terror dashed from side to side of their wide pens, suspecting that some vast hawk was hovering over them preparing to swoop down. As they flew over Cologne he could recognise the Nazi standards fluttering from roof and turret. He did not feel that he was in the air at all. He felt that he was in some gigantic yacht moving down the smooth waters of a canal, with the land stretching wide and far on either side of him. It was no fear of personal safety that clenched and unclenched his fingers. It was another fear. The *Normandie* had sailed on Wednesday, it would dock on Monday, early on Monday morning. It was now late on the Friday afternoon. Would or would not the *Hindenburg* get him to New York on time?'

It was exciting to be travelling on the *Hindenburg*. I looked forward to talking about it afterwards, but I cannot say that I enjoyed it. There was nothing to do on board and the accommodation was very crowded. My cabin was minute and I shared it with another passenger. There were two main lounges, one a dining room, the other partitioned into a music room and writing room. There were only six armchairs. There was a small bar downstairs which was the only place in the ship where one could smoke. I am a nonsmoker so I did not feel deprived. But there were so many passengers who did want to smoke that I did not feel justified in occupying a seat unless I was actually drinking. One passenger, a chain-smoker who had to consume two short drinks an hour, was in bad condition by dinner time. The promenade deck was short and very narrow. There was scarcely room to pass the passengers who were standing by the slanting windows. There was nothing for them to look at but the sea. Unless one had the luck to find one of the chairs in the drawing room free there was no alternative to reading on a narrow chair in the dining room, and waiting for the next meal with the clock every five hours going back half an hour. The only official entertainment late in the first afternoon was a tour of the ship down the long narrow backbone, 'the cat walk' that, running from one end to the other of the ship, supported the vast network of stays and girders, along which the crews' and officers' quarters were ingeniously concealed. The meals were heavy and Germanic for which, without exercise, I had little appetite. I felt uncomfortably gorged.

Those two days were as long in their passing as any I have known. Once travel by aircraft had been established I cannot believe that the airship would have attracted many passengers. One only saved three days. In the following summer, several Britons who had seats for the Coronation thought it would be chic to return for it by the *Hindenburg* so that they could remark casually during the procession 'on Saturday in New York'. They saw the ceremony on the screen.

Donita was waiting for me at Lakehurst. We had no plans apart from an invitation to spend a week-end with the Brandts. But as I have said earlier I learnt at the Algonquin that Carol had been forced to return to England on Vincent Sheean's account. I had left New York before she returned. There was at that time no air-conditioning in the Algonquin. I cannot remember there being any anywhere in New York. Families went into the country with exhausted fathers and husbands catching a train down on Friday afternoons. Everyone grumbled about the heat but New York had a special charm of its own then that it now has lost. You sought cool balconies. There was talk of 'summer wives', of the girls who had to stay in offices and felt abandoned over the week-ends. Today New York is far too cold in the summer. You get hot and damp in the streets, then you go into a refrigerated restaurant and catch a cold. You have to carry a pullover. I preferred it the way it was.

I spent three weeks in America. I was due back in early August for A. D. Peters' cricket tour in Bath. I spent most of the time at the Atlantic Beach Club. It was delightful there. Friends came out from the city in the evenings. Vetlugin came out twice accompanied by a 'summer wife'. We talked intermittent shop. In the middle of our political discussion – there was to be an election in November – he would suddenly interject 'What about a story about an American girl married to an English peer who . . .' I went back to England with half a dozen sketches in my portfolio.

It was an idyllic time. It was Miami all over again. It was better than Miami, in many ways. Donita and I knew each other so much better. We had more in common. We were better friends, and yet, and yet, there was a feeling, a doubt, a question, 'what next?' I'd ask myself.

Nothing stays static, there has to be progression or retreat. What was this leading to? In Miami when we had talked about my next visit, there had been the unspoken underthought 'Come back in July then we'll be able to see what all this is about.' Well here we were in July and what was it all about?

We were having a fine time. We promised ourselves another fine time in January, perhaps in the West Indies. Then in January would we find ourselves planning for another meeting in July, on the French Riviera maybe? One playground after another; was that to be the pattern? A month or so together then my going away to write the stories that would support each new playground. Was that how it was to be? It was fine by me. Was it fine by her? She had her own life, her own career. She was writing weekly articles for the *New York Woman*. Soon another paper would recognise her talent. She had a genuine flair for the personal interview. She was at the start of her career. Soon she would be an editor, soon . . .

Sitting in front of our cabana at the Atlantic Beach Club we planned out our future hopefully. There was ample reason to be confident. This was so fine; this was so very fine, why worry when it was so fine. And yet . . . and yet . . . there was that niggling question, never put into words, at the base of both our minds. 'What next?'

It was while I was at Atlantic Beach that Franco's Moroccan troops landed in southern Spain. The news did not seem to be of any immediate or personal importance. It was happening a long way off. It seemed of very little moment compared with the news of Edward VIII's holiday in Venice with Mrs Simpson, of which the American papers were full and of which no news had yet appeared in England. Even in England the significance of the invasion was only recognised by a few close watchers of the omens. Spain had always lain outside the radius of English interests.

For me at Edrington the autumn of 1936 proceeded at

what had come to be seen as its habitual pace. Joan had decided to build a nursery by adding a storey to the wing over the dining room. As that would take two months we closed Edrington and rented a house in Cambridge Square. It was very comfortable with ample nursery space. We let our flat in Hill Street but I maintained my perch in Abbey Road. There was a study in Cambridge Square but I always found it hard to work in the house where I was living, so every morning after breakfast I took a bus up the Edgware Road like any 'city slicker' going to his office. I was working very hard. I had sent *Red Book* a synopsis for a 50,000 word one-shot which I planned to have finished before Christmas.

We had a varied and amusing time in London. We saw friends, we went to shows, we entertained and were entertained. It was, as it proved, the one time when we lived a conventional domestic life in London, a part of London's life. I wish we could have done it oftener. London was where I belonged but Joan would never have enjoyed a life without the children; she needed a garden for herself and them. Even though she was having a good time in London, she counted the days until the building at Edrington was finished. She was a wonderful mother to them, they were a great happiness to her. Once she was to say, 'I suppose I ought to go on some of your trips with you, but I don't want to miss any of their childhood. They are little such a little while.' But for me those two months in London were the only two when I led the kind of life that six years ago I had pictured myself leading as a married man.

By now everyone was talking about Mrs Simpson. How long would this pretence of secrecy be maintained, with references to the scandal in the American press being cut out of papers before they were put upon the British bookstalls? One American paper had a cartoon of a crusty English Tory reading a copy of *Time* from which half a page had been excised. The caption ran 'Our King is having a ripping time'.

When the story finally broke it was hard to believe that it was really happening; it was even more difficult to know what was happening. It seemed at one point as though a solution would be found. One night the *Daily Express* published a late-night issue headed 'Crisis ended' and its issue next morning showed photographs of the paper being read in London night-clubs. But the tragedy pursued its course to the inevitable climax.

In retrospect it is possible to see the whole thing as a piece of great good luck for the country. But to very many it was a great, great shock. We had all our adult lives looked forward to Edward's reign. He would stand for youth, for the new ideas, a counterblast to the hidebound reactionists. We had been prepared to follow him with unquestioning loyalty. We could never feel in that way about his brother. The Scottish children in the streets were singing 'Hark the Herald Angels Sing, Mrs Simpson's pinched our King'.

And all the time the concern about the Spanish war was mounting. For instance, Helen Gosse was saying, 'The King shouldn't have had a scandal at a time when the country ought to be united against Franco.' I thought that a silly thing to say, and I still think it was. But it was the kind of thing that people were saying then. Opposing sides were taken as violently as they were to be twenty years later in America about McCarthy. Families were divided and young men were joining the International Brigade in the same spirit of crusade as their fathers had enlisted in 1914. Men like John Cornford were dying as Julian Grenfell had.

America was later to devise the label 'premature anti-Fascists', and it seemed to me that many of the supporters of the Loyalists were active, not so much for the sake of Spain's welfare but as a weapon against the English Establishment. Writers are usually left-wing and when Nancy Cunard conducted a symposium among writers as to whether they were pro-Franco, anti-Franco or neutral, the vast majority were anti-Franco. Of those who were pro-

Franco I can remember only Geoffrey Moss. There were only six neutrals, of whom Evelyn and I were two.

I could not see that the Spanish Civil War was any concern of England's. I could see no reason for regarding the Spanish Government as sacrosanct. For over a hundred years Spanish history had recorded a succession of revolutions, *coups d'état* and *pronunciamientos*. The government that Franco had attempted to overthrow was no more the sacred expression of the people's will than any of its predecessors. If Franco had not intervened, the moderates would have been soon out of office and a Communist minority would have taken over. What I had seen in Russia had not made me enthuse over a Communist dictatorship. I would as soon live under Mussolini as under Stalin. My absorption in the American scene prevented me from identifying myself with either Spanish party. What F.D.R. was doing in Washington was to me so much more interesting and important. The slogans of the hour seemed to be misleading. Unite against Fascism and war, indeed. Why should Fascism be identified with war? Why should an Englishman have to take sides in a Spanish quarrel?

I had expected the autumn of 1936 to be as exciting as the spring had been. In a sense, it should have been under the same basic situation, with myself working on the *Red Book* stories that would finance my return to New York. I did not like being on the side line. The Hastings were active raising funds for the Spanish prisoners of war. They had been to Madrid. I felt very out of it listening to their talk. I would think to myself 'Only another 15,000 words of that *Red Book* one-shot, then there'll only be that novelette to do and I can book my passage to New York.' February was the provisional date. Soon I could start making plans.

On a Sunday morning in December I put a telephone call through to New York. 'I've finished my one-shot,' I told Donita. 'Where do you think we should go in February?'

There was a pause, there was a change in the tone of her voice. 'I can't be sure of any trips in February,' she said. I knew at once, I guessed at once, that something had happened. There was someone else. 'I was just going to write to you,' she said.

The letter arrived ten days later. He was a sculptor called Roy Sheldon. He had lived and worked in Paris during the twenties. He had been forced to return to New York because of the Depression. He was in his early thirties. They were going to be married after Christmas. It all sounded very suitable. It now did not matter whether or not I wrote that *Red Book* novelette.

Later, quite a little later I had a long talk with myself. 'It was bound to happen sooner or later,' I told myself. There was nothing real in it for her. I could give her a good time for a month, then leave her to her own devices. It was not enough for her.

I looked ahead. This was the first time that this had happened, but it would not be the last. My life was in two parts, my English life and my New York life. They were separate and distinct. Probably my New York life would become more important, I would spend more and more time there. But I'd remain an Englishman, I'd never break my English links.

'You're bound to fall in love again,' I told myself; 'there's a special affinity between American women and yourself. It'll be the same thing over again. What'll you do when you feel it happening? Will you draw back? There's always a point when you can draw back. That point once past, you can't. Will you draw back in time and save yourself the dreary empty feeling that's making everything seem pointless to you now? Will you think it worth it?' That was the question that I asked myself. Was it worth it? Had it been worth it? 'Moon over Miami.' Yes, I knew it was, I knew it had.

CHAPTER 9

The Pre-War Months

The firm of Hill and Peters did not survive very long. Early in February, Peters asked if I was still planning to go over to New York. 'Oh yes,' I said, 'I need to have a talk with *Red Book*.'

'That's fine, I'm planning to go over too.'

'To see "Berengaria" again?'

Crossing on the *Berengaria* last spring he had fallen in love with an American divorcée. For some time before I had known her name we had referred to her as 'Berengaria'. Now that I did know her I still used the nickname. He shook his head. 'Not altogether; I've got to replace Carol.'

I was surprised. 'Why?'

'Too many of my women clients find that she's more than they can stand.'

I have never asked any of his clients what the trouble was. I suppose the phrase 'more than they can take' about sums it up. It embarrassed them to have their work handled by a 'prima donna'.

'I'm not leaving her,' I said.

'I didn't think you would.'

Peters found a replacement in Harold Matson, who has remained his US representative ever since. Carol started her own business under the name Carol Hill. It was a small firm for a few carefully selected clients. They were delighted with her.

In retrospect the next thirty months appear to have been lived under a cloud; but that was not the impression that they gave as we were living through them, not to me at least. The lights may have been going out all over Europe, but life in England seemed to go on very much the same. There was no last time feeling. Every week-end we had guests. We never thought a time would come when there would be no housemaid to unpack their clothes, who would come into the drawing room after lunch with a request for 'Mrs Kennerly's keys'. There was no inflation yet. The pound bought what it had always bought. I bought two new suits every year. I captained the MCC Sussex College tour. In 1937 I was Vice-President of the Odde Volumes, but I declined the Presidency in 1938 as I wanted to make a tour of the West Indies. October 1939 was the time to go into the Chair.

Every time I went to New York Elinor Wolcott Gibbs gave a party for me. I added to my acquaintance there, Dorothy Parker and Russell Molony, among others. John O'Hara paid two visits to London. In 1938 he came to Ladies Night at the Odde Volumes. I had a box that year for the Lord's Test Match and Francis Meynell brought James Thurber round to it. The *News Chronicle* had commissioned him to write an article and he drew an entertaining comparison between the wickets and the match game that he used to play in Bleeck's with Wolcott Gibbs.

I was to see quite a bit of John O'Hara, both in New York and London. In early days he was drinking heavily – 'having trouble with the sauce' was the way he put it – and everyone warned me that sooner or later I should find him in one of his moods. 'Get ready to duck under the table when the plates start flying.' In 1936 he went on a long racket, sleeping in the day, waking up in the early evening, moving from one bar to another. His friends would report his progress and condition to one another, 'I've just seen John in 21. He was looking awful, unshaven with a dirty collar.' That would be at noon. Then at two in the morning another report would come. John O'Hara was in Tony's now.

'How is he?'

'Fine, shaved, very spruce with a fresh starched shirt.'

Finis Farr in his biography of him has many anecdotes of his moods. But I was lucky with him. I always found him delightful company. He would drop me notes: Peel's was closed: where should he get shoes in London? He had read in Charles Graves' book on London's clubs that men of note could be elected to the Athenæum without delay under the special dispensation of Rule III. 'I have been a card-carrying snob all my life, how about me under this rule of yours?' Finis Farr's full-length portrait of him should be read in conjunction with Brendan Gill's sketch in *Here at the New Yorker*. One cannot tell how his novels and short stories will appeal to a new generation. On his tombstone is inscribed 'Better than anyone he told the truth about his time, the first half of the twentieth century. He was a professional. He wrote honestly and well.' The words are his own; they are not unjustified. He was very much of his day and hour; he had an exceptional ear for dialogue and it is hard to stop reading when one has been caught up with his pace of narrative. His sex scenes are highly inflammatory. He was on a big scale. He may well prove to be the man of whom critics will write in 2000, 'John O'Hara was the mouthpiece of the first half of the twentieth century.'

In October 1938 I was elected to the Athenæum. It was the last thing I would have expected for myself at the time when this present narrative begins. Early in 1936 I received a fan letter from Douglas Ainslie saying that he had the greatest admiration for my novels and that he would like to tell me how much he admired them across a dinner table, that he expected to be in London for two weeks in the following month. On what day would I dine with him at the Athenæum?

I knew very little about Douglas Ainslie. I do not know a great deal now, except that he was a distinguished man of letters, some ten years younger than my father, who mostly lived abroad. *Who's Who* informed me that his father had been a diplomat, that he had been a diplomat, serving in the embassies in Athens, the Hague and Paris. I had met him once, however, in 1920 when Norman Davey asked me to dinner with himself and his friend Jack Yule. I cannot remember anything about the dinner except that it was at the Orleans Club, that the menu had been ordered in advance and that the food and wine were excellent, as they always were when Davey was in charge. I thoroughly enjoyed myself and was surprised when Davey a few days later apologised for Ainslie's rudeness to me.

'I wasn't aware of it,' I said.

'You weren't? It was very obvious; I was most embarrassed.'

What I supposed had happened was that Ainslie had taken no particular notice of me and that Davey, who was very touchy where his own dignity was concerned, would have been offended if a senior man of letters had paid so little attention to him. I who have no great sense of dignity was content to enjoy an excellent dinner and listen to my elders.

A little later I was to find a reference to myself, though not by name, in one of Ainslie's books. In 1919 I had given two lectures in the Aeolian Hall on 'Our Public Schools'. There had been a discussion after the second lecture during which I had been asked what I thought of co-education. I had answered that I thought it admirable for such boys as were unequal to the hurly-burly of a public school. An attractive young woman rose to ask what girls had done to deserve the company of weaklings. That got a laugh and on the following day the episode was reported in the *News Chronicle*. This anecdote Ainslie had recorded in his book. Either he had attended the lecture or he had read the account of it in the *Chronicle*.

I wondered if he would refer to our first meeting when I was his guest. He did not; he had clearly forgotten the incident, and I presume at Norman Davey's dinner he had either not heard my name when I was introduced to him or it had conveyed nothing to him, and he could not be bothered to exert himself on a nondescript young man of twenty-two who had not impressed the company with his conversation.

I could not have expected him to recognise me from that one meeting. In the course of sixteen years I had lost nearly all my hair. Nor for that matter did I recognise him. Sixteen years is a long time.

I enjoyed my dinner. Ainslie was a gracious host, and I am susceptible – who is not? – to flattery, particularly from a distinguished man of letters. I have not been exposed to so very much of that. I cannot remember much of what he said, but I got the impression that the future of the English novel was in good hands. I cannot remember what we ate – the food at the Athenæum did not in those days attain a very lofty standard – but the wine list has been always good, and I remember we drank right through the meal a heavy sweet white wine; I think, a Barsac. It was a curious choice. I have never at any other time except once rather recently on the Rhine, drunk a heavy sweet white wine right through a meal, but it was very good. It had a mellowing effect and by the time we were ready for our port, I was wishing the world well.

'Why aren't you a member of this club? You ought to be.' he asked.

It had never occurred to me to ask any of my friends to propose me. I had thought the Athenæum was too scholarly, too official and too formal for me. I thought moreover that the selection committee would look askance at the author of *The Loom of Youth*.

I pointed this out to Ainslie.

'Nonsense, nonsense,' he said; 'too many people have that idea about the Athenæum. They think it stodgy but it isn't. It may have been once, but isn't any longer. We need people like you. We must put you down right away.'

He beckoned to a waiter. 'Will you please bring down the Candidates Book.'

I cannot imagine what reception a member would receive today if he asked a club servant to transport the heavy Candidates Book from the Drawing Room to the Coffee Room, but there was no servant problem then. The heavy leather book was spread upon the table.

'Here we are; here's our page. Quite a long waiting list, but that won't worry us. Now for your particulars?'

I woke next morning as I have on so many other mornings wondering to what exactly I had committed myself on the night before. The Athenæum and myself did not seem a suitable juxtaposition of component parts. At the same time it would be pleasant to be a member. I had been impressed by the fine building with its wide curving staircase, and now that I was down in the Candidates Book I did not want to have my name removed. I did not want to have 'withdrawn at candidate's request' scrawled across my page. That usually was taken to mean that the candidate had realised that he was likely to be blackballed. I had better find out first what chance I stood of being eventually elected.

I wrote to Sir Alan Barlow, who stood as high in the counsels of the Athenæum as he did at the Savile. He was reassuring. 'There is no reason,' he wrote, 'why you should not join the Athenæum. I will warmly support your candidature if you promise not to resign from the Savile.' So I let my name stand.

Whether or not Douglas Ainslie did anything to support his candidate I do not know. I never saw or heard from him again. When I was elected two years later I wrote him a note of gratitude, but he did not answer it. It was altogether a curious incident.

In the same month, October 1938, I was initiated into Freemasonry, being elected to the Savage Club Lodge. I had joined the Savage Club in January 1919, but when I joined the Savile in 1922 I resigned from it. E. V. Lucas has written that a man should never resign from a club. 'It is,' he said, 'an insult to your fellow members, to the men who

have elected you.' I wish I had read this dictum before I
resigned. I had an idea that a man did not need two clubs. It
is possible today when club subscriptions are so high that a
man cannot afford a secondary club. But club subscriptions
were not high in the early twenties. I could easily have
afforded a second club; in fact most Londoners did. Galsworthy described Soames Forsyte as having two clubs, one
of which he put on his cards and never used and another
one to which he went two or three times a week. The
Forsytes were great club men. When one of them wanted to
see a cousin or a nephew he called for him at his club, usually
to find him in. There were no telephones it may be remembered in the period of *A Man of Property* and they were
not in general domestic use in the days of *In Chancery*. It is
hard for us today to imagine an existence without a telephone. How difficult the plotting of a novel. I soon regretted
that I had left the Savage and when I remarried and spent
most of my time in England I rejoined.

I was sponsored into Freemasonry by Cecil Palmer, the
one-time publisher, a member of Clifford Bax's cricket XI
and one of my closest friends. It was he who proposed me
for the Savage Club Lodge.

Very few men can give a satisfactory reason for becoming
a Mason. Self-interest is not permitted as a reason. I suppose
that what usually happens is that a friend whom one trusts
says 'I think this is the thing for you.' That is how it was in
my case.

Very few Masons say much about it in their autobiographies. The vows of secrecy are very strict. But Tolstoy's
War and Peace gives the layman as much information as he
needs. When I worked in Military Security in Baghdad, I
noticed that our 'Top Secret' files contained one on Masonry.
One night when I was Duty Officer I took out this file. I was
curious to learn how the Iraqis who were Masons, conducted
themselves during Rashid Ali's revolt against the monarchy
in 1941. The file contained only one document, a typed copy
of the pertinent chapter in *War and Peace*. As these details of

the initiation ceremony are general knowledge I can therefore refer to my own initiation. My feelings when the bandage was removed were not unlike Peter's, different though the ritual had been. During the ceremony, I was blindfolded. After being in darkness for half an hour the lights dazzled me. There were a hundred or so members on the raised seats above the floor, some of them I had known for ten, fifteen, twenty years. Their eyes met mine, there was a new warmth of welcome there. I had not known that they were Masons. I was meeting them now on a whole new basis. It was one of the most movingly dramatic moments of my life.

It is one of my great regrets that I made so little progress in the craft. I have never understood what it was all about. Masonry requires a great deal of patient study which I could never give to it. From September 1939 onwards I was in the Army. In Baghdad where there were two flourishing lodges, I joined the Lodge of Iraq and was raised there to be a Master Mason. I enjoyed the dinners and the meetings. I felt I was meeting on closer terms some of the more prominent members of the community and on my return to London I attended several meetings of the Savage Club Lodge. Their banquets were very special with the special characteristics of the Savage Club weekly dinners, with members providing excellent entertainment. But my visits to England rarely coincided with Lodge Meetings. There is no Lodge in Tangier today, and though I have joined a lodge in Gibraltar, the difficulties and cost of getting across to meetings are considerable. I have never fully entered into the privileges to which I am entitled.

1937, Coronation Year, was the last carefree year, or carefree at least for those of us who failed to recognise the fate that had become inevitable. Many of us would not believe that the world would be so mad as to plunge itself into war. We had always been assured that there would have been no war in 1914 if Germany had realised that Britain would honour its guarantee to Belgium, and in spite of the Spanish

Civil War, Munich was a long way off. In March I went over to New York. I travelled by the *Europa*, second class, in order to obtain the material for a magazine short story – *Good Housekeeping* took care of it – on the problems of a girl travelling second class when her beau was travelling first.

I was met at the docks by Peters. He wanted to get me committed to a scheme of his own, before I had committed myself to anything on Manhattan. 'Berengaria' was once again in the ascendant. He wanted to convey her for a honeymoon to Cuba. For that he needed an alibi. He wanted to be able to tell his wife that he was accompanying me to Cuba to organise a series of magazine short stories. All my expenses were to be paid. 'Won't cost you a penny, old boy.' It would have been churlish of me to have said anything but 'Yes', yet, I think, I earned my keep.

Peters and 'Berengaria' would start in on daiquiris at half-past six. By eight they would be in an anapæstic mood, ready 'for a siesta'. They would not reappear until eleven, ravenous for dinner. Which was fine for them, by Spanish hours. But I would find myself in an elevated mood with nothing to do about it for three hours. Yes, I think I earned my keep.

I returned to England in time for Evelyn's wedding to Laura Herbert. It was a most happy occasion; the bride looked so young and lovely and Evelyn was so patently in love with her. The dark period was over. For eight years he had lived as a divorced man, unfree to marry. An impossible situation and yet if his wife had remained faithful to him would his great gifts have developed in the way they had? He would never have left her alone while he made those long trips to Abyssinia and British Guyana. Her health would not have let her accompany him. He could not have written *Black Mischief* and *A Handful of Dust*. Would eight years of domesticity have given him the material and inspiration for two novels of equal but different quality? I thought of Elizabeth Barrett Browning's 'Half a beast is the great God Pan'. 'The President of the immortals' is concerned only with the talent, with the genius that he has implanted being developed to its fullest degree; he does not care what suffering the artist endures in the process or inflicts on others. He gives the artist neither the life that will make him happy nor one that is in keeping with his own natural instincts but the one that will give him the incentive to create good books.

I had returned to London that spring with a comfortable bank balance. I had been planning to take Donita on an expensive trip. As those reserves had not been touched I decided to give a party for Stanley Rinehart and his wife Fay Yeatman in the River Room of the Savoy. There were some eighty guests.

That party had several dramatic consequences. Margaret Lane asked if she could bring Doris Langley Moore 'and can we come in fancy dress, we are going to a fashion display dinner'. They made a dramatic entrance, in eighteenth-century costume. I had never seen Margaret, a very beautiful woman, look more radiant. It was the first time that she had met Hastings. Today she is the Countess of Huntingdon.

I asked Vyvyan Holland, at that time a bachelor, whether he would like to bring a guest or would prefer to campaign independently. He asked if he could bring Margaret Rawlings. Charles Morgan was among the guests. His romance with Margaret Rawlings had been one of the more prominent episodes of the previous couple of years. It had been conducted with such little privacy that everyone knew that it was 'off'. That night, however, re-meeting unexpectedly, they danced together with such appreciative abandon, that three days later 'everyone in London' knew that it was 'on' again.

Vyvyan, abandoned, took Dorice Fordred home. This was a project that I had tried to foster for quite a while. I thought that they were right for one another and I knew she liked him. I was surprised at his not doing anything about it. 'Why didn't you years ago?' I asked.

'I thought she was having an affair with you,' he said.

Englishmen do not hesitate to make advances to their best friends' wives but they are cautious about their girl-friends. More than one man has asked me if the coast was clear as far as I was concerned. American men have, I have observed, no such qualms where girlfriends are concerned, but they are punctilious with wives, unless their intentions are really serious.

That summer Joan and I did not go to the South of France but in January we went to Morocco. For a year we had been hoping for another child but without success. We wondered whether a change of setting might not prove propitious. At that time P & O and the Dutch line operated a three-and-a-half-weeks' package trip to Marrakesh. You caught a P & O liner from London and a Dutch ship back from Tangier. Passengers to the Far East preferred to begin and end their trips at Marseilles, thus both saving time and avoiding the turbulence of the Bay of Biscay.

On the way out we took a night train from Tangier to Marrakesh; on the return journey you travelled by day, spending one night in Rabat and one in the Minzah hotel in Tangier.

We chose this trip largely because Jean Morley Kennerly was wintering in Marrakesh. I was also curious to see Tangier; it had a romantic appeal for me. As I have told in my *Early Years* I fell in love in 1927 with an American married woman I had met on a ship between Tahiti and San Francisco. She was due to return to Tahiti in July. I promised to meet her there. In June, however, her husband received a cable from Max Blake, the American Consul General in Tangier, asking them to spend the summer there with him. I was prepared to change my plans and go to Tangier instead, but the scheme was not confirmed, and in mid-June I caught from Marseilles the *Louqsor*, an intermediate class French cargo ship for Tahiti. On the third day out I saw on my left, high on a cliff, the white and blue houses of Tangier. I have seldom seen as lovely a city. Instantaneously it laid a hold upon my heart. What a place for a love affair. In Tahiti ten weeks later, Ruth and I wove it into our dreams of a future which we knew to be foredoomed. One day, we said, we would have a villa there. In the novel *Nor Many Waters*, which I wrote that winter and dedicated to her as a birthday present, I spoke of the dream city of Tangier. Instinct must have warned me of the part it was to play in my life.

It looked every bit as lovely on this January morning. We arrived at nine o'clock; our train was due to leave at ten at night. In those days there were no docks, only a breakwater. We had to go ashore in rowing boats. Our tour tickets included the services of Thomas Cook. Our luggage was deposited at the Minzah hotel where we were to lunch later. A guided tour of the Kasbah was awaiting us.

It was the first time I had been in a Moorish city. We were fascinated by the high arches and the narrow streets, by the one-room shops, by the bustle and animation. We saw a snake charmer and a conjuror. We walked down through the Medina to the Petit Socco, where we paused to take mint tea.

The Petit Socco is small, narrow, picturesque, lined with cafés. At this time both the Spanish Loyalists and Francoists came to Tangier on their leaves. One side would sit on the one side, the other opposite. They would ignore each other with decorum, then they would go back to their separate armies and kill each other. That seemed very civilised and Spanish. Tangier was a free port in an International Zone, and the steep narrow street that ran from the Grand to the Petit Socco was lined with money-changers who announced their rates of exchange on black boards outside their shops. The peseta and the franc were the two main currencies in which one settled one's accounts. Commodities highly taxed elsewhere, like alcohol, were very cheap.

In the early afternoon we drove outside the town. The

fields were brilliant with blue irises. I had never seen and have never seen anything equal to it. Today you will not see that splendour. The flowers are pulled out by small boys by their roots and sold. Today you will only see an occasional privately owned field which has not been despoiled. There is such a one at the American School.

We went down to the station early and settled into our sleeping-car. As the train passed the frontier into Spanish Morocco I drew back the curtain of the compartment and was surprised and rather alarmed to see that the whole sky was a brilliant orange. I could not think what it was. I wondered flippantly whether the Francoists had not staged an immense Auto da Fé and were burning Communists. In view of the political atmosphere there might well have been some such outbreak. I was relieved when the train passed into French Morocco. Two days later I read in the press that there had been an Aurora Borealis and that the sky had been aflame right down to the Sahara. There was no precedent for such a conflagration.

The Mamounia in which in a few years time Churchill was to spend his convalescence is still one of the world's great hotels. It was then exceptionally charming. It was fairly small, it was French, and the ochre-brown walls as a background to the groves of date palms delighted the eye. The climate was perfect, dry and warm. Marrakesh has been a subject of many articles and travel films. Its beauties are familiar. Its bazaars are covered and kept cool by palm branches, through which the sunlight strikes in sharp bright angles. The market place with its superb mosque in the background is today crowded with charabancs and cars, but then it was as it had been for centuries, the gathering place for innumerable singers, conjurors, snake-charmers, fortune tellers.

That year a typhus scare had frightened away the tourists, so we had the golf course to ourselves. The Glaoui was an enthusiastic golfer, and each day two different greens were put under water so that the course was always in good repair. It was only on days when the Glaoui wanted to play himself that the whole eighteen holes were open.

Jean Morley Kennerly, who had been for reasons of health resident for some weeks, was and is a very social lady. Her husband, an American, was one of the directors of Faber and Faber. She and he were two of our best friends and were constant week-end guests at Edrington. She had a number of friends in Marrakesh who entertained us. One of her friends, a French officer attached to the Foreign Legion, allowed us to use his horses. A cousin of Jean Kennerly's was married to the British Vice-Consul Bryce Nairn, who later as Consul was to be usefully active after the Casablanca Conference. She was an excellent painter and became after the war a sketching companion for Winston Churchill. Nairn was to be Consul-General at Tangier when I came there in the 1950s. He has now made his home in Marrakesh.

It was a happy time and when the time came for us to leave, it was almost certain that the main purpose of the trip had been achieved. Our Dutch ship on the return journey stopped at Lisbon. The cathedral there has a special wall seat on which, the superstitious are agreed, you can make one prayer that will be surely granted. Joan wished for a son. Her wish was granted in October.

Many years later we were to tell Peter this. He was delighted. His brother and sister, Andrew and Veronica, who were only a year apart, were so very much a team that he felt left out. They used to talk of 'the days before we had Peter'. He did not feel he had been really wanted. He would have preferred to belong to a larger family. After the war he paid a visit to his Uncle Evelyn and returned with some resentment, 'they're six, why are we only three?' In a family of six he would have found a companion. It was then that we told him about Morocco. 'What,' he said, 'you went all that way for me?'

When the lease of our flat in Hill Street expired in the previous October, Joan had decided not to renew it. She did not like living in two places. She would prefer when she came up to London to stay at Fleming's. In consequence we did not come up to London very much during the spring of 1938. Joan loved Edrington and she loved being with her children. But I kept on my perch at Abbey Road.

During the spring and early summer I worked on a novel that was published in October with the title *Going Their Own Ways*. It was not a very satisfactory book; it did not have a central plot, with one character or group of characters taken direct from A to Z, one chapter leading to the next in terms of time and interest. It had instead a central theme with various different characters, several of them scarcely known to each other, illustrating various aspects of the marriage problem. I worked into it a number of stories including a one shot that had appeared in *Red Book*. It was readable. Stuff that appeared in *Red Book* had to be that, but it was not a unified whole.

The author of chronicle novels was in an awkward position in 1938. I did not know where and when to set a novel. If I wrote a book about the contemporary scene, if the hero in chapter one, in June 1937, walks down Piccadilly wondering whether he should or should not ring up the girl he had met the previous evening at a party, I should be writing about a person who was worrying about Mussolini and Hitler because his personal life depended on what was happening in Berlin and Rome; that would involve political arguments and discussions which might be out of date before the book was finished. It would be impossible to write about contemporary characters without telling the reader how they felt about the various issues of the day. If on the other hand the story were to start in 1930 and the story was to cover three or four years, the reader might well think, 'does it matter what this character does in 1930 because in 1938 there may well have been an international conflagration that will deny all significance to events that took place in 1933'. The only solution was to choose an action that took place within the course of a few months as

Galsworthy's Forsyte novels did. There was no scope, in fact, for the chronicle novel. Next time I decided, as I corrected the proof of *Going Their Own Ways*, I would find myself such a plot or else set the story outside England, in the West Indies for instance.

In June 1938 the Saintsbury Club was entertained in Paris by the Club des Cents, an occasion which A. J. A. Symons celebrated in a ten-page brochure 'When club meets club'. Thirteen of us accepted the invitation and lest that number should seem inauspicious, Barry Neame, 'mine host' of the Hind's Head at Bray, joined the party. We were invited to bring wives. All of us with the exception of Vyvyan Holland were married, more or less, but Lord Lymington – now Lord Portsmouth – was the only one who elected to bring coals to Newcastle, and he it must be noted in extenuation had very recently exposed himself to the vicissitudes of matrimony – *en seconde noce* I need hardly add.

We were dined in the Bois du Boulogne at the Restaurant du Pré Catalan. The British Ambassador was the guest of honour. I had the honour of being seated next to André Maurois. As an *amuse gueule* we had smoked salmon with a dry champagne. The first course was *cantaloup frappé au vieux ports*. A *consommé de volaille* was followed by a *timbale de homard Newberg*. The white wines were a 1934 Alsatian and a 1927 Château Palmer Blanc from Cantenac; a wine which rarely appears upon the market and of which A.J. wrote: 'It has a Sauternes' nose but an unexpected quality of flavour, quite independent of the sweetness behind.' The two red wines were Mouton Rothschild 1928 – what would a bottle of that fetch today? – and a Beaune 1923 – a great, a very great wine. It surprised us all that so great a wine should be called Beaune *tout court*. I had hoped then for a big Sauternes but we had two 1928 champagnes. I still hold 1928 to have been the greatest of champagne years. What majesty Krug exerted then! The Heidsieck was in jeroboams, the Perrier Jouet in double magnums. The dimensions of the two bottles were identical. A.J. was reminded of Fowler's remarking on another vexing question: 'China is porcelain and porcelain is China. There is no recondite difference between the two which are indeed not two but one.' A.J. did however maintain that there is such a thing as what he called 'a platonic jeroboam' which holds six bottles and is to be found only in Bordeaux. I have been assured that that statement is correct.

Our entertainment did not finish with the banquet. On the Sunday afternoon we were taken to *'le grande steeple d'Auteuil'* before which we were regaled with a champagne lunch at the Pavilion Royale in the Bois. Its chief feature was *ortolans des Landes*. I had never tasted their succulence before nor have I since. They were served on paper envelopes on which they had been cooked. We were instructed in how to eat them. Holding the bird by the head, you take the whole of the body into your mouth biting through the neck, and then chew gently, rejecting such morsels as prove tough.

The day closed with a supper by the river, with champagnes '23, '26, and '28.

I flew out from Heathrow airport in a very small machine, that rocked uncomfortably in the wind. There were no customs and security arrangements that I recall. I motored there with Andrew and Veronica. They were allowed to go inside the machine in which their father was to fly.

CHAPTER 10

Munich and After

My younger son Peter was born on October the 13th. What should have been a peaceful time for Joan was filled with harsh anxiety. The Munich crisis happened so quickly, and came on us so suddenly that everyone was dazed.

It lasted less than three weeks. On September 15th Chamberlain was on his way to Berchtesgaden. Within a few hours he was back. Two weeks later the French army was half mobilised, the British navy was completely mobilised. On September the 27th Chamberlain was on his feet in the Commons. For an hour he was telling the House what it already knew. There was no hope. Then a note was passed to him. The expression on his face changed. A new situation had arisen, he explained. There was to be a meeting in Munich of Daladier, Mussolini and Hitler. He would attend it, he would leave next day.

I recall unco-ordinated moments. I travelled up to London from Reading by the same train as Storm Jameson. She was carrying a copy of her new novel *Here Comes a Candle*. I did not get the significance of the title. 'Here comes the candle to light you to bed,' she reminded me. 'I hope,' I said, 'that it's not going to prove appropriate.'

Then there was an evening at Silchester, when all the male members of the village were summoned to the church hall to assemble gas masks of which a large quantity had been distributed to every village. It was not too easy to slip the rubber mouthpiece over the metal clasp; one's fingers began to ache.

And then suddenly the crisis was at an end and Neville

Chamberlain was waving the document that had been signed by himself and Hitler. 'Peace in our time.' 'Peace with Honour.' There were very few who were not abundantly relieved. The 'premature anti-Fascists' were, of course, indignant, so were a few traditional conservatives. Vyvyan Holland gave a party shortly after 'the great betrayal'. One of his guests was a newspaper magnate. They all said the same thing: that we had only postponed the war for a year; that in a year's time we would be only slightly less unprepared. I did not agree. I thought we had to convince not only the world but – and this was more important – ourselves, that we had done everything within our power to avoid war; that there was no alternative to calling Hitler's bluff. In the meantime there was nothing to be done but carry on with our own lives, taking such steps as might be appropriate to fit ourselves individually for wartime service.

It was announced that an emergency reserve of officers was to be enrolled. I sent in an application, with letters of recommendation from Sir Arthur Willert and my publisher, the head of Cassell's, Newman Flower. A few weeks later I received the information that I could not join the Emergency Reserve because I was already a member of the Regular Army Reserve and as such would receive instructions when and if I was needed. This was a great relief. I was on the RARO because I had been to Sandhurst and thus had held a regular army commission. In 1919 when I opted for civilian life I transferred to the Reserve. In 1921 when there was the threat of a general strike, I was recalled to the colours for seven weeks; and every so often during the 1920s I would receive a note of instruction telling me where to report in the event of a general mobilisation. This present confirmation of the fact that I was still on the War Office's books was a relief to me; it absolved me from responsibility. I could relax and let the Army do what it wanted on my account. I arranged an immediate trip to the West Indies.

In 1928 and 1929 I had visited Martinique, then the Leeward Islands, Antigua and Dominica, after that Barbados,

Jamaica, Trinidad and Haiti. This time I booked to the Windward Islands; to St Lucia, Grenada and St Vincent. I had hoped that one day Eldred Curwen would come on another trip with me. He was the ideal travelling companion, but two years earlier he had fallen in love with a divorcée, Peggy Bainbridge. They had not married, because under her divorce agreement she would have lost her alimony, but she had taken up residence in the Villa Marina. In the course of the summer I had deplored this fact to my cousin Helen Gosse. 'It won't be nearly so much fun without him,' I had said.

'Why don't I come instead?' she said.

'Why don't you?'

It never occurred to me that she would. She was still linked with Aylmer Vallance and I did not believe that she would want to be away from him for several months. She had taken a cottage near Aberdeen for the summer and Aylmer had gone down to see her for long week-ends. It was not a very satisfactory arrangement. But because of the scruples of the authorities at the *News Chronicle* she did not want to live with him openly in London.

'It would do us good to be away from one another for a time,' she said; 'then we can make up our minds about each other.'

There were still divorce problems on his side.

'Give me all the particulars about your trip,' she said.

The Munich crisis intervened and I presumed that she had thought no more about it. I was very surprised when I learnt from my travel agent that she had paid the deposit on her passage. I kept believing that she would cancel it. She was a highly erratic creature. But the days went by and the letter announcing her change of plan never came. Finally on a grey November morning there she was, on the London docks, with what seemed to me an uncomfortably large amount of luggage.

I viewed the luggage with dismay. It was going to complicate my own planning considerably. How responsible was I going to be for it and her? In all the travel plans that I had made or thought about, I had never pictured myself as travelling with a female on platonic terms, for I was confident that those would be the terms on which we would remain. As indeed we did. Well, I had got to make the best of it. It would be a new experience, anyhow.

As I have already said, she was Amazonian. John Fothergill said of her in his *An Innkeeper's Diary* that she made a cathedral seem crowded, and our ship – a British one – was small. When she was in the bar, other passengers would hesitate about coming in. In the dining room we sat at the doctor's table; she had suggested that we should get a table to ourselves. But I had overruled her. I wanted to meet other passengers, to become part of the ship's life. She agreed, reluctantly. But later she was to admit that I was right. The doctor was a very charming man of the world, and he took an instantaneous liking for Helen. 'I'm glad you stuck to your point,' she said. 'You usually do, don't you?'

'Whenever I can get away with it,' I said.

'I'm glad you do. It'll make this trip a great deal easier. The trouble about John' – John was her husband – 'was that he never stuck to his point. And he was right more often than not.'

The weather worsened as soon as we were out of the comparative shelter of the Channel. Once in the Atlantic the sea became really rough. I did not miss a meal, but I spent most of the day in my cabin, buttressed by pillows. I had brought Proust to read. C. S. Forester was aboard. Helen was a great admirer of his work, particularly *The General*. His wife was prostrate with seasickness. Helen and he played chess most of the time. On the third afternoon she admitted him to her cabin. Next day she regretted it. 'He's being such a bore,' she said. 'He keeps telling me how marvellous I was.'

'What's wrong with that?' I asked.

'I wasn't marvellous at all. If he thinks that that's the best that I can do, I feel insulted. I hope the sea calms down and his wife comes on deck.'

The sea did calm down, but it was not only Mrs Forester whom it released. For the first four days while the ship groaned and creaked and rattled, four men had played bridge in the bar solidly between one meal and the next. One of them was a very personable Englishman in his early thirties. He was tall, strong, handsome. As a crowning glory he was a redhead. Most of the passengers had felt curious about him. On the fifth day he joined in the ship's life. He had followed a wise technique. 'Don't get involved with anyone during the first days on board. Keep to yourself, see who is around. Then go into action.' He had marked Helen down as the lady most likely to prove congenial. He found her a welcoming prey.

From then on I found myself in somewhat the same position that I had been in Cuba with Peters and 'Berengaria'. I was expected to be a constant escort who vanished at appropriate moments. On board that was an easy enough role to play. But it was less easy when we reached Grenada, when I wanted to get about on my own, and make the contacts that would provide me with material for my books. Helen's redhead had come out as the representative of some international import–export firm. He was bound for Trinidad, but in the meantime he had contacts in Grenada and St Lucia. Helen had made no definite plans to return to England. I was to sail for Boston on Christmas Eve, aiming to spend three weeks in New York before going back to England. Helen planned to continue her romance. In the meantime she considered it my cousinly duty to smooth out circumstances for her redhead and herself.

I cannot deny that it was with a deep sense of relief that I waved her good luck at St Lucia when she eventually took off for Trinidad. Yet at the same time I had to admit that I had had a better time in the Windward Islands because of her. People liked her and when they did not exactly like her, they were fascinated by her. There was more fun going when she was around. I got asked to parties that I should not have been, had she not been there. In Grenada she had told the

Governor that she was an avid fisherman. He lent her his
fishing rod. She was never to use it once and oh, what a
cumbersome article it was to move from one island to
another, down one gangplank after another. It was typical
of her making a nuisance of herself, but also of her so en-
dearing herself to people that a Governor would be ready to
entrust to her, a complete stranger, a presumably treasured
possession. Yes, I undoubtedly got more fun out of that
trip because she was with me. I was very fond of her. I
have very few blood relatives. I had seven maiden aunts,
and one of my two uncles emigrated to the USA while the
other, a naval officer, died young, married to a Tasmanian.
The Waughs and the Gosses were very close. Edmund's
daughter Tessa was a bridesmaid at my mother's wedding.
Helen died tragically young, having eventually married and
then divorced Aylmer Vallance. She had a son born towards
the end of the war whom she called Tito. She asked me to
be his godfather. 'Fine,' I said. 'When's the christening?'

'I don't mean to have him christened.' Which also was
very typical of her.

I travelled up to the USA on one of the Lady boats, an
admirable Canadian line that plied between Montreal and
Port of Spain. It stopped at all the British islands. I paid on
it my first visits to St Kitts and Montserrat. It gave me my
first realisation of how akin the islands were, how similar
and how different, with their distinct histories and backgrounds derived from their frequent changes of hands
during the eighteenth century when the British and French
fleets had fought for their possession, and when they had been
so important that in 1763 England had nearly given Canada
back to the French in exchange for Guadeloupe. St Lucia
and Grenada were to become the islands that I visited most
frequently after the war. Grenada is exceptionally beautiful.
It was there that Twentieth Century-Fox laid most of the
filming of my novel *Island in the Sun*. Darryl Zanuck sent
scout photographers down to help him select locations.

When he saw the photographs of Grenada, he said at once, 'This is the place.' It also had the attraction then, of being the one island without any colour prejudice, all the white planters having been killed during the Napoleonic Wars.

When I left England I was not sure how long I should be able to afford to stay in New York. I presumed that my West Indian visit would prove expensive, as indeed it did, and I did not want to hurry it. I was hoping to find material for a novel, so that I was relieved to find waiting for me in Dominica in a large batch of mail a note containing the welcome news that *Red Book* had bought the last story I had sent them. I should be able to stay three weeks – just the right length of time.

My novel *Going Their Own Ways* was published during my visit; Carl Carmer had a book coming out in the same week and Farrar and Rinehart gave a joint birthday party for us. Elinor Gibbs, whose second child was due that spring, gave a party for me. Janet Kirby was there; her marriage was on the rocks and she was being courted unsuccessfully by Alan Rinehart, whose marriage was also on the point of disintegration. Mary Roberts Rinehart was very hopeful that Janet would rescue her favourite son and at the last-day lunch party that she gave for me, Alan and Janet were my fellow guests. I had not been in New York for twenty months and there was a constant meeting of old friends – Katherine Brush, Erin O'Brien Moore. I met and made friends with Ursula Parrott. Donita and her husband were now running a flower shop. She was later to write an entertaining book *Say it with Flowers*. Roy Sheldon's attempts to support himself as a sculptor, though he had real talent, were not proving successful. It had been one thing to be a Left Bank sculptor in 1928. It was quite a different thing to be one in New York in 1938. I had a suspicion, which was to prove correct, that the marriage would not last very long. I saw quite a lot of her. I had an encouraging evening with Voldemar Vetlugin. *Red Book* wanted more stories from me.

As usual in New York I felt all my batteries recharged. I

had been away too long. My morale was low. I was running out of ideas. *Going Their Own Ways* was not nearly good enough. In the public library at St Lucia I had spent a morning reading an almanack that gave a résumé of the last year's books. The references to me were far from flattering. What, I wondered, was the point of going on. Why not retire and become a country squire? It was the only time when I have had this feeling. Three days of New York cured my despondency. John Farrar, the Rineharts and Carol Hill gave me back my confidence.

Not surprisingly, having been away for twenty months, I had no emotional involvement in New York, and the likelihood of forming one at such notice was not great. I sought solace at Polly Adler's. Polly Adler in the twenties and thirties was New York's most famous 'Madame'. She has told her own story in *A House is not a Home* – I have written about her in *A Year to Remember*. Her fortunes were beginning to ebb by 1939, but her club was still a cosy rendezvous. It really was a club. You sat at an oblong table with Polly, her staff and one or two male clients. There was no solicitation. You sat around, you danced, you ordered drinks, no pressure was put upon you if you did not want to play. You took leave of your hostess, just as you would at a cocktail party. Finance was never mentioned. But at the door a tall handsome dark girl handed you a bill. It was usually less than you expected. Drinks were a dollar apiece. I found there, this time, a delightful blonde from Georgia, who was called 'Deep South'.

Delightful though she was, however, I felt that I wanted to take a more romantic *au revoir* of the USA. War was imminent. When should I cross the Atlantic again? So much had to happen first. There was in California a young German-American woman, Lucia – with whom I had been very happily in love in London. She was married then; but the marriage had broken, she had returned to the USA, got a divorce and had remarried. I had kept in touch with her and her last letters had suggested that her marriage was not going well. She had been a very good friend of Vyvyan Holland. He was twelve years older than I, as I was twelve years older than she. He had been a father confessor to her. She had told him that this second marriage of hers had never been consummated. 'I don't give it another year,' he said. I called her up. Her voice was warm and welcoming. 'I was thinking of coming out to see you,' I informed her.

'Why don't you?'

'If I did, would I have a chance of seeing you alone?'

'There wouldn't be much point in your coming out here if there wasn't.'

'If I booked a suite in a hotel, could you come to lunch with me?'

'Why not?'

It was a risk. I was well aware of that. I had not seen her for thirty months. Two people can become strangers in that time. But it was worth the risk. I had time for a four-day visit.

It was a bad journey out. Winds were contrary. We were grounded in the Middle West for half a day. We landed late at half-past ten. Lucia had come to meet me with her husband. As we stood together by the baggage counter, I felt as much in tune with her as I had in London. It all seemed yesterday. 'I've booked you into the Beverly Hills hotel,' she said.

'I can't think why he can't stay with us,' her husband said.

'Oh, Alec's funny that way. He doesn't like staying in other people's houses.'

He was tall, dark, athletic, handsome. He was under thirty. He was also rather rich. Vyvyan Holland's story seemed incredible. 'That's what you would think, isn't it?' she said. 'You wouldn't say, would you, that I was difficult about those things?' Within the year she had gone to Reno. Ten years later he married again.

'I'd give anything to see her,' she said, 'and find out if he was the same with her.' But she never did. He died rather young.

Next day she came to the hotel. We lunched in my suite. It was just the way it had been in London. We went down to Palm Springs for the week-end.

On my last evening in New York, Frank Case gave a cocktail party for me at the Algonquin. Frank was in tremendous form. He had just published his autobiographical *Tales of a Wayward Inn*. It was not a best-seller, but it was doing well and was being widely and well reviewed. Now that Prohibition was ended, the hotel was making money. Frank gave me a free hand to invite whom I liked. When would I see them all again, I wondered. Afterwards I dined alone with Elinor Gibbs. She was keeping early hours because of the future baby. I went on to Polly Adler's. Next day in my cabin there was the yellow envelope of a cablegram: 'Come back to us soon Polly and Deep South.'

On my dressing room table that night there was a tumbler with a red rose in it – and a note from Donita. Every day there was a red rose there, with a different note. She records this in her book *Say it with Flowers*.

I was travelling by a German ship, the *Hansa*. I had written a couple of articles for the North German *Lloyd* magazine and got a reduced rate in settlement. I also wanted to remind myself before the curtain fell of how many pleasant sides there were to the German way of life. There was one passenger in particular of whom I was to think during the years ahead. He was young, strong, blond, the perfect Nordic type. It seemed so wrong, so very wrong that we should be on different sides from men like this. In 1956 I was to meet him on a French ship bound for the West Indies. He seemed unchanged and had a young and pretty wife. He had come through untouched.

On the journey I wrote a story called 'Soldier From the Wars Returning'. It described an officer returning to England in 1918 after eight months in a German prisoner of war camp. A son has been born to him in his absence. After a scene of maladjustment between his wife and himself, they achieve harmony. They go into the nursery and look at their sleeping son. They look forward to the year that will give them their reward for all they have endured during the war, the year when their son will be entering the heritage that they have earned for him, the year 1939. Carol sold it to the *Saturday Evening Post*, the only story that I ever sold them.

I returned to Edrington to the news that Arthur Yencken, who was now in the Embassy in Rome, had invited us to spend a couple of weeks there with them. It was the first time that I had been to Rome. It was cold and showery in England, but there the sky was blue and the air was warm. The gardens were bright with mimosa. The Yenckens ensured that we made full use of our time. They had arranged that we should attend a succession of sightseeing tours arranged by an Italian countess. We were included in all the invitations that were sent to them. We went to a number of affluent palazzos. I was fascinated by the beauty and elegance of the Italian women. We played golf most days. It was an excellent course, a little confused by the reprisals that the authorities had taken against Britain, changing the measurement of the holes from yards into metres, so that a hundred-and-thirty-yard short hole would be marked as just over a hundred. One under-clubbed oneself. Count Ciano had just taken up the game. He played with feverish keenness and a complete lack of skill. He went round the course with a caddy, by himself. I saw him once on a pulpit tee, drive off seven balls in succession. They went in all directions, then he flung his club down the fairway. It was the only projected object that went straight. I felt that this was a hopeful sign. I knew how one-tracked the mind of the embryo golfer can become. I did not believe that anyone so infatuated with the game could give it up for the sake of war. With Mussolini in love and Ciano the slave of golf, there was surely a chance that Italy would remain a neutral.

Yet it was no longer possible to believe that war with Germany could be avoided. The 15th of March had been prophesied as the *dies irae*, and *Punch* on the 15th came out with a cartoon of John Bull waking that morning to the sight through his bedroom window of a midget of alarm scampering into the distance. But the prophets were correct. The Germans marched into Czechoslovakia.

Shortly after this England signed a treaty of mutual defence with Poland. The country on the whole was in agreement, though a few opponents asked where and how England proposed to defend her ally.

In April I received a form from the War Office asking whether I would volunteer to return to the Army for three years to help in the training of the new Armies. I volunteered. The secretary of the Authors' Society lived in the next village to Silchester and was a good friend of mine. He told me that he had been asked to supply the government with the names of twelve writers who would be useful members of a propaganda bureau. He told me that he had put my name on the list. I asked him to take my name off. Propaganda had got itself a bad name in the first war. I remembered Siegfried Sassoon's satires. I wanted to serve as a soldier.

At about this time one or two of my contemporaries, among them Alan Pryce-Jones and Hugh Mackintosh, were taking a War Office course in military intelligence. I did not know about this at the time. I wish I had. I was clearly too old for combat service. I should have sooner or later been drafted into some kind of staff work. By joining that course I would have got in on the ground floor; but perhaps, as a novelist, I got more out of my Army years by doing from time to time whatever the authorities decided. I shared the common lot.

And so the spring turned into summer, and everyone behaved as though September was not heavy with omen. In April the Saintsbury Club held its dinner as though there were no interruption threatened. The Baron de Marchiennes invited us to cross the Channel in September and allow the Belgian gastronomes to entertain us in Brussels as the Club des Cents had in Paris the year before. Compton Mackenzie asserted that he would go.

I was a member of the Royal Literary Fund Committee and attended its annual banquet. The Prime Minister, Neville Chamberlain, was the guest of honour. Still held generally in high respect, he was very pompous and self-satisfied. How soon he was to be an object of derision. The chief speaker was Dorothy Sayers. She had been invited because it was believed that as a writer of detective stories she would provide light entertainment. Far from it. At some length she told an anecdote about her cook. 'I am sure this will amuse the Prime Minister,' she said. The cook at the end of the anecdote had remarked that 'that there 'itler is so fidgetty'. Then she delivered a ten-minute philosophical address which did not contain the opportunity for a single smile – no question of a laugh.

At the last meeting of the Committee before the war, one of the applicants for a grant was Dylan Thomas. The transactions of the Committee are confidential, but all this happened a very long while ago. Myself I felt that at such a time a young man should have been able to find some remunerative public service. I knew very little about him. Eighteen months before, Joan had been at a party at which he was one of the guests. It was a warm evening and he had stood on the balcony, throwing his cigarette butts into the street below. One of them landed in the open car belonging to Joan's escort and burnt a hole in the seat. At Committee meetings the books of the applicants are spread out on the table. One of the senior members of the Committee – not a man of letters – picked up a collection of Thomas's poetry and read out one of the poems in a derisive tone of voice, 'I don't call this poetry,' he said. The application was refused. J. B. Priestley was indignant and wrote to several members of the Committee, arguing that poetry could not be judged if read in that manner, asking that the question should be re-opened, that the poems should be sent to Walter de la Mare – a member who had not been present – asking him his opinion of the literary quality of Thomas's poetry. I do not know how the matter ended. It was the last meeting I was able to attend till the war was over.

In June the Sette of Odde Volumes celebrated Ladies' Night in Bath as guests of Adrian Hopkins, Philatelist to the Sette, who as Mayor of Bath had been very active in restoring the Assembly Rooms. It was a sumptuous occasion. Twenty-five years later the occasion was repeated. And Hopkins created a trust with the Bridgwater Building Society to enable the Sette to celebrate fifty years after the first, the third visit of the Sette to Bath 1989. 1989. If I am still around I shall be ninety-one that year. Maybe I shall make it.

That summer the West Indies sent over a cricket side. I had a box for the Lord's Test Match. It was the last first-class cricket match that my father was to watch.

J. B. Priestley's wife was active in support of an orphan's home, the St Pancras House Improvement Society, and to raise funds for it J.B.P. organised a cricket match between actresses and authors. The authors' side included Joyce Carey, Peter Fleming, A. P. Herbert, Cecil Day Lewis, C. S. Forester, V. S. Pritchett, R. C. Sherriff, A. G. Macdonell. The actresses under the captaincy of Joyce Barbour included Celia Johnson, Angela Baddeley, Ursula Jeans, Jill Esmond, Cathleen Nesbitt, Margaretta Scott. A. G. Macdonell acted as a broadcasting announcer.

That summer Terence Rattigan had running a play called *After the Dance*. It was not one of his most successful plays, but it had some very moving scenes. It dealt with a group of Bright Young People who tried to continue the spirit of the twenties into the thirties. The hero was a man who aimed to be a novelist but never really worked at writing, who made it a half-time occupation. This play affected me. I felt it was true of me, that I had not for the last few years really worked at writing, spending too much time in London, going to parties there and not waking up quite fresh next morning. I resolved to cut down my visits to London, only going up for special occasions. I had found

a plot for a new novel. A West Indian planter from one of
the smaller islands – an amalgam of St Lucia, Grenada and
St Vincent – would fall in love, on a holiday, with an English
girl fifteen years younger than himself. To her, coming out
to the West Indies would be a very great adventure. She
was not in love with him, in the way that she had expected
to fall in love one day, but she was attracted by him, she
liked him and respected him. For a while she was reasonably
happy. Then she became bored. She decided to have a baby,
but it died in childbirth. She was warned that she must not
attempt to have another. She has nothing to look forward
to. Her husband is asthmatic. His condition worsens. She
had not noticed his condition at first, but now she feels that
for the best years of her life she is committed to the nursing
of an invalid. She will be left in early middle age, a widow
in a country where she has no roots, with no relatives, with
no tried friends. When she is in this mood a young Englishman arrives who has come out to prospect for a company
that wishes to build a luxury hotel in the West Indies. Her
husband owns a piece of land that would be suitable. He
encourages her to act as a guide for the young man, 'Show
him round the island; point out its attractions; make him
want to recommend this island and our site.'

She takes her role so seriously that the young man falls in
love with her. Light-heartedly she starts an affair. It changes
into a searing passion. He goes to New York to consult with
his employers. He returns with one of the directors, and his
daughter to whom he is clearly considerably attracted. My
heroine is terrified. Such a marriage is so clearly the right
thing for him. How can she hope to hold him? If only she
was free. She drifts into a desperate state of mind. Her
husband's health grows worse. His coughing night after
night tears her nerves to pieces. Life has become a torture
to him. At least she tells herself that it has. She begins to
find herself wishing that he was dead. How much better off
everyone would be. She is certain that if she were free, the
young man would marry her. One evening after a party,

her husband falls asleep while she is at the wheel. She leaves the engine running and shuts the garage door.

Up to this point it would be a straightforward story. Then it would become a detective story. I had never written a thriller. It would be fun to try one. I could have the representative of the company with whom the husband had insured his life, come down to the island to investigate the case. The widow would feel he was suspicious. The reader would never be told whether or not he was suspicious. The story would be told entirely through her eyes. The agent had many causes to feel suspicious. The heroine would gradually become certain that she was suspected.

The novel was, in fact, a range-finder for *Island in the Sun*.

It would be an exciting book to write and what a relief to have characters who were not worrying about Hitler and Mussolini: a book that would not date. In the end the woman would decide to commit suicide. She drives her car down to the beach. She swims out to sea. In half an hour's time it will all be over. She is at peace for the first time for weeks; so at peace that she wonders why she is letting herself be frightened into such a desperate action. What made her think that that prosaic insurance agent suspected her? A guilty conscience, that was all it was. How stupid she is being. She changes her mind. She swings round in the water and swims back to shore. But Fate is merciful and the waves are stronger.

I worked on the book steadily during the summer. By the end of August I was half-way through.

That spring A. D. Peters moved his Adelphi offices from Adam Street to Buckingham Street. It was a charming seventeenth-century house, but his business was smaller then than it is now, and the house was too big for him. He asked if I would care to take over, as a flat, a couple of rooms on the first floor. He was anxious to have a tenant whom he could trust not to 'snoop around' when the offices were closed. He would rent me the flat at two pounds a week and this minute rent would be deducted from my account with his firm. There would be a resident housekeeper who would serve breakfast and tidy up the flat, attending to the laundry. It was a tempting offer. The lease of my flat in Abbey Road was shortly falling due, and in October we as a family were to sail to Australia for the winter. Joan had rented a house near Melbourne in Sorrento. I should be away from London for six months. It would be an economy and a convenience. Adelphi was nearer to the parts of London that I frequented and I did not need more than a perch there. I did not need anywhere that I could entertain; just somewhere that I could keep some clothes and ask an occasional friend in for a drink. I accepted his offer. My acceptance was to have dramatic consequences for me later.

The flat was very small: one reasonably sized room, a bedroom that was really only a passage leading to a bathroom, with barely space for a single bed. After the war when the business enlarged it was John Montgomery's office for many years. It had charm and it had distinction. The walls were panelled; it had a fireplace of which photographs appeared in architectural books about 'old London'. There were some wooden bookshelves built into the corner of the wall beside the fireplace. It was easy to make it look attractive with a few pictures and the bookshelves filled.

At that time there was a picture gallery in Brook Street that rented pictures at so much a month, with an option to buy. For a month I had over the fireplace a very decorative flower picture by Matthew Smith. I could have had it for £60. It would be now worth a very considerable sum, but I preferred to it a Cedric Morris of a small group of birds for which I eventually paid £25. I already had at Edrington another picture by Cedric Morris. I always admired his work but I do not think his pictures have ever fetched high prices.

I played a good deal of cricket during the summer. I turned out regularly for the village side. Cassell's ran a touring eleven under the captaincy of Desmond Flower and this year as in other years they brought down a side to Silchester. We had a buffet lunch for them at Edrington and the day was warm and dry. I was a member of the Berkshire Gentlemen and played three or four times for them. One of the matches was against the Berkshire Regiment. The regiment was captained by Miles Dempsey, with whom I had played several times for the Chiltern Ramblers in the twenties. I sat next to him at lunch. Douglas Jardine came into the mess in the evening. He was in the Territorials.

I captained the MCC Sussex College tour. The weather was bad, and the last – and usually the best – game against Eastbourne College had to be cancelled, but we had some good cricket and some convivial evenings. Most of us stayed at the Metropole. I arranged to have a nucleus of the same players in the side each year. A. D. Peters, Keith Falkner, J. B. Wyndham, T. G. Grinter, A. N. A. Boyd. One of the Colvills came as 'our Professor'. We agreed to come on the tour next year. My parents went to Worthing for their summer holidays and they came over for the Lancing and the Brighton College matches.

On A. D. Peters' tour at Bath we played on the familiar grounds – Melksham, Trowbridge, Lacock, Box, Corsham. I cannot remember much about the actual matches. We did fairly well, as far as I can remember. Well enough for us to feel that we could tackle another tour next year. None of us were getting any younger. There was no new blood coming in. We were slow in the field, and there was a preference for half-day matches. Several players had dropped out over the last years. Sooner or later we should feel we were not equal to taking on the stronger town sides and should have to concentrate on the more rustic villages. We suspected that a tour would come when we should lose match after match with humiliating scores against us and when individual players would break down with strained backs or knees. Cecil Day Lewis came down for the first time for this tour, and something went wrong with his shoulder after the second match. When Clifford Bax resumed the tours in 1920 many of the players, survivors from 1914 who did not lead very active lives, found themselves 'breaking down'. Soon this would be happening to us. Within three years or so there would come the final tour which we would begin with fallacious optimism and gradually realise that the time had come to 'call it a day'. We should be very reluctant to face the facts and we should probably attempt one tour too many. We should be very loth to give up all that went with the tours, the good talk, the reading of the morning paper by the swimming pool, the morning beer at Forte's; the four-handed games of chess in the evening. We were lucky to be saved that by the war. In 1946 there was no question of our starting again.

The last match was against a military establishment near Corsham where Evelyn records in his diary 'six thousand civilians were at work storing explosives in fifteen miles of subterranean trenches under the ground'. My parents were staying with Evelyn at Stinchcombe, and Evelyn brought them over to watch the game. Evelyn reports that I 'made a good score and took some wickets'. Afterwards Evelyn drove me back to Stinchcombe for the week-end. It was the first time that I had been there. It was a beautiful house, with many lovely things in it. Evelyn was very happy over its embellishment. Much of his time was spent in excursions to sales. His diary is full of references to articles that he and Laura bought. Evelyn was very active in the garden; on the Sunday after attending Mass he changed into football kit and transported earth in a barrow from one part of the garden to another. He was leading a life in tune with his own nature. For how long, I wondered. In his diary for that day he wrote, 'War seems more probable' and on the Tuesday, August 22, he wrote, 'Russia and Germany have agreed to a neutrality pact so there seems no reason why war should be delayed.' I remembered how on his wedding day I had reflected that the failure of his first marriage had contributed to his development as a writer. I had thought then that Fate twists a writer's personal life so that his talent shall have its fullest scope. 'Half a beast is the great god Pan to make a poet out of a man.' Would history repeat itself under different circumstances? His marriage to Laura was firmly based, but would this domestic happiness be permitted to continue?

On his desk was the manuscript of his new novel. He was happily and confidently at work on it. In his subsequent letter of dedication to Alexander Wolcott he was to say that he hoped it would be his best book. But it was to be published as 'work suspended'. In exchange the next six years were to give him the material for *Put Out More Flags* and *Sword of Honour*. The war created in him the mood and series of moods that produced *Brideshead Revisited*, and sent Evelyn to Hollywood where he was inspired by Forest Lawns to write *The Loved One*.

Seeing how happy Evelyn was in his home and marriage, in view of the fact that that happiness had been won by seven years in an emotional wilderness, it seemed cruel that the happiness should not have been continued, but the great god Pan willed otherwise.

It was a great piece of good fortune that I should have that opportunity of seeing how very real that happiness was, and with our parents with us.

On that week-end a neighbour brought round for a pre-lunch glass of sherry the delightful Diana Holman Hunt, a granddaughter of Holman Hunt and consequently a cousin of ours, whom we had never met before. Holman Hunt married one of the daughters of our great-uncle, a London pharmacist.

Evelyn says of me that 'Alec was increasingly, abnormally inarticulate and engrossed in his profession.' This puzzles me. It is the only critical remark he has to make of me in the entire book. And I wonder what exactly he means by it. Does he by 'inarticulate' mean 'indistinct in speech'? There was a time when people, particularly Americans, complained that I mumbled and I have been on my guard against this tendency. I thought that by this time I had conquered it, or does he mean that I was imprecise, employing awkward turns of phrase. And why should he at this point call attention to the seriousness with which I took my writing? He must have been always aware that I was at pains to do my best. I do not think I have ever talked much about what I was writing, unless the people I was with were interested and that was not very often.

On the Monday morning I returned to London. Eleven days later the German tanks crossed the Polish frontier.

They were a strange eleven days. War was inevitable and I think everyone was relieved that it had come at last. One could not go on living from one crisis to the next. It had to be settled one way or another. Nobody had any doubt that we should win. Nobody except Vyvyan Holland. He had come down to Edrington for a few days of golf and wine tasting, Joan having taken the children to Sandwich to the Guildford Hotel for two weeks of sun and sand. 'How can we guarantee Poland's neutrality? How can we protect them, where, what with?' After listening to him patiently for a while I said, 'Do you remember how violent you were a year ago over our not going to war?'

'That was different,' he said.

'And shall I tell you what the difference is? Next month *The Importance of Being Earnest* is due to open at the Queen's Theatre for a six weeks' run. If there is a war all theatres will be closed.'

'You mustn't say things like that to me,' he answered.

As it happened theatres opened far earlier than anyone had expected. *The Importance of Being Earnest* was a great success. It was a superb production with John Gielgud, Edith Evans, Gwen Ffrangçon Davies. Instead of being taken off after a six weeks' run, it was kept on right through the winter.

In the Edrington guest book, Vyvyan has written 'Crisis Time' and he has put down his scores at the Calcot Golf Club, 78 and 79.

Our golf and our consumption of port were cut short, however. Joan decided to come back from Sandwich, to get the house ready for whatever might befall it.

'I suppose I should cancel our passage to Australia,' she said. The cancelling of that trip was one of the things in my life that I most regret. I was greatly looking forward to seeing Australia in her company. I have a feeling that I would have been excited by the country and by its problems, that I would have found plots and themes there, that it would have been an inspiration. Perhaps I might have made Australia instead of America 'my other country'.

At the end of August my father always spent a few days with us at Edrington. He usually came alone. My mother did not like to leave the poodle, which would have caused friction with Joan's dachshunds. His birthday was on August 24th, and when possible he came down for it. This year he came a little later, on Tuesday the 29th.

The weather was richly autumnal – mist in the morning, then the sun breaking through, with full summer heat by noon. It reminded my father of his boyhood; of his father going out to shoot. He had planned to stay until the Saturday, but the probability of war had by now become a certainty.

'I don't like to leave K alone at a time like this,' he said. He went back on the Thursday evening.

The next day German tanks moved into Poland. It was a question of hours now. But no official instructions had been given to the public, so in the evening Joan and I motored over to dinner at the Hind's Head at Bray. It was to prove the last time I dined there. I still have a copy of its wine list and now and again I read it nostalgically. What a parade of clarets. Margaux 1923 at 18/- (90p) a bottle, Mouton Rothschild 1924 at 20/- (£1.00). And in terms of Burgundy, Richebourg 1923 at 12s 6d, (62½p), Corton Grancey 1929 at 17/- (85p). Mine host Barry Neame died during the war. I have not had the heart to go there since. The food was as excellent as the wine. Joan and I did ourselves well at our last pre-war dinner.

We left as dusk was falling. No instructions about a black-out had been issued, but it was soon clear that an unofficial blackout had been imposed. The street lamps were unlit. We had to switch on our lights. Several times on the drive back indignant voices shouted at us, 'Put out those lights.' But we had no alternative. Next day the papers carried full instructions.

Our head gardener was the air-raid warden. During the morning he discussed with us the thickness of the library curtains. 'I don't think they are thick enough, sir,' he said. When we moved into Edrington, there had been black under-curtains but they were, we had thought, unsightly, and we had told the previous owners that we should not need them. The idea of a blackout had not occurred to us.

On the Sunday morning we did not go to church. We stayed at home to listen to Neville Chamberlain's broadcast. We had three cottages, across the path behind the kitchen garden. The head gardener's, the chauffeur's, the under-gardener's. I took my elder son, Andrew, down into the cellar, to collect three bottles of champagne. 'We'll take these bottles round to the cottages so that they can drink to the country's luck.'

At each door I made a little speech. Andrew handed across the bottle. 'He'll remember this all his life,' I thought. He did not, though. When in April 1946 he returned from Aus-tralia whither Joan had taken the children in June 1940, he had no recollection of it. What he did remember, was an occasion a year earlier when he had overheard, in the garden, Joan and I talking about the war. 'I don't see how we can keep out of it,' Joan had said. He had slunk away behind a hedge and wept.

You can never tell what children will remember. When Andrew and Veronica came back to Edrington, their first act was to rush up to the nursery, to see if there was still on the ceiling the stain where they had once thrown up some water. Neither Joan nor I remembered the incident.

'Did they ever talk of it in Australia?' I asked. She shook her head. Was it a secret that they had shared or was it at the very last moment that one of them had said, 'I wonder if there's still that stain on the ceiling where we threw up the water and Nannie was so mad at us?'

On the Tuesday morning I received a letter from the War Office, containing a railway warrant and instructions to report in uniform to the barracks in Dorchester, in two weeks' time.

CHAPTER 11

Back into Khaki

To celebrate my seventy-fifth birthday in July 1973 my English publishers W. H. Allen gave a dinner party for my new novel *The Fatal Gift*. It was fifty-six years since my first novel had been published. That is a long time to remain active in the arena. In my speech of reply I attributed my literary longevity to luck in many ways, but most of all to the actual date of my birth. Only a man born between November 1894 and November 1899 would have been old enough to serve in the first war and young enough to serve in the second. For any other career this would have been an unlucky birthday: the man born between those dates would not have finished his education, he would have started adult life at a great disadvantage; and then just when he had got over that handicap, he would, unless his work was of such importance to the war effort that he could claim exemption, have been back in the Army for six years, with his career interrupted at what might have been a critical point. For a novelist, however, mine was a lucky fate. I had the experience of commanding men in battle, than which there is no more important masculine experience. I developed quickly. I had written a novel at an age when I should have been a sixth former concerned with Greek iambics. I got a five-years' start. And then twenty years later when I was beginning to wonder whether I had been so lucky after all, there came this calling-up notice on the second day of war, with what was to prove a six-years' break in mid-career.

There were moments at the end of 1938 and the beginning

of 1939 when I had asked myself whether my contemporaries and I were not the seed that had been cast upon stony ground, that we had no roots in themselves, that we had come up too quickly. I had been granted a breather that I badly needed.

It was as I have already said through having been at Sandhurst and a regular officer that at the end of the war, I was enrolled in the regular Army Reserve of officers. Others who were not so graded found it difficult to get back into uniform. The period of 'the phoney war' was a troublesome time for the man of forty. Evelyn, who was not yet thirty-six, took two months going from one source of influence to another; and Evelyn had access to a great number of influential people. The early pages of his war diaries describe his efforts. The majority of his contemporaries abandoned the attempt and settled for some form of civilian occupation. Evelyn refers in *Put Out More Flags* to those who 'had taken out an insurance policy against unemployment by joining some military unit in the past'. Basil Seal's brother along with many others had joined the territorials 'as part of the normal obligations of rural life. They were now in uniform with their problems solved. In later months as they sat idle in the Middle East, they were to think enviously of those who had made a more deliberate and judicious choice of service, but at the moment their minds were enviously at rest.'

That was how I found myself. With what relief I opened the door of the orderly room at Dorchester, saluted a room that contained only two corporals and announced that Lieutenant Waugh was reporting for duty, sir!

In the first war through being seconded to the Machine Gun Corps, I had never joined the Dorsets, and when I had been called up at the time of the coal strike in 1921 I had been sent to the Machine Gun Corps base at Shorncliffe and thence to guard the docks at Newcastle. So that I did not now find myself among old comrades. I did however find myself in a familiar atmosphere.

The barracks at Dorchester had ceased to be the depot of the regiment and become instead an Infantry Training Centre for the newly joined recruits. I was posted to a specialists' company, my particular job being to train a section in the handling of the tracklined Bren gun carrier. I can imagine no job for which I was less well fitted, as I not only knew nothing about the insides of a car, but did not possess a driving licence. I protested when my assignment was explained to me.

'But how can I do that, when I can't drive a car?'

'That doesn't matter,' my company commander told me. 'You don't have to teach those fellows how to drive. You've got to see that your corporals and your sergeant teach them properly. Though I suppose that while you are out there, you might take a lesson or two yourself.'

'Out there' was Bovingdon, the bleak stretch of common that Thomas Hardy had called Egdon Heath and that was now a tank training area, and to which half my section went to take instruction, while the other half remained in Dorchester, being instructed in such barrack style activities as map-reading, musketry, and drill. One day I would stay in Dorchester. The next I would go out to Bovingdon, where I was an honorary member of the Tank Corps mess, and where I lunched rather better than I did in Barracks. On my days in Bovingdon I drew a half-day travel allowance, which was slightly more than my lunch cost me.

It was a cosy job. I was on my own. It had variety. I got to know my men and like them. On my second day at Sandhurst all the new cadets were bidden to write an essay on their first impressions of the RMC. It was the way that the officers learnt what the new draft was like. I learnt subsequently that my essay had impressed authority. As five months earlier I had been finishing *The Loom of Youth* that is not perhaps surprising. I followed the same procedure with my section. It was a help to me.

I did not make any progress in my studies of the mechanism of the Ford V8 engine though I had ample opportunities of doing so. At Bovingdon there was a hall filled with section-alised models of carburettors and the like. 'Is there anything that you'd like me to explain to you, sir?' my sergeant would say. I would shake my head. 'I think you made it very clear to us this morning.' And so he had, but to me there was all the difference in the world between the sectionalised model of a carburettor, and the greasy object that was concealed behind the crankshaft. I did not think that my NCOs should waste on me the time and care of which the other ranks stood in need.

I did, however, feel that I ought to possess a driving licence, so during my Christmas leave at Edrington I asked the local garage man to refresh my acquaintance with the rules of the road. On my return to Dorchester, I asked my company commander to give me a test. 'All right,' he said, 'I was planning to go to Bovingdon tomorrow. You can drive me out.'

I got him there safely. 'That'll do,' he said,' 'I'll sign your form.' But on the return he said, 'You don't mind, do you, if I drive?'

That showed me what he thought of my performance at the wheel. I have never driven a car since, and I have managed well enough without. But I wonder if it has not had any effect on me psychologically. For most men a car is an element in the technique of courtship. The heroes in my novels never drive out the heroines on lonely roads to see the sunset; they try to manœuvre them back to flats. *Island in the Sun* is, I think, the only novel of mine in which there is love-making in a car.

For the first ten days at Dorchester we were under can-vas, then we moved back, half of us into billets, the others into the mess. I had a room in the mess which was much handier and much more comfortable than a billet. Coal was provided. Within three weeks I was settled into the fam-iliar routine of peace-time soldiering, with week-end leave twice a month. Sometimes I went to Edrington, sometimes Joan joined me in London and we went to the theatre. The phoney war was now established. I had reported at Dorchester in the belief that I might be posted away at any moment; but like most of the reservists I was now on the strength of the ITC and I pictured myself training batches of new recruits indefinitely, with a new group joining us every month.

One morning the senior Major in the mess was indignant because his boiled egg was stamped 'From Holland'.

'In an English mess, we should have English eggs.'

That was how life was then. None of us guessed that in eight months' time, as far as England was concerned, there would be no Holland and no eggs.

The first battalion of the Dorsets was in Malta, the second was in France. When it sailed in the first week of the war, the small group of Junior NCOs and officers that it left behind as a training cadre contained two young subalterns of three years' standing, who had joined the regiment on the same day and had been the closest of friends ever since. They were a lively and popular couple who had contributed considerably to the gaiety of local society before the war. In the second week of October they felt that some effort should be made to resume that gaiety. The war had not started yet. One might as well enjoy oneself until it did. They decided therefore to hold a small evening party. They knew a number of young women in the neighbourhood who were beginning to feel bored. There was also a house called Conygar, six miles out of Dorchester, that belonged to Charles Boxer, who later married Emily Hahn. Boxer was in the Far East but his sister-in-law was living there – his brother Myles Boxer was in France. She was an attractive woman in her early thirties. She had as guests two lively young women in the ATS who were serving as orderlies in the Officers' Mess. Conygar could be a good base for parties.

These parties were to be on a modest scale. Hours, the Colonel insisted, must be early. They started at six and ended at ten-thirty. There were sandwiches. There was dancing. Whisky was in short supply – we mostly drank gin and lime. Rose's Lime Juice was at that time very popular in England. Its sales were backed by an astute advertising campaign in which a peer in bed was saying to his butler who called him with his morning tea, 'I'm surprised to feel so well this morning, Jenkins. It was a big night, you know.'

'That's because you were mixing Rose's Lime Juice with your gin, milord.'

And in point of fact Rose's Lime Juice and gin do mix very well.

The first party was a success. Others swiftly followed. Everyone was in a party mood. For several months the country had been living under heavy strain. It had been impossible to settle down to anything in that atmosphere of uncertainty. On September 3rd we had thought, 'Now it's come. Now we can get on with it.' When nothing happened, we felt let down. We talked of 'the bore war'. At Dorchester we were in the mood for parties, we were in the mood to meet new people. Our old lives had ceased. We were anxious to find out who were the other inhabitants of this new world to which we were committed; with whom we were to share this new existence.

That first autumn was a period of discovery, that had its own special, particular excitement. A number of other houses were open to us. The director of the West Country brewers Eldridge and Pope had been at the same preparatory school as I. We ourselves from the mess organised returns of hospitality. It was a strange, self-contained universe. We were on an island. All round us was the embattled world; but here outside it within a seven-mile radius of Dorchester we were self-sufficient. It was a curiously personal, curiously unreal world. We were curiously at peace; and in this unreal world we began to fall in love.

It was a *drôle de guerre* and it was a *drôle d'amour*. It bore the same relationship to a real love affair that the Maginot Line did to actual fighting. It was unadmitted, undeclared.

We never saw each other alone. With petrol rationed, transport had to be carefully organised: as many crammed into one car as a car could hold. We met at parties. We made plans for the next party. We now and again talked on telephones. There were admitted preferences but that was all. We had a vague prescience that sooner or later this *drôle d'amour* would have to end, just as the *drôle de guerre* would have to end. We were in no hurry for that to happen.

Myself, I was no exception. She was to be, twenty-five years later, the heroine of my novel *The Mule on the Minaret*. I called her Diana then. I will call her Diana here. She was twenty-seven years old, unmarried, the daughter of a retired and knighted admiral. She was very tall: when we danced, I used to move at an angle to her, my left arm hanging free. Once in London fifteen months later we were guests at an Anglo-French officers' dance at the Dorchester. She was dancing with a Frenchman so much shorter than she, that the couple looked ridiculous. 'What a pity that that woman is so tall,' I overheard one of the guests say. When they came back to the table, I recognised that he was three or four inches taller than I. Yet I never felt ridiculous when I was dancing with Diana. I suppose that because I did not, she herself felt quite natural, whereas she would feel awkward dancing with a man of five foot eleven.

She was dark. She had blue eyes. I will not say that she was beautiful, but she had radiant moments, when she seemed transfigured. She was a Scot. She was indomitable. She had great courage. She was incapable of anything mean or petty. She was one of the finest people I have ever known. She had a deep contralto voice. Talking to her on the telephone was a date.

We met regularly through the autumn. We were asked to the same parties. Once or twice we went to a cinema, taking tea first at the Judge Jeffrey's Rooms, then dining afterwards. When she was drinking red wine she would hold the glass between her hands.

She had not yet found the kind of war work that would

prove congenial, and had some half-time employment taking Red Cross classes. But in mid-December she went up to London for a week and returned with the news that she had been taken on at Passport Control, the cover name for MI6.

'That means we shan't see you any more,' I said.

'Not much, I'm afraid. I've now got to start looking for a flat in London.'

I had an idea. 'I've got a flat in London I can let you have for a pound a week.'

That would be a bargain for her; and a convenience for me. The flat was no use to me and even £2 a week was an expense when I was living on a Lieutenant's pay. 'I think that's a fine idea,' she said.

A quite different time was to begin for me. With Diana in London, Dorchester lost much of its appeal, and with Diana in London I now had an impulse to go up there myself. It would be fun to take her out to dinner and a theatre. If I was to yield to that impulse I would need more money. I remembered my half-finished novel. It needed another ten weeks' work. When I delivered the manuscript, Cassell's would pay me half the advance – £300. I suggested to Peters that he finance those ten weeks by paying me £5 a week until I had finished it. Peters agreed. I set to work.

I had in the first war found the conditions of Army life conducive to novel writing. My body was occupied but my mind was free. I got up at two o'clock every morning and wrote until reveille at half-past six. I went to bed at half-past eight. I have seldom written a book with more excitement. The conditions were precisely those which I had described as ideal four years before, separated from one dear to me, thinking at the end of each day's stretch at writing: 'I am two thousand words nearer her.' The last page was sent off to be typed in mid-April. Another week and the typescript would be back to me. A week of revision and Cassell's would have the book. Summer would have begun. How often would I be able to get up to London? There was a

train for the West that left Waterloo at 4 am. It reached
Wool Station that was two miles from Bovingdon at ten to
ten. My Bren gun carriers could meet me there. They and I
could manage a full day's work. It looked a very reasonable
project. I might be able to go up to London to dine with
Diana at least once a week. And every third or fourth week-
end I could be in London. Such was the project that I held
before my eyes, in those early mornings as I sat at my bedroom table, the small handwriting steadily blackening page
after page.

Was it a reasonable project? I thought it was. It might have
been. I was never to find out. On the third Saturday in
April the Orderly Room at Dorchester received instructions
that on the Monday afternoon at 3 pm Lieutenant Waugh
was to report to room 308, at the Northumberland Avenue
hotel. What on earth was this about: how had it come
about?

And that was something I was never to find out completely. I presented my credentials at the hotel. I was met at
the barrier by a corporal whom I recognised as the Middlesex slow bowler Powell with whom I had played a number
of MCC matches against schools. 'You're for France, sir,'
he informed me. France? But why? In what capacity?
Surely not to help train the drivers of Bren gun carriers.
Powell took me down a long passage to a room that
was occupied by a number of army secretaries in uniform,
tapping at typewriters. A middle-aged captain wearing a
red and black brassard on his arm came in. 'We know each
other,' he said, 'don't we?'

I had met him at Murren at the Grand Palace Hotel in
January 1926, when I had gone as the guest of Arnold Lunn,
to obtain material about skiing for a projected novel. He had
been one of the chief figures in the Kandahar Club.

'Of course,' I said.

'We've had quite a job finding you,' he said. 'There's no
need for me to ask you any questions; you're identified.
I'll take you in to see the Major.'

The Major was in a barely furnished room with two sub-alterns. Everything seemed very improvised and crowded: the place had been a hotel, after all, seven months before. One of the subalterns was a young man with whom I had played cricket with the Chiltern Ramblers. It was curious that three of the first five people I met, I should have known already. The Major was friendly, burly and middle-aged.

'So we've run you down to earth at last. That's good. I think we've got a nice assignment for you. Know Ewan Butler, don't you?' Ewan Butler. I am bad at names: I did not think I did.

'You don't. Well you soon will. Capital fellow, capital fellow. Nothing to stop you going across right away is there?'

'I've all my things at Dorchester.'

'You have? Well that's a nuisance. You'll have to go back to fetch them. How long will that take? A day, two days? You can go down this evening. Bring it all back tomorrow. Report here on Wednesday morning and we'll have you off on Thursday.'

On that Thursday morning I caught the 11.30 train from Waterloo. My parents came down to see me off. Catching this particular train that I had caught so often on my way back to Edrington, it was hard to realise that this was not an ordinary routine journey. It did not seem that I was starting a campaign, in uniform, in wartime. How different had been the catching of that leave train from this same station in February 1918.

'You look so young in uniform,' my mother said. I took off my cap, to retain my seat in the compartment. Balding and bare-headed, I looked more than forty. 'The years pile on now,' my father said.

The train stopped at Basingstoke. Joan had brought the children down to the station to say goodbye to me. I handed over to them a suitcase and my cricket bag. I wondered when I should need that cricket bag again.

CHAPTER 12

The BEF Again

I was bound, though I did not know it, for Arras, where GHQ was stationed. Its code name was 'Brassard' and the word 'Arras' must never be mentioned on the telephone. I was provided with a sheaf of documents that I had to present to a succession of RTOs. Each RTO in turn tore off the appropriate sheet. I was described on these sheets as IO Writer (Intelligence Officer Writer). So that was what I was. But what that signified I was never to discover even when I eventually reached Brassard, and it took me a day and a half to get there.

I had crossed the Channel in one of the usual steamers and the usual steward brought me tea and biscuits in the morning. Le Havre looked as it always did, with large invitations to transatlantic passengers to 'say it with flowers'; I was still part of the familiar 'between-the-wars' world. But after Le Havre I was back in World War I, dawdling across northern France in an unheated second-class carriage. 'When I eventually arrive I'll find out what it's all about,' I thought.

I did not, though. I was not expected. At least I was not expected to arrive on that particular day. It was only known that I was supposed to be on my way. I found in the office to which I was directed the Captain in Charge of the Section, Ewan Butler, and Lord Gerald Wellesley – who was later to become the Duke of Wellington – and with whom I was to share a desk. 'What am I to do at that desk?' I asked.

'You'll soon find out. All in good time,' they said. They

would check me into a hotel; in a day or two I would be found a billet. And in a day or two I would be found a mess: till then it would be a question of looking after myself in restaurants. In the meantime they would take me out to dinner; to a very good dinner too: with champagne to finish up with. 'You'll find a lot of old friends here,' they told me.

The office hours were 8 till 1 and 4 to 7 with one afternoon off a week. There was no period for exercise or recreation. Indeed during the winter when the weather had been bitterly cold, the health of the staff suffered through lack of exercise and over-eating. There was no occasion for the junior officers to leave their offices. They had no business to transact with other sections. There were no conferences to which they were summoned. They had nothing to do all day except read and write.

There was a good deal to read. We had both the London and the Paris newspapers. We were encouraged to make extracts from the French papers to use in our reports. We were a branch of public relations and part of our job was to keep relations good between British troops and the civilian population. Domestic adultery was a constant problem. The Poilus in the Maginot Line were worried about the way in which their womenfolk were conducting themselves with the Tommies who were billeted in their homes. There were also the incidents in which civilians were injured by cars and trucks driven by military personnel. Lists of these occurrences were prepared and sent to the administrations concerned. The preparation of these lists devolved upon Gerald Wellesley. When we found such an incident ourselves, we would mark the paper and pass it over to him. Occasionally we were given a particular assignment. The section was asked for instance to prepare a case for banning the circulation overseas of two publications likely to lower the morale of the troops – Claud Cockburn's *This Week* and Oswald Mosley's *Action*. As Cockburn was a cousin of mine, I asked if I might be given the Mosley dossier. After a morning's study of the file, I could not see how any sensible man could be discouraged from doing his duty by Mosley's pleas for a police state. But I made the arguments in favour of banning *Action* as persuasive as I could. By the time GHQ were ready to take action, there were no British troops in France to be corrupted.

Such definite assignments were unusual, however. I was an IO Writer and my job was to write. Ewan Butler had been *The Times* correspondent in Berlin. He was an excellent journalist and since the war has written several quite successful books, but he had not been trained to organise other people's work. 'Write what you feel like,' he instructed me.

'What happens to the stuff?'

'We send it to the Press.'

'What Press?'

'The French Press, first. Then back to London. Everything we produce goes back to the War Office.'

The DMI was Mason Macfarlane, who after the war stood for Parliament and defeated Brendan Bracken at the 1945 election. Under him was Gerald Templar, who was to become CIGS after the war. They were two inspiring chiefs. I wrote a series of five articles on the methods of training in an ITC, to prove to the French how thoroughly and efficiently the British were training their recruits. 'That's just the stuff,' said Butler. I was congratulated by both Templar and Mason Macfarlane. I was excited at being on the General Staff. I was very anxious to do well.

I devised the idea of writing a serial story about a young British officer who fell in love with a French shopgirl. His romantic and honourable behaviour would improve the general image of the British in French eyes. I have forgotten the plot. It was the kind of thing that in the twenties I had sold to the *Daily Mirror*. I wrote three instalments. The idea of writing fiction was a new one. Butler was delighted, 'We must try and place this with some French paper.'

'How will we do that?' I asked.

'That's not our job. The public relations section will look after that.'

And that, of course, was the trouble about our section. There was no machinery by which its productions could be got into print and distributed to the public to which it was addressed. In the Middle East later in the war there was a large public relations department which issued its own magazine, and daily and weekly newspapers. It was a very efficient department, run by professionals. But there was nothing of that sort then in the BEF. I do not think that anything I wrote at Arras was ever printed. Sooner or later I should have realised this and my enthusiasm would have evaporated. I have never worked for a studio in Hollywood, and I have never known how script writers manage to keep up their spirits, working on stories that are never filmed. Six months at the most would have finished me, I expect; that would eventually have happened to me in Arras, but in the meantime my morale stayed high.

I had also the typescript of my novel to correct. I could not, I felt, bring it to the office and correct it at my desk, under the scrutiny of Gerald Wellesley, so once again I found myself getting up early in the morning at my billet. It required about ten days' work. On the fifth day half of it was finished. I took it to the censorship department.

'What's this?' I was asked.

'A novel.'

'What about?'

'Adultery in the West Indies.'

'That should be all right. Is it spicy?'

'Slightly.'

'Then I'll look at it myself.'

Another five days and I brought him the second half.

'Here's the rest of it,' I said.

'Good, I enjoyed the first half.'

'Has it got off all right?'

'Of course. No security risk there. I could send this instalment off unread. But I had fun with the first half. I'd like to know how it all turns out. Extraordinary the things you chaps can get away with nowadays.'

In 1940 *No Truce With Time* seemed quite a daring book. 'I'll have it off tomorrow,' he assured me. But that was on May the 9th.

That night air raid warnings went for the first time. There was the sound of guns. I fancied I heard one or two explosions. Next morning the town looked as undisturbed as it had every other morning but on the mantelpiece in my mess was a notice instructing 'all GHQ Officers to report to their offices directly after breakfast'. The balloon had gone up all right.

Gerald Wellesley had stretched out on his desk the table plan on which he had been at work the night before. In the following week a large inter-allied dinner was to be held in Lille. Gamelin was to attend it. Wellesley had been a diplomat in the early stages of his career. General Gort had ordered him to draw up a table plan in terms of protocol. 'I don't suppose I shall need this any more,' he said.

He had a map of Arras on his desk. He was marking the places where bombs had fallen during the night. 'My billet is here. Bombs fell here, here, here and here.' He joined the crosses with his pencil. 'My billet is in the exact centre of that area.' The hotel where I had stayed on my first night was one of those that had been hit.

The photographer who was attached to us came in.

'Any instructions for me?' he asked.

'You bet I have,' said Butler. 'You drive up to the frontier and start taking photographs.' He looked round the room. 'You might as well take Waugh with you,' he said.

It was a bright, sunny day; the rolling countryside was fresh and green. Would tanks be churning up that greenness in a few hours' time? We passed through Douai. I had spent four days there in the first war after being captured. A factory had been bombed. Nobody seemed to be taking steps to get it back into operation. My companion took photographs. We reached the frontier shortly after ten. The barrier was still across the road. There was quite a number of cars parked in a side road. An American radio man I knew – a member of the Savage Club – was standing by his microphone. He had a cameraman beside him.

'I'm to report the raising of that barrier,' he said. 'It'll be quite a moment.'

I lay in the grass and waited. Ten o'clock passed, half-past ten, eleven, five past eleven. Then the barrier went up. The drama of the moment lay in its complete absence of theatricality. Nothing was happening, yet everything was happening. The barrier was up. Once again Britain and France and Belgium were allies in the face of war. That barrier would not be lowered till the war was won . . . and when would that be?

We did not that day go very far into Belgium. We drove as far as the first town, Tournai, and took photographs of the first lorryloads of troops being welcomed by the Belgians with boughs of flowering shrubs. We were back in Arras by dinner time. But on the Saturday we went back early, with instructions to stay the night in Brussels.

We knew by now that German tanks had struck deep into northern France. They were not yet engaged with British troops but their effect on the civilian population was manifest. We booked rooms at an hotel facing the railway station, and the trains going south were crowded. We passed car after car headed south and west. Many of them had mattresses strapped on to their roofs, as a protection against bombs. We called at the British Embassy and saw a Second Secretary. We asked what newspaper offices we should visit. He handed us a copy of one of the morning papers. Most of it was filled with empty columns. The censor had been busy. The communiqués were printed in large type, alongside the new wartime regulations; the sale of alcohol was prohibited: only beer and wines were to be served in restaurants. 'I doubt if there'll be any Monday papers,' we were warned. The Embassy itself was clearly packing up, ready to move south.

We lunched in a restaurant in the big square. It was half-full, but talk was muted. The proprietor offered us an aperitif. 'You are the first British officers to honour my restaurant,' he said. I wondered if we should be the last. Belgians had always specialised in Burgundy. We asked him what we should order. He brought us an undated Beaune. It had not the majesty of the Beaune 1923 that I had drunk twenty months earlier with the Club des Cents but it was very good. So was the lunch itself. I wished that the Saintsburys could have accepted the Baron de Marchiennes' invitation in the previous autumn.

Cafés closed at ten o'clock that night. No one was on the streets. We went into one of the largest hotels. Two men were sitting reading in opposite corners of the lounge. I wondered who they were and what they were doing. I supposed that until three days ago there were Americans on business trips in Brussels.

Next morning we drove further east. We went as far as Louvain. It was Sunday and the shops were closed. At a kiosk beside a bus stop there were signs of a precipitate departure – an abandoned meal, dirty plates, a half-finished bun. In a public garden we found a section of British troops digging trenches. A Belgian policeman objected when we took photographs. He marched us to the officer in charge, who examined our passes with suspicion. 'I don't think you should be in forward areas like this,' he said. Forward areas. So that was where we were. Had the battle advanced that far? 'I think we'd better be turning back,' I said. We might find ourselves confronted with an advance patrol. We were unarmed. I did not want to spend another war in a prison camp. We drove back through Lens. Young girls were parading the streets proudly in their white first communion clothes.

I returned to Arras to find GHQ in a process of dispersal. Half the staff had gone forward. I began to wonder whether the manuscript of my novel had been sent to London. I called round at the censor's office and found it closed. Where had it moved to? No one whom I could contact knew. Ourselves we were told to await orders. We had nothing to do. I wrote an account of my trip to Brussels that was typed and sent back to London. I saw no point in continuing my *Daily Mirror*-type serial. The sun shone. We sat in deckchairs in a garden that contained a small artificial pond which we had recently stocked with trout and goldfish. We wondered what would happen to the fish if we retired, as it began to appear certain that we should. Might it not be humane as well as pleasant to let the water out of the pond, scoop up the fish into a bowl, take them round to the mess and instruct the cook to make a *friture*? For a whole morning we sat there in the sun, arguing out the problem. We were so absorbed in our debate that we did not realise how absurd it was, that in the middle of one of the greatest battles in the history of the world, a section of Intelligence Officers should spend a whole morning debating the fate of a pondful of infant fish.

In the late afternoon we learnt that our chief, Mason Macfarlane, had been put in charge of a large body of fighting troops named Macforce, that he had taken Gerald Templer with him, and we were now under Public Relations.

Next day we were told to entrain that evening for Boulogne. We arrived there early in the morning. At Arras strict security had been placed on the presence there of Brassard. No such security was employed in Boulogne, a town presumably honeycombed with spies. As our train drew up in the station a loudspeaker announced that all GHQ officers were to report to the Imperial Hotel. It was not surprising that within a few hours German planes had made the Imperial their target.

Luckily it was a concrete structure. Gerald Wellesley and I were sharing a room on the sixth floor. We had just gone to bed when the raid began. We got out of bed and stood on the balcony to watch a plane circle over the town. Then it loosed a stick of bombs.

Even at Ypres in 1917 I had not seen so much blood shed;

Alec Waugh in May 1936

Alec Waugh's Christmas card to New York, 1936

Andrew Waugh with his mother. Christmas 1933

Alec Waugh in 1946

Edrington, 1938

Andrew and Veronica Waugh with
their mother in Australia, 1943

At a New York cocktail party, 1947, with Michael Arlen on the extreme right

In search of copy Alec Waugh goes to a Butlin's Holiday Camp in August 1947. Alec Waugh is on the extreme right

Alec Waugh with Charles and Barbara Addams at Doubleday's party for 'the Lipton story' held in the New York Yacht Club, 1950

Midshipman Andrew Waugh, 1952

Veronica Waugh's wedding to Christopher Keeling,
September 1955

Quentin Reynolds' party in Tangier, March 1956. From left to right: Alec Waugh,
Quentin Reynolds, Daphne Fielding and Beverley Nichols

Alec Waugh with Virginia Sorensen. Macdowell Colony, 1958

British Consul General in Boston. Darcy Edmondson (extreme right) gives fund-raising party for Macdowell Colony. Virginia Sorensen, Alec Waugh and James Ramsay Ullman

Peggy Mann, author of *A Room in Paris*

Alec Waugh in Malaysia, 1964

Alec Waugh in Tangier, 1966

Peter Waugh

With James Dickey at Alec Waugh's seventieth birthday party in
Alexandria, Virginia

a number of men were killed, a number wounded: among them was Roger Machel of *The Times* with whom I had dined earlier in the evening. One of the wounded men was screaming. A lorry carrying petrol was ablaze. Among those on the spot was Colonel Medlicott, originally of Anglo-Persian Oil and now in charge of Public Relations. His daughter Yvonne worked in the same office as Diana. The sight of that blazing lorry gave him an idea. Later in London when a group of oil men was deciding how, in the event of an invasion, to prevent oil from falling into German hands, Medlicott remembered that blazing lorry –

'Why not,' he suggested, 'burn it offensively. Flame-throwers, oil bombs, things like that.' That was the germ of the subsequent Petroleum Warfare Department, of which I was to be Staff Captain for a year.

One of the bombs landed on the Imperial, just below my window, smashing a hole in it. My room was a shambles, windows and door blown out. I had been told that aviators after a plane crash immediately get in a plane and fly it, otherwise they will lose their nerve. I had an idea therefore, that if I were to keep my nerve now, I should be well advised not to go below into the shelter. I did not relish the idea of a further sixth-floor residence, but luckily the previous residents had left behind them in the general commotion of retirement, not only a pile of blankets but a collection of 'curious' books that I should have been shy of reading in public. I selected the most lurid one and swept the glass out of my bed. In London a few months later, I seemed no more perturbed during the air raids than anybody else.

Our section had been accorded a small office in the town. There was no mess for us to join but we were issued with a consignment of iron rations so that we could picnic in our office. We had no work to do except to provide the BBC with a daily news bulletin on the progress of the battle. 'You might do it today, Alec,' Butler said.

We had received no intelligence summaries from strategic headquarters which had gone forward when we 'retired'.

'Say what you like,' Butler instructed me. My only source of information was the BBC announcements and a local paper the *Pas de Calais*: after studying the map I decided to draw a parallel between the present situation and the Battle of Naseby. I compared Hitler's tanks with Rupert's horse. 'Now as then,' I concluded, 'infantry will decide the day.'

We had brought our suitcases with us from the Imperial Hotel.

'We are going to Paris to form a new headquarters there,' Butler informed us. In the meantime we were to move into new billets in the town. Eventually I found myself sharing a vast ormolu double bed with Gerald Wellesley. 'It's only for one night,' Butler said.

That afternoon we learnt that the only road to Paris had been cut. Later, walking along the waterfront, I passed the Duke of Gloucester walking in the opposite direction, with Colonel Medlicott. His presence reassured me. If he was here, the War Office must know that we were, too. We were not abandoned.

On the Wednesday morning we were told to be at the docks by one o'clock, carrying one small suitcase. The docks were littered with discarded army blankets. It was then that I realised the extent of the rout in which I was involved. Troops must be in a bad way before they discard blankets.

The bombing on that last afternoon was heavy. In spite of the instructions to bring only one small suitcase, I had brought a heavy suitcase too. As I lay out on the docks I wondered if I should rearrange my kit so as to get it all into the one suitcase. I had a pair of new brown shoes in the small case. I had difficulty in fitting them into the bigger case. The bombing became more intense. I was beginning to get frightened. 'I can't be bothered with this,' I thought. 'If I have to, I'll leave the small suitcase here.'

'Now don't be a fool,' I adjured myself. 'You are now on the docks at Boulogne, being bombed. Nothing matters except getting your body on to that boat out there. But tomorrow afternoon you'll be in London. You'll need those shoes there.'

The cross-Channel steamer that was to take us back was anchored some fifty yards away. We were to be rowed out to it in a succession of small boats. Our journey from Arras had been impeded by the responsibility of a wooden box – the size of a small coffin – that contained, Butler assured us, valuable secret documents. It had been a nuisance then. It was a nuisance now. It was awkward to handle and now at the very last moment as it was being lifted up the gangplank, it slipped out of Butler's hands: it crashed back into the boat and slid into the water, the light wood splintered and the sacred contents floated out to sea.

Eventually the last small boat took off, and at this final moment a fireman who had been on duty there decided that he had had enough of being bombed and jumped into the boat. He fell as he did so. From the expression on his face he looked as though he had quite hurt himself. I always wondered what happened to him. He arrived in England without military status, without presumably any papers of identity, without any luggage in his bright fireman's uniform. As likely as not he spoke no English. What did happen to him?

Among the refugees from Arras that I found on board was the censor to whom I had handed the typescript of my novel. I asked him if it had got back to London. 'No,' he told me, 'but it's quite all right. It is in a big black box in Amiens.' I think this was one of the silliest remarks that I have ever heard.

CHAPTER 13

London after Dunkirk

It was on the 23rd of May that I was evacuated from Boulogne. Nine weeks later I was posted to a month's intelligence course at Swanage. Those nine weeks were as crowded and disorganised as any that I have known. I have not kept my pocket diary for that year and I cannot recall the exact sequence of events. To begin with Ewan Butler and myself were posted to the War Office to work in the Public Relations Section. There was an idea for getting out a magazine for the troops still in France. There were several old friends in the Section, such as Denzil Batchelor and E. G. Boulenger; the atmosphere was congenial, but we had barely begun to work out a rough draft of the magazine when it was decided to form a new GHQ BEF south of the Loire, and Ewan Butler's section reassembled at Aldershot Barracks to await sailing orders.

We spent a morning there, during which we were issued with a great deal of equipment, including an excellent pair of binoculars that I still possess. Then Butler asked whether we could not go back to our homes, provided we left our addresses, so that we could be recalled at a moment's notice. This was on a Monday. It was on the Friday morning that the first steps to form the new GHQ had been taken, and during the week-end it had become very doubtful if this new GHQ would ever be assembled. At the end of the week the project was definitively abandoned and we were told to report each day at Chelsea Barracks for new instructions. I was to wait there for two weeks. At the beginning there were some twenty of us. One by one we were posted to other units. Finally only Gerald Wellesley and myself were left unposted. At the end of the week I was left alone, with orders to report on the Monday morning to Holland House, which was among other things the central bureau for unposted officers. I was welcomed by a very friendly major. 'How long is it since you have had any leave?'

'Not since Christmas.'

'Then I think you had better take a week's leave now. After that I have a very pleasant little PT course for you at Hendon. Report there at the Police Barracks on Monday week, nine o'clock: take gym shoes and shorts and a number 3 iron.'

I remained there till I was sent on the intelligence course at Swanage.

In fact, during that crowded two months, when the country was alight and rejuvenated with the Dunkirk spirit, with Winston Churchill's oratory, with Herbert Morrison's 'Go to it', with J. B. Priestley's Sunday evening broadcasts, no one in the country can have made a more negligible contribution to the War effort.

In other respects, however, a good deal was happening. Though the typescript of my novel was buried in a big black box in Amiens, I still had the manuscript of the last quarter. I got it retyped, revised and sent off to Cassell's. I did the final revision in the Library of the Athenæum. I was nearing the last page when J. C. Squire came across to me, his face wearing an excited look. 'Did you hear Winston on the air last night?' he asked.

'I did.'

'Terrific, wasn't it terrific? I sat right down afterwards and wrote a poem. I'll show it you.'

He pulled from a bulging pocket a crumpled piece of paper. It was an eight-line poem, two four-line stanzas. It looked pretty good to me.

'Fine,' I said. 'It's fine.'

'I think so too. I took it straight down to *The Times*. Took a taxi there. No point in waiting till today. I couldn't better it. One knows about these things. It's coming out tomorrow.'

He looked over my shoulder. 'What's that you're working on?'

'A novel.'

'You're working on a novel?' He looked amazed and rather shocked. 'To be working on a novel, at a time like this.'

In the first war girls gave white feathers to young men who were not yet in uniform. In this war a quadragenarian in uniform was given what amounted to a white feather for employing his time frivolously, at a time of crisis.

I put the manuscript into a large envelope and took it across the Strand to Peters' office. Two seventy-five pounds, less the money Peters had advanced me. A hundred and fifty, say, in my account next week, I would give a party. I had not been to a London party for a year.

While as a soldier I was being moved, purposelessly and profitlessly from one desk to another, my personal life continued its familiar routine. I dined at the Savile, I visited my parents, I took a net at Lord's. We had week-end guests at Edrington. Then Joan decided to go back to Australia.

'We aren't doing any good here. We're useless mouths. I can't bear the idea of the kiddies not getting enough to eat.'

'You're very wise,' I said. The plans were carried out speedily. There was a week-end at Edrington, just like every other week-end, with Evelyn ringing up to ask if he could bring over Laura and a brother officer and his wife to dinner. He was stationed in the neighbourhood. His unit was on the move. 'Are you going to the Middle East?' I asked. 'No, no.'

He did not tell me where he was going. But later I realised that he must have been bound for Dakar. It was the first time that I had seen him in uniform. He looked very fit and soldierly. The Morley Kennerlys were with us that week-end. During dinner on the Saturday the police rang up to ask if Morley was with us. As an American citizen his movements were being watched.

Early on the Monday morning I went back to London, to my waiting at the Chelsea Barracks, planning to invite the Lovat Dicksons down for the next week-end, but that evening there was a message from Joan that her ship was to sail on Friday, that she was catching a train from Euston on the Thursday evening.

I could not believe that it was happening so rapidly. I took two more days' leave. My father and mother came down for the Wednesday night. He was beginning to look and feel very old. It was almost certainly the last time he would come to Edrington. My elder son Andrew was about to be seven years old, Veronica to be six. They would look quite different when I saw them next. I was saying goodbye to their childhood. They showed no particular excitement about going away. They did not feel that they were beginning a big adventure.

I sat by Joan while she packed her trunks. We had always made mild fun of my Uncle George, my mother's half-brother, an amiably eccentric clergyman. He had three years earlier sent us a Christmas present, a passport photograph of himself. We had thought it funny, because we had thought him funny, and there had grown up between us a silly, but at the same time amusing, game – in the way that family jokes are amusing to the family – of passing this photograph backwards and forwards between ourselves, in an envelope containing tickets for a Test Match say, or in an official Jury summons. I now, when Joan was out of the room, slipped the photograph into the pocket of a light spring overcoat. It would be a nostalgic surprise for her when her fingers encountered it in Melbourne on some December morning five months hence.

The fact that the police had rung up Edrington to ask if Morley Kennerly, an American citizen, was staying there was typical of a new atmosphere of suspicion in the country. The threat of invasion was in the air. The danger was believed to be very actual. Both Richard Church and Hugh Walpole on the same day in early June began their review of the week's books with the reflection that it was strange to be sitting down at a familiar desk doing a routine review of books that might never appear because the country had been invaded. Authority was on the alert and the examples of Norway, Denmark, Holland were being studied. The danger of fifth columnists had to be kept in mind. In those countries there had been many disaffected citizens ready to welcome the invader. In England there had been the British Union of Fascists and a society called 'The Link' that had sympathies with Germany. There were a great many refugees from Germany, some of whom must have been planted by the Nazis. Steps were taken to ensure that there were no German sympathisers at large. A law called 18B allowed the police to hold without trial British subjects who were likely to constitute a security risk. Mosley and many of his henchmen were arrested. A great many Germans and Italians were deported, some of them in ships that were to be torpedoed in mid-Atlantic. Savatoni from the Savoy Grill was one of them. English girls who had love affairs with Germans and Italians were cross-examined by MI5. They were warned that if they did not tell all they knew, their fathers would be informed of their peccadilloes.

Defeatist talk was threatened with prosecution. Duff Cooper as Minister of Information attempted to organise 'The Silent Column' for those who were resolved not to discuss the war. It was in this atmosphere that I celebrated the delivery of my new novel. The party was held in a friend's flat in Chelsea. I asked about thirty guests, among them several friends whom I had not seen since the war began. I intended it to be a lively occasion; it should have been, and in the main it was. Cocktail parties were not all that common at the time and there was no lack of champagne. Unfortunately two of my guests became involved in an altercation – Diana and A. G. Macdonell.

A.G.M. was one of my oldest and best friends. I was

one of the characters in *England, Their England*. He was a delightful fellow, but he was quarrelsome and choleric. One of my friends nicknamed him 'The Purple Scot'. I do not know how he and Diana drifted into their altercation. Pétain was the subject of it. I did not overhear any part of it. But a girl who did overhear it said that Diana's defence of Pétain was outrageous. I can well believe it. She was always ready to defend the unpopular point of view. But she did not lose her temper, whereas Archie did. She remained aloofly contemptuous.

Among the guests was Aylmer Vallance, by now a Lieutenant-Colonel in the Censorship Department. Macdonell went over to him, protesting so I was told afterwards, that 'that girl over there' was talking the most dangerous nonsense and that she should be stopped. Aylmer asked me who she was. Colonel Medlicott was in the room and if I had realised what was happening, I could have asked him to intervene. I could not believe that anything said at a private party could lead to complications. But in the agitated atmosphere existing at the time anything could happen. Vallance found out where she was employed and reported her to her chief. A.G.M. was at that time writing a 'talk of the town' piece in the *Bystander*. Next week he included in it a full account of the whole incident. The authorities at Passport Control were as annoyed about the paragraph as they were about Diana's behaviour at the party, and she was fired.

I was furious. It seemed to me that both Macdonell and Vallance had behaved outrageously; that the laws of guest and host entail certain sacred obligations. I wrote and told them both that I took my leave of them.

I never saw Macdonell again. In October he had a heart attack in his bath and died. I once after the war passed Vallance in Fleet Street and we cut each other. He was by then divorced from Helen. He died several years ago.

It was awkward for Diana to be fired in wartime from an organisation like Passport Control. It was a black mark on her dossier. She worked for a short time in an undistinguished capacity in the Ministry of Aircraft Production, soon resigned from it and went into documentary films, in which she quickly made a name for herself. For me too, the incident had repercussions.

Early in the autumn Vallance was moved from Censorship to the War Office to take charge of the Department of Public Relations to which I had been attached on my return from France. If I had not had that row with him, he would certainly have offered me a post in his department. We had been good friends for a dozen years; and apart from my cousinship with Helen, he had employed my pen on one or two special assignments for the *News Chronicle*. Moreover I was the right kind of man for his department. Soon after he had taken it over, Denzil Bachelor, who did not know about my row with him, suggested that I might like to join them. Vallance smiled wryly. 'I don't think he would,' he said.

There were many times during the next two years when I regretted my row with him. I did not indeed find the right niche for myself in work for which I was fitted by taste and training till November 1942, when I was posted to Baghdad to the DSO's office – a branch of MI5. I often wished during those thirty months that I were employed congenially at the War Office, but in the long run it was a great piece of luck for me that I was not. If I had been in Vallance's department, I should almost certainly have stayed there as Bachelor and Boulenger did, right through the war; I should have missed my years in the Middle East which added a dimension to my interests, and I should never have had that experience with police methods that I made use of in several of my novels. Professionally, I got much more out of my war than Denzil Bachelor did out of his. I have been consistently lucky as a writer, and to me as a writer, my row with Vallance was a lucky break.

I was, of course, a difficult man to place. I was too old for my rank. Majors in their thirties were reluctant to have under them a man who was their senior in civilian life, and

I had no technical knowledge which would have been of use in one of the new Ministries. Nor had I any contacts with the kinds of men who were running the intelligence services. SOE was recruited from White's and Buck's, not the Savile and the Athenæum. When I eventually found a posting, it was in a most unlikely capacity, as Staff Captain to the Petroleum Warfare Department. I owed this appointment to the concern for me of Diana's friend Yvonne Medlicott whose father, on his return from France, was made Deputy Director General of the Petroleum Warfare Department, a new branch of the Ministry of Mines which was examining the offensive uses that could be made of oil. Yvonne told him that I was at a loose end, 'Couldn't you find some use for him?' she asked.

'I don't see why not,' he said. 'We need a new Staff Captain. Our present one's quite hopeless. Alec's a cricketer, isn't he? He should be all right.'

I was at that moment at Matlock, the new intelligence centre, on a security course. He rang me up that night.

'When does your course end?' he asked.

'Saturday morning, sir.'

'What will you do then?'

'Await a posting, sir.'

'Have you anything definite in mind?'

'Not yet, sir.'

'Then you might as well come to us. I can't explain to you what it's all about. Not over the telephone, at least. We're inventing a lot of gadgets; someone has to write them up for the Home Guard. You could do that, couldn't you?'

'I think so, sir.'

'Fine. Fine. You'll be our Staff Captain. Call round here on Monday morning at 10 o'clock. I'll put you in the picture.'

It was on Tuesday, September the 12th that I had that conversation with Colonel Medlicott. The London blitz had begun on the previous Saturday.

CHAPTER 14

Love in the Blitz

When I came up to London for my interview I was faced with a personal problem. If I was to be stationed in London, I should need back my flat, but Diana was still living there, and I was by now desperately in love with her, whole-heartedly committed as I had only been once in my life before, with the American Ruth of whom I told the story in *The Early Years of Alec Waugh*.

This was altogether different. Ruth was several years older than I; Diana was fourteen years younger. Ruth was married to a man very many years older than herself. Diana had no ties, while I was married but with Joan in Australia. There was another great difference between the two romances. Ruth was in love with me. Diana was not. I was, however, so committed that this scarcely mattered. The French cynic has said, 'The one loves. The other accepts love.' I was getting so much that I did not complain because I was not getting more.

Diana enjoyed my company. We had good times together. In August after I had finished my intelligence course at Swanage and I was awaiting posting, we had gone for four days to Chagford, to the Easton Court Hotel. Those four days are one of my richest memories. I was overjoyed at the prospect of being in the same city as Diana. Since she had left Dorchester at Christmas we had only been together for brief intervals. But the rearrangement of our lives was going to be a problem.

It was a period when nobody could look very far ahead. My first Sunday in London – September the 17th – is still

honoured in RAF annals as the day when 157 planes were
shot down in an afternoon; it was, though we did not
know it, the decisive day in the Battle of Britain. All that
afternoon, a warm and sunlit day, the blue skies were
laced with the white trails of circling aircraft, with the
white puffs of bursting shell. Once a machine with its wing
shot off dived in a spiral to the ground. Was the invasion
that Hitler had threatened, that Churchill had prophesied in
his speeches, going to take place? Was all this only a prelude?
Was London going to be reduced to rubble? No one could
look far ahead. One accepted the readiest solution, and the
solution that A. D. Peters suggested was very reasonable.
The housekeeper at No. 10 had decamped on the third day
of the blitz, never to reappear. Peters, whose wife and
daughter lived in the country and who had stayed occasional
nights on the second floor, was now permanently employed
in the Ministry of Food and had moved into Howard Marshall's flat in Hill Street. Howard was also in government
employment. There was a minute flat at the top of No. 10
that had been let to E. M. Delafield. Peters suggested that I
should return to my flat, and that Diana should move up
into his flat. Diana suggested that she should bring Yvonne
Medlicott to share it with her. The three of us would take
over the kitchen for such meals as befitted the picnic
existence that we proposed to lead. The office staff, run by
that admirable backbone of the firm, Miss Stephens, would
see that someone came in to scour out the house each
morning. Some mattresses were moved into the cellar, in
case the bombing became too intense. It was a reasonable scheme: in terms of Bairnsfather's first war cartoon,
'If you know of a better 'ole go to it.'

It is never without nostalgia that nowadays I visit Peters'
office. What a strange time it knew the autumn and winter
of 1940–1. At 9.30 every morning Miss Stephens would
arrive to open up the office for the two or three members of
the staff, the accountants and the packers – I have no idea
how many of them there were – and for W. N. Roughead,

the ex-Scottish Rugby International who was still debating whether to join the Navy, his age group having not yet been called up. For eight hours the work of the office would be conducted in a sepulchral calm. In peacetime there had been a succession of callers, clients, writers needing to discuss their plans, to be encouraged or to voice complaints. But during the blitz, no one came up to London without good reason. Many writers were engaged in war work. Books were being written and published, short stories marketed, but no one was taking much concern about it. It was a question of telephone calls and letters and the despatch of packages. By six o'clock the office would be closed.

Then at quarter past six a whole new life would begin. Diana, Yvonne and myself would be back from our offices. Gramophones would be turned on; friends would arrive; Diana and Yvonne were often attended by a cohort of Free French soldiers. Diana's two brothers were in the Royal Navy and sailors on leave would call in unexpectedly. After shepherding a convoy across the Atlantic they would need to be enlivened. Then the bombing would begin. There were quiet evenings, of course, there were many quiet evenings, but to A. D. Peters, who would look in occasionally, it seemed that his office had become a night-club.

London had glamour during that first winter of the blitz. It was an empty city, but it was still an English city. Austerity had not yet been felt. Clothes rationing did not start till the summer of 1941. People still looked smart. The streets were not shabby though they were littered with broken glass. You could eat well. Wine cellars were still well stocked. There was a sense of pride in having provided the first check to the German menace. One felt oneself to be at the centre of big events. When I went into the country for the night on a tour of duty, to Winchester or Swanage, I did not get the long sleep I had expected. I felt restless, wondering how things were in London. Many Londoners have told me that they felt the same.

You could get about at night, though taxis were hard to get, unless you were coming out of a restaurant and could command the services of a commissionaire. Tubes went on running, though the tube stations had become dormitories. Authority had at the beginning attempted to prevent those who were not passengers from taking shelter in the Underground. But authority was powerless against popular demand. The public took over the platforms and the corridors; the passengers built bunks, set up toilets. Every night people would go down to their allotted places with blankets and pillows. It was a remarkable feat of self-organisation.

Standing on the platform, as often as not alone, I noticed something that I never had before, that you can tell when a train is coming, not by its sound but the feeling upon your cheeks of a breath of cool air that had been displaced by the coming train.

There was no lack of quiet gaiety that winter. During the first two weeks of the blitz, most of us were a little dazed and kept in touch with the three or four close friends who lived within walking distance, but we soon discovered who else in London was in no mood to spend evenings underground. Good friends became better friends, Betty Askwith, Brenda and Paul Willert, Theodora Benson, Primrose Codrington, A. D. Peters, Howard Marshall, Vyvyan Holland – we were all of us in our different ways employed in some kind of war work. We were ready to welcome relaxation, and we had many festive evenings at Hatchett's, Boulestin's and Simpson's.

Luckily I was in funds. In late October, *Red Book* bought the serial rights of *No Truce With Time* for five thousand dollars. For a year I could be self-indulgent. Every Saturday night I spent at Highgate, at my parents' house. I went into my office for a couple of hours. There was never anything to do, except answer an occasional telephone call. I would leave at half-past eleven. My mother would come into London. We would meet at the Lyons Corner House in Coventry Street for brunch: take a tube back to Golders

Green and see a film at the Ionic Theatre. Then take the 210 bus to Hampstead Lane, getting there in time for a late tea with my father.

They were cosy evenings. My father was in excellent spirits; his deafness was a good friend to him, he could not hear the bombing. He was now again Chairman of Chapman and Hall, Philip, later Lord Inman, having felt that he could not be chairman of two firms, Chapman and Hall and Methuen. My father was kept busy. He had manuscripts to read and to report on. He attended monthly board meetings. The firm was doing well. Paper was rationed and books sold out automatically. Henrietta Street had ceased to be a worry for him. His friends visited him regularly. And on Sunday mornings E. S. P. Haynes would walk over the heath with a friend and drink a couple of glasses of the tawny port of which he kept a store at 14a. After tea I would return to Buckingham Street.

In early January, through John Codrington, who had been a contemporary of mine at Sandhurst, I joined Pratt's – a unique superclub in Park Place that is situated in a basement, in what was originally the kitchen of a house, a considerable attraction during air raids. Its one sitting room is filled with a large open cooking range. Its dining room table has only twelve seats at it. It is very intimate. It serves good grill-room types of meal. Its members, at dinner, usually drink vintage port after a tankard of beer. There is always good talk there. There are many references to it in Harold Nicolson's *Diaries*. It added a great deal to my enjoyment of life that winter.

And all the time there was Diana. My absorption in her increased every week. I knew that it was foredoomed. It could not last. As she was not in love with me, she resented the situation in which she found herself. It had been one thing to go down to Chagford for four nights and picnic on the moors. It was quite another to have me about the place all the time. She felt trapped. It had been one thing to have a cubbyhole to retreat to when the bombing was a novelty; but now that the bombing had diminished, or rather now that Londoners had got used to it, she wanted to live her own life independently. She was a very independent person. She was bored with her employment at the Ministry of Aircraft Production. She was itching to shake her shoulders and be rid of everything. She was under strain. She was often irrritable and short-tempered. It had been a mistake no doubt to make the experiment of communal living, but during the early days of the blitz you had to make snap decisions, and decisions once made you had to stick to them. It was a problem by which as the war progressed more and more people would be fretted. They would be immobilised by war conditions. They would drift into situations and then could not get out of them.

I knew that Diana was irritated and resentful. Once, so as to ease the strain on her, I went to live at the Savile for a week. But I could not bear to be away from her. And even as it was, the good times were so very good, for me and I think too for her. She has told me that she too, can remember nostalgically evenings in that first winter when we would sit on our return from work, sipping sherry. The sirens would go. The air would be loud with the explosions of anti-aircraft fire. There would be the dull thud of bombs. Sometimes the house would shake when one fell close. The roar of aircraft overhead would get upon our nerves. 'Let's get out of this,' I'd say.

Boulestin's was only a few yards down the Strand. It was underground. Its cooking was as good as ever. Its cellar was well stocked. At this time it was quarter empty in the evenings. One did not need to book a table. Our favourite table was the one at the end, on the left-hand side looking down the room. It was good to settle back into one's seat, with a menu in front of one, knowing that one was going to enjoy an excellent meal and that for two hours one had not to worry about bombs. Boulestin's had at that time a number of half-bottles of a delightful Sauternes, a Château Rayne-Vigneau. We always ended our meal with one. We felt very close to one another as we sat there sipping the cool sweet wine, letting its richness seep along our veins. The bombing earlier in the evening was a bond. We shared if not actual danger, at least the sense of battle. Later on we would have to go back to see what skies held for us; but for the moment we were safe, soothed by good food and wine; together.

At last the half-bottle would be finished. 'What's it like outside?' I would ask the waiter as I paid the bill. Perhaps he would shake his head. 'Not too good,' he'd say. Or else he'd smile, 'Pretty quiet now.'

More often than not it would be quiet, but once on a noisy night we came round the corner of Duke Street to find the street cluttered with rubble, the air raid wardens active with fire hoses in the ruins. The explosion had been so fierce that the front door of No. 10 was open, the lock having given way. Only once was it as bad as that. But bad or good, we had had those two hours, in the calm and safety. We had had that final half hour sipping the rich Rayne-Vigneau; those few hours, scattered over those few months were as good as anything that life has brought me.

Early in February, Cassell's published *No Truce With Time*. I had a small dinner party at Simpson's to wish it luck – A. D. Peters, Howard Marshall, Philip Jordan, Diana and Yvonne Medlicott. Every writer has one book, somewhat a favourite, that he feels never has had the luck it should. *No Truce With Time* is that book for me. I wrote it with great excitement. It was a new kind of book for me to write. It told an exciting story. It was serialised in *Red Book*. Later MGM bought the film rights. Michael Arlen and Richard Aldington worked on the script. But just when it was to go into production the war ended and the project was shelved. Its film title was to have been *Diamond Rock* from the name of the barren piece of island that a group of British sailors held for four years during the Napoleonic Wars. The sales of the book were adequate, but not more than adequate on each side of the Atlantic. Routine sales; and the press was adequate, but not more than adequate. There was no enthusiasm about it anywhere. Paperbacks, except for Penguin in England, had scarcely started in those days. It was never issued as a paperback in the USA but it was twice in England, at different intervals, and in England it was recently issued in a library hard-cover edition. But it never 'caught on': no one has ever said to me, as they have invariably said, at some time or other about all my other books, 'By the way, I read an old novel of yours the other day. I rather liked it.'

And yet surely the fact that it was bought as a serial by *Red Book* and by MGM as a film, proves that it has basic merit, as a story.

It came out, I suppose, at the wrong time. It is timing that counts, in writing as in everything. My first novel, *The Loom of Youth*, came out in 1917 at exactly the right time when after the failure of the Battle of the Somme and the sustained mismanagement of the war, the country was ready to criticise the training of the class that ran the war. And in 1956 *Island in the Sun* came out exactly at the right time, when the aeroplane had brought the West Indies within range of tourism, and in Britain's Colonial Empire 'The wind of change' was bringing demands of independence. But in 1941 no one was interested in the West Indies, no one was going there. And with England at war, and the USA on the brink of war, there was no reader identification with the problems of a young woman, married to a West Indian planter several years older than herself, childless, who had nothing to do in the morning but lie on a long chair on a verandah and wait till it was time to go out to coffee.

The timing was wrong. 'It never took off' as the phrase is now.

'It's something that can't last,' I had said to myself about Diana and myself. I had prayed that it would last long enough to end without a break, for me to be posted overseas. There had been some talk of my going to Gibraltar, or for Diana to find some form of war work out of London. But it did not turn out that way. Shortly after Easter, Diana went with Yvonne to an evening party. There was 'a stranger across a crowded room' and that was that. There was nothing for me to do but make my exit with such dignity as I could summon.

CHAPTER 15

Posted to the Middle East

I moved out of Buckingham Street into a flat on the eighth floor of the White House, a new building by Great Portland Street Station. Scarcely anyone wanted at that time a flat on the top floor of anything, so I got a one-room flat for £108 a year. It was very small. But it had a kitchenette; I made it personal with books and pictures. I felt myself there. And there was a bus that ran straight to the Athenæum where I breakfasted every morning, before walking across the park to my offices in Queen Anne Square. It would suit me very well till something else turned up.

That something turned up very soon. By now my presence with the Petroleum Warfare Department had become unnecessary. Colonel Medlicott had said on that first telephone conversation, 'Write things up for the Home Guard.' I was to perform a good many odd jobs as Staff Captain for the PWD but 'write things up for the Home Guard' was the one thing I did not do. The Minister of Petroleum was Geoffrey Lloyd, youngish, vigorous, ambitious. He had as his Director-General Sir Donald Banks, who had had a distinguished career in the Post Office, and as a territorial had reached the rank of Brigadier. He had just been evacuated from the BEF. The department was feeling its way. It had ample funds at its disposal. It could experiment in a way that a routine service unit could not do. It was to have a distinguished war record. Later on it invented 'PLUTO' (pipe line under the ocean) to carry oil across the Channel, and it created a device for dispersing fog at airports. But in the winter of 1940 and 1941 it was mainly concerned with the defence of road blocks and strong points that the Home Guard were building. One of its favourite weapons was the hedge-hopper. An enemy tank advancing along a lane was to spy a couple of petrol barrels. They looked innocuous enough, but behind the hedge would be another barrel filled with explosives, that, operated by a sentry twenty yards away, would leap over the hedge and land upon the tank, igniting the barrels that were lying in the path. We also devised a flame-thrower that could be attached to a Bren gun carrier.

Our most ambitious project, however, was an attempt to set the sea alight. In the first war there had been a widely believed rumour that Russian troops had been shipped to England and conveyed as reinforcements to the Western Front. In the second war it was believed that German invasion forces had been entrapped in a sea of fire. There were reports of Germans with badly burnt bodies being taken into hospitals behind what came to be called the invasion ports; there were reports, too, of the Germans preparing a special kind of fire-resisting uniform. In the propaganda leaflets that our aeroplanes scattered behind the German lines there was a cartoon of a section of German soldiers in a small boat that had been set alight, with the caption 'look how our captain burns'.

It is impossible to know how these rumours started. If there had been such a weapon, our department would have heard of it. It has been conjectured that while some Germans were rehearsing an invasion exercise, a bomb from one of our aircraft fell into some waters where a British ship evacuating troops from Dunkirk had been sunk and there was oil on the water which the bomb set alight. It is not a provable story, but the Germans appear to have believed that we had such a weapon. Anyhow the PWD set about experimenting with the project.

We had an installation at Swanage. We had oil tanks on the high ground behind the beach; pipes under the water carried the oil some fifty yards out to sea, where the oil was spread out in a circle to be there ignited. Up to a point our attempts were successful. We produced films to show that this could be done. I wonder if those films are to be seen in the Imperial War Museum. I was in control of the film section. We employed the Shell Oil Company's film unit to make the pictures and some of them were highly handsome. They showed the oil seeping under the water, spreading in a circle, the wick was fired, a line of fire spread outwards to the circumference, then the whole circle was ablaze, a column of flame towered into the sky, crowned by wreaths of smoke. It would have been a barrier through which no landing craft could have passed, and it was our suggestion that we should construct such installations at all the beaches where landings were expected. The trouble about the scheme was the difficulty of setting and keeping the sea alight. Security instructions on factories where oil is stored stress the inflammability of oil, but it is a different matter when you are trying to start a conflagration. Oil is very reluctant to burst into flame when you want it to.

This was abundantly proved on an occasion which became known as 'black Wednesday'. The department held an exhibition to which a number of very high-ranking officers were invited. Elaborate security measures were taken. I with my Shell Film unit went down the night before. We prayed for fine weather, and woke with relieved anticipation, to grey skies which did not hold the threat of rain. Unfortunately it was a windy day, a big sea was running, and of the four columns of fire that were expected to rise from the water, only one caught alight and that in a very minor fashion. The visiting red hats were not impressed. The department argued that if the sea was strong enough to dowse the flames it would capsize the landing craft. This argument did not seem valid to the chiefs of staff and the project was abandoned. It must have cost a great deal of money, but our department was in an exceptional position. It was not part of the naval, military and air force establishments, answerable to the Treasury for its disbursement of every shilling. It was an independent body, empowered to make experiments and present the results of its experiments to the chiefs of staff. There was no check on its expenditure.

The extent and variety of its experiments ensured that I, as its Staff Captain, should lead a varied and interesting life. A Staff Captain like a G3 is usually a dogsbody, and so was I. But I was a dogsbody who was constantly on the move. The filming of these experiments involved me in excursions. We had an experimental station near Southampton to which I used to drive down with our cameras every ten days or so. We had demonstrations that involved my staying the night at Winchester. We also had some defence installations near Norwich which involved a two-day visit. Our films were shown to 'high-ups'. Geoffrey Lloyd our Minister was, as I have said, a man of youth and vigour, highly ambitious and efficient, he liked to have his opposite numbers aware of what he was doing. I would be in attendance at these film showings.

Every so often there would be a demonstration. I remember in particular one in late October, in Wiltshire, near Heytesbury, about ninety minutes' drive from London. It was a perfect autumn day, misty and chilly in the morning, with the sun breaking through about ten o'clock, with the mist dispersing; the air was warm and the countryside green and glistening. The scene for the display was set in a green valley; the ground had been carefully arranged beforehand so that there were no obvious signs of the various engines of death that were shortly to reveal their malice. The camera crew and I sat half-way up the hill, munched our sandwiches and consumed a bottle of Beaujolais, waiting for the arrival of the distinguished guests. There were not a great many of them, but they were certainly distinguished. Queen Mary was there. I cannot remember if a buffet tent had been set up for them. I rather fancy that it had not; that they had lunched somewhere else. I do not think that chairs were provided for them. They stood in the sunlight watching.

It did not last long, half an hour at the most, but it was an impressive display, explosion after explosion, burst after burst of flame, superb colour effects of red and orange, a thin mist of smoke, the smell of cordite; then as a final *feu de joie*, an explosion in mid-air that served no purpose, a superb firework that burst high in the sky, a gigantic flowering of red and orange with the ground below it that an hour earlier had been so smooth and green and soft, scorched, torn, blistered, and littered with scraps of metal; a miniature battlefield.

And just at that moment, on a path behind us appeared a solitary horseman. He was tall, handsome, in his late forties, Siegfried Sassoon. I remembered that he lived near here. This was presumably one of his routine daily rides. He had had no warning of this demonstration. He reined in his horse, he looked down at the familiar valley, so long loved, now so unsightly. He looked at the group of red hats who were preparing to take their leave. What thoughts must have been passing through his mind? His war poems more than anyone's had shocked the world into a realisation of what modern war was like. He had made his protest. He had believed that because of that protest and the protest that it had inspired in others, war had been exiled from the councils of mankind. Yet here it was again, twenty years later, and on his very doorstep and there grouped together watching it, were the staff officers whom he had satirised. Though we had not met so very often, we had been quite good friends. I had not seen him for some years. I was on the point of running up to greet him, but I checked. Better not maybe; who could tell what thoughts were passing behind that handsome mask. Better leave him to his thoughts. I never saw him again.

That was in late October; and during the rest of the autumn and through the winter I was kept usefully busy with the PWD. But by the summer it had become clear that the projected invasion of Britain had been abandoned and after the invasion of Russia, the department turned its attention from the Home Guard, 'hedge-hoppers' and the like, and concentrated on far more ambitious projects which were far too technical for me.

I had introduced Arthur Calder Marshall, who had just been commissioned, to Colonel Medlicott and room was found for him in the department. We sat across a desk from one another and I confided my perplexities to him. 'I don't know what any of this is about,' I said.

There was a commodity called a 'conical canister' which amused us with its indelicate implications, for whose transportation I was responsible. 'I've no idea what they are,' I said. 'I don't know whether you send them by a despatch rider or in an army lorry. I've got to get out of this.'

I made enquiries at Intelligence Corps Headquarters and learnt that the Free French Forces needed interpreters. An appointment was made for me. On my way to it I met Anthony Powell on the steps of the Athenæum. He was in uniform, a captain. I had not seen him for some time.

'What are you doing here?' I asked.

'I'm on leave, but I've come up to be interviewed as interpreter for the Free French Forces.'

'So have I,' I told him.

'Good luck to us,' he said.

It would be pleasant if we were to be in the same command. Without knowing him at all intimately, we had been casual friends for fifteen years. He was gracious, easy, sure of himself without being self-assertive, a good mixer without 'bonhomie'. He had, unlike so many of his contemporaries, been heterosexual from the start, like Peter Quennell. While Peter was involved with Cara Pilkington, on whose account he was sent down from Oxford, Tony was involved with Nina Hamnett, a liberal education.

In *The Soldier's Art* he has given a description of his interview at Free French Headquarters. He was needed as an interpreter at battalion level, and was asked to translate into French a document 'specifying current regulations governing the issue or non-issue of rations to troops in the field'. 'At first sight,' Powell wrote, 'the prose did not seem to make much sense in English.' The examining officer shook his head over the subsequent translation. But he was anxious to be co-operative. 'Perhaps it's only written French you're shaky in ... Now let us postulate that the 9th Regiment of Colonial Infantry are on the point of mutiny. They may be prepared to abandon Vichy and come over to the Allies. How would you harangue them?' Powell's hero was forced to admit that he would have to fall back on English, and he rejoined his unit.

My interview was very different. An agreeable colonel asked me some questions about myself and my military career up to now. Then he began to talk to me in French. My accent is not bad. I went to a preparatory school, Fernden, that specialised in French, particularly in French pronunciation. We had to distinguish betweeen grave and acute accents over the letter 'e'. For lunch we had a table at which only French was spoken. In the Easter holidays we were taken for two weeks to Boulogne. My French was not ostentatiously grammatical, my subjunctives were elusive, but I felt at ease talking it. I talk it in fact as fast as I talk English. I could not have passed the test that was applied to Powell but I was not required as an interpreter at battalion level.

After a couple of minutes of talking French, the colonel went back to English.

'Do you know what we are looking for?' he asked.

'No,' I told him.

'We are sending out a reinforcement to Spears' mission to Syria and the Lebanon.'

'That's wonderful.'

My eyes must have brightened and my voice glowed. Syria and the Lebanon. Where I had never been before. What an adventure. I do not know if the colonel had had any doubt about my appointment. If he had, I suspect that it was that glow in my voice, that brightness in my eyes that turned the scale in my favour. Some men of forty might not have wanted to be posted so far from home.

'We are sending out about twenty of you,' he explained. 'You'll be going out by ship, of course. Your convoy's leaving two weeks from Sunday. I wish I could offer you some leave but we'll have to put you in the picture. So perhaps you'll spend your mornings in this office reading up the files. There's going to be a publicity section to this mission. That's what we had in mind for you.'

Publicity. At last I was going to have the kind of job for which I was fitted by taste and training. So I spent a succession of contented mornings putting myself in the picture. I knew, of course, roughly what had been happening in the Levant during the summer, how British, Australian and Free French Forces had dispossessed the Vichy French during a brief, but fierce campaign, but I knew none of the details arranged between de Gaulle and the British in the person of Oliver Lyttelton as to the future administration of the country and the eventual independence into two separate kingdoms, of Syria and the Lebanon. I also spent several hours in the library at the Athenæum, reading General Spears' two books *Liaison* – an account of the first battles of 1914, and *Prelude to Victory* – an account of the campaign in front of Arras in the spring of 1917. I had not met Spears, though I had been at a charity public dinner at which he had spoken during Jubilee year.

My last lunches at the Athenæum were enlivened by the fact that the wine committee had decided to reduce the price of its champagne, because it was feared that the wine might go off in quality. Among the wines that were reduced was Krug 1928. What a wine that was. Several of my friends profited from this opportunity.

On the last Friday of September, Hamish Hamilton, now a prominent personality in the Ministry of Information, gave a big cocktail party to celebrate the tenth birthday of his publishing house. It was a nostalgic occasion for me. I was there, as myself, in *propia persona*, as Alec Waugh, the novelist. When should I be doing that again? Some of the guests there I was never to see again. I had a long talk with Hugh Kingsmill, Sir Henry Lunn's second son, who had been a fellow prisoner of war at Mainz, of whom I had been very fond, but from whom I had drifted out of touch. His books had never received the recognition that they had deserved; he had grown bitter and was resentful of those of his friends who had been luckier. We had a very genial talk that evening. I also had a very pleasant talk with Mrs Belloc Lowndes, who had been one of my first friends when I came back from a prisoner of war camp in 1918. She was a most generous woman. There is a picture of her in Hugh Walpole's *Fortitude*. She was intensely interested in the commercial side of writing, she knew how every writer's stock stood upon the literary bourse; how big an advance he and she was getting from what publisher. She was absorbed in the relations between authors, editors and publishers. She had the instincts of an intriguer. Leaning across a lunch table at the Ivy she would whisper 'are you happy with Heinemann?' as another kind of woman in another context would have whispered 'does your wife really understand you?' But she was never malicious, never mischievous. She never made mischief. She gave young writers, as Hugh Walpole stressed in *Fortitude*, advice that was an admirable mixture of literary and commercial commonsense. She would give tea parties for visiting American editors to meet English writers. She was always looking for an opportunity to do something for other writers; very often succeeding. She brought the right people together. She was the last person that I talked to at Hamish Hamilton's party. She hurried across to me just as I was leaving.

'Tell me about Evelyn,' she said. She was particularly interested in Evelyn, as a fellow Catholic.

'He's just back from the Middle East,' I told her. 'He was at Crete. I'll be seeing him tomorrow.'

'Give him my love. I pray for him in his marriage. We regard marriage as a state of grace, you know.'

It was the last thing she ever said to me.

I spent my last night at my parents' house. My father used to describe himself as 'the old sentimentalist' and this was an occasion that could have been sentimentalised. In all human probability it was the last time that the three of us would dine together. I was likely to be away several years, and he was seventy-five, but he treated the evening as though it were any evening. We did not make an occasion of it.

The Saturday was warm and sunny. I was catching a ten o'clock train for Glasgow. I had my sleeper booked. I was giving a small goodbye party in my flat at the White House: I had asked the Calder Marshalls to dinner afterwards at Le Perroquet. At the last moment I had invited Diana too. I wanted to leave a friendly memory behind me.

Evelyn was due for lunch. My mother had said that she would like to prepare some sandwiches for my party. In the morning we went up to the grocer's and made appropriate purchases of small rolls and paste. You could always find appetising commodities in the Highgate shops. The tradition of good service had been maintained. There was also a quite good bookshop. I bought an omnibus Arnold Bennett. It contained *Lord Raingo*, which I had never read. It was to make a good companion for the journey. I suppose that *Lord Raingo* has been out of print for many years. I never see references to it. But it only just missed being a great book.

Evelyn arrived shortly before one. He looked very well and smart. On the journey back he had finished the novel *Put Out More Flags* of which he had written the first part on the way out. He had returned via Trinidad.

'What a long way round,' I said.

'So's everything today.'

'Did you go to the Queen's Park Hotel?'

'I didn't go ashore. Someone had to stay on board. As I'd been there already I volunteered.'

I would find a lot of old friends in Cairo, he told me. The main trouble, he warned me, was the difficulty of cashing cheques.

I asked him if he could come to my party. He shook his head. He had been commissioned by *Life* to write an article on commandos. He had got special permission to write it from Brendan Bracken. He had better get it finished before he went back to duty. His diaries have no entry for this week-end.

I have hardly any recollection of my goodbye party. I cannot remember who was there and who said what. Vyvyan Holland told me that our good friend Peter Smith-Dorien was in Beirut. He had been brigade major to General 'Jumbo' Wilson in the attack on the Vichy French. He was now a Lieutenant-Colonel in Spears' mission. A. D. Peters' wife Henrie Maine was at my party. She told me that her brother, who had travelled with me on the *Aquitania*, was a captain in Spears' mission. 'In ten weeks you'll be living in an elegant flat in Beirut,' she told me.

That was the first indication that I had of the kind of life that was awaiting me. I had not pictured an officer on an overseas campaign living in an elegant flat anywhere. I had thought of barracks and canvas as his portion. Those two incidents I remember: nothing else.

But I do remember very clearly the dinner afterwards at Le Perroquet in Leicester Square with Diana sitting beside me on the banquette and Arthur and Ara Calder Marshall across the table. Diana and the Calder Marshalls were good friends. Ara was working on documentary films and Diana, rid now of the Ministry of Aircraft Production, was shortly to join her in a career in which she was to achieve quite a measure of success, during the war and after it.

We all felt very close to one another. I could not believe that it would be several years before we should meet again. I could not believe that between Diana and myself there had been those harsh moments only five months back. It might have been this time a year ago.

I cannot remember what we ate. Food was still good in London then, particularly at Le Perroquet. We drank champagne. The clock moved on.

'I must ring my parents and say goodbye,' I said.

'The party was a great success,' I told them. 'Your sandwiches made all the difference.'

I returned to the table to find a fresh bottle in the bucket.

'We thought we'd like to contribute a final bottle,' Ara said.

Diana's hand lay on the banquette between us. She raised two fingers, an invitation to have it held. The bottle emptied. 'Time to be on my way,' I said. The Calder Marshalls went back to their flat. Diana saw me to Euston Station. There was no air raid. There had not been one for several weeks. The station had an empty look.

'I'll join you at the train,' the porter said. The train seemed a long way off. We found my compartment, and waited for the porter. He took a long time coming. 'Let's go and sit down,' I said. 'He's bound to find us.'

We sat down on the bed. We had nothing to say to one another; yet we had so much to say. 'I'd better go and see what the porter's about,' I said.

Nothing was happening on the platform. I went back into the compartment. 'No sign of him,' I said. 'But he's bound to turn up, I haven't tipped him.'

At that moment the train began to move. It happened so quickly that we were helpless to do anything. We stood in the corridor, looking at the gleaming rails. 'Well, here I seem to be,' she said.

The conductor was benevolent. 'The first stop is Crewe,' he said.

'When do we get there?' I asked.

'Quarter past three.'

It was now quarter to eleven.

'Can she stay in my compartment?' I asked.

'I don't see why not.' There was no club car on the train.

'Will you call us when we get to Crewe?' I said.

'For sure.'

We went back to the compartment. Four hours and a half in this narrow compartment that was almost entirely occupied by a narrow but comfortable bed. There was no real alternative. We looked at one another, then she laughed. 'Do you make a practice of seducing your women in this way?' she said.

CHAPTER 16

The Middle East

The incident of my luggage was typical of my first fifteen months in the Middle East. I do not know what happened to my valise. It was not in the van at Glasgow. I had to go on board right away. The RTO promised that the valise when it arrived would be safely delivered to the ship. 'We don't sail for three days. It's bound to turn up.' But it never did. I thought myself in a desperate predicament. I had only an overnight suitcase and I was launched on a campaign that would last several years. How on earth was I to manage? As it turned out I managed very well. One usually travels overweight. I had no occasion to 'dress up'. Two shirts are all that anyone needs. I could sleep nude while my one pair of pyjamas was being washed. In Cairo there was an officers' shop where I bought battledress and generally filled up the gaps in my wardrobe. I needed a tropical kit.

When I returned to England forty-five months later, I was to discover that my valise had found its way to Edrington. It contained a great deal that I was then very glad to have. Clothes rationing was in force, and I was delighted to find a supply of underclothes, pyjamas, cricket shirts and two pairs of formal shoes. I also found the field glasses that had been issued to me in Aldershot when I was posted to return to the BEF. I have them still and they accompany me regularly to Lord's. Had I taken them to the Middle East they would have certainly been requisitioned and despatched to the western desert. When I unpacked my valise in England in 1945, I thought I had been lucky in having mislaid it in

Euston Station. Everyone was better off except for the untipped porter. I felt sorry for him. He must have been put to quite a lot of trouble getting my valise redirected. That is why I say that the loss of my luggage was symbolic of my first fifteen months in the Middle East, with what seemed at first to be disastrous, turning out in the end for the general best.

In *His Second War*, I have given an account of my experiences in the Middle East. In addition, in a long novel called *The Mule on the Minaret* I told the story of a university professor of my own age, a veteran from the first war who was posted to Spears' mission when I was, in September 1941. It is not autobiography, and Diana who is the heroine of the novel was never in the Middle East. But the pattern of the professor's career was much the same as mine although I never rose above the rank of major, whereas the professor finished up with red flannel on his lapels.

I will not repeat myself. I will not tell the same story twice. Another equivalent of the untipped porter was a misunderstanding between London and the Cairo headquarters of Spears' mission. When London learnt that a new branch of Spears' mission would be required to administer the new territory that had come under British influence, it assumed that officer reinforcements would be required. Cairo never explained to London that it could find all the officers it needed on the spot. Spears' mission (Syria and Lebanon) could not wait. It set about recruiting new 'missionaries' from the pool of momentarily displaced officers that had accumulated at Cairo as a result of the campaign against the Vichy French. The roster was practically filled when Beirut learnt that twenty prospective 'missionaries' were about to sail from Glasgow. Beirut cabled immediately 'stop them'. But it was too late. We were already on our way.

We arrived on a Sunday evening to receive instructions from the RTO that we were to spend the night either in army barracks or at Shepheard's Hotel, at our own expense, and report next morning at headquarters. After seven weeks in confined space, four to a cabin, we accepted the luxury of Shepheard's and settled down contentedly to the prospects of a gourmet meal and the protracted study of a wine list.

Those prospects were fulfilled, but just as we had decided on the choice of wines, one of our number recognised a familiar face, a gunner captain who had been on an intelligence course with him in England. He came across to us.

'Are you the benighted pilgrims for Spears' mission?' he enquired. We were, we told him.

'Then let me offer you my sympathies; it's a fool's mission that you're on. Your places were filled five weeks ago.'

Next day we were received at headquarters by a major whom I had met two years before on the French Riviera. We were warmly welcomed. 'It was a bit of a shock when we learnt that you were coming out,' he said. 'We've had six weeks to decide what to do with you, and we've found occupation here for more than half of you. The remainder will go to Beirut.'

I was one of those who was destined for Beirut. 'There's a chap called Tweedie who's placing press representatives with the various consulates. He's at Beirut now. He's signalled that he wants you up there.' I arrived to find that he had returned to Cairo on the previous evening.

I was warmly welcomed – one always was warmly welcomed – in the Middle East – by a *chargé d'affaires*, a senior officer from the Anglo-Sudan Service – a very hand-picked group, most of them of ex-university athletes – 'Blacks ruled by Blues' was the phrase for them. I had met him already, at Edrington, a neighbour having brought him round for drinks one evening.

'I'm so glad you've come,' he said, 'though I'm afraid you won't be here long. Tweedie's got just the thing for you. In Tehran. I'm sorry you missed him. He'd have explained what it's all about. He'll fix it up for you in Cairo. In the meantime you might stay here. We've a vacancy on our establishment for a staff captain. You might as well fill that, though there won't be anything for you to do except to take your share as duty officer. We ought to hear from Tweedie in a day or two.'

But we did not hear from Tweedie in a day or even in a week or two. I spent the mornings in the library at the American University reading Persian history.

I started to grow restless. 'Couldn't we ask Tweedie what's happening?' I asked. Cables were exchanged. Tehran was hanging fire, but I was not to worry. It was all under control.

The days went by, became weeks and then a month. I became more than restless. I wanted to make my contribution to the war effort.

'Couldn't we nudge Tweedie's elbow?'

'He's a very busy man, you know.'

'Yes, but even so.'

This time the nudge did produce an answer. The Tehran project had fallen through, but Tweedie was sure that something else would turn up soon. The *chargé d'affaires* and I looked at one another. 'What now?' I asked.

'Would you like to go back to Cairo?' he asked.

'To do what there?'

'Join the pool.'

I shook my head. Those were icy waters. It would mean the surrendering of my third pip. 'What's the alternative?' I asked.

'Well, you are on our strength as our staff captain. Why don't you become that? I'm sure there are lots of odd jobs we can find for you.'

Back to the start, in fact, exactly where I had been in the PWD. A dogsbody, dealing with technicalities with which I was unfamiliar.

I attended inter-allied conferences, where we discussed the transportation of various materials and stores.

'And now, Captain Waugh,' the English chairman would say, 'perhaps you will explain to our French colleagues what it is we want.'

'I'm afraid, sir,' I would answer, 'that I don't know what these things are in English, let alone in French.'

I was clearly the wrong man for the job. But I did not see what I could do. A temporary captain must not become unposted, with loss of rank and insecurity of employment. Anything might happen to an unposted subaltern.

And I was, I had become well aware of it, a difficult man to place. I had some good friends in Cairo, but they were too high up to be of use to anyone placed as lowly as myself. Walter Monckton, for instance, with whom I had played quite a little cricket, who had been a fellow member of the Odde Volumes, and Dick Casey, the Minister of State who was married to a cousin of Joan's, and who had stayed at Edrington; Dick Casey was very hospitable to me when I was in Cairo. But he was far too high up to be of any practical assistance. What I needed was an equivalent for Alymer Vallance and there was not one in the Middle East.

In the meantime I was in many ways having a good time. I had made friends with R. A. Usborne, the SOE man in Beirut, the future author of *Clubland Heroes*. SOE funds had provided him with a comfortable flat and he invited me to share it with him. Usborne was a Carthusian, a Balliol man, a cricketer and a footballer. He has a keen wit, and a scholarly talent for light verse. He was excellent company. And today, before I come to London, he is the first person with whom I make contact, in advance. We had very good times and Beirut was a delightful city. It was pretty, with gracious Turkish-style rectangular houses, with tree-lined avenues, backed by majestic mountains. Spring was on its way. I never knew what Usborne was about in his cloak and dagger role, but he was involved with a number of Lebanese with whom I was brought into contact, and whom I met in their own homes. I made friends in particular with Charles Ammoun, later to be the Lebanese ambassador to the United Nations, and his sister Blanche, a painter and a poet of international distinction.

It was part of my duty to keep contact with the French.

The mission had no mess, in order that we should be free to entertain and be entertained by our French opposite numbers. This was a new and exciting experience for me. It is not easy for an Englishman to meet the French in that way in France. Whenever possible I had travelled in French ships, but my acquaintance with the French themselves was limited to the role of fellow passenger. My close friends in France were the barmen, the bar girls, the sailors on the waterfront at Villefranche. There was a great deal of party-giving in Beirut. Life had been grim after the fall of France. The Vichy French had imposed an atmosphere of mourning. There had been no dancing in restaurants. But now Beirut was under the rule not of a defeated but a victorious army. There was no need for austerity and gloom. Spears had been appointed minister to Syria and the Lebanon, and he was in London receiving his instructions. But his wife, Mary Borden, the novelist, was at the residence and saw to it that we had a merry Christmas.

At the dinner that she gave I sat next to Anita Leslie. We had a cordial time and a few days later I rang up and asked her if she could have dinner with me. She would, she said, be delighted. 'At the St Georges then at eight o'clock.'

On the chosen evening I found her at a desk writing a letter. I was a minute or two early. I went across to her. 'Please,' she said, 'will you excuse me. I want to finish this. Alec Waugh is calling for me in five minutes.' She had no idea that she had been sitting next to me at the Christmas dinner. We had never met before, but she probably knew that I knew her father. We moved in the same worlds and she had thought it natural that I on arriving in Beirut should ask her out to dinner.

That experience taught me quite a little about myself. Because I am not unknown, I expect a fellow dinner guest to know something about me; I therefore make no particular effort to make an impression. My books have already introduced me, for better or for worse. I relax. But I realised now

that a young and attractive woman could not be expected
to take an interest in an unknown captain, forty-three years
old, without a shining personality. Anita had been gracious
and agreeable at the Christmas dinner – she could not be
anything else – and she was a delight to look at but she had
not put herself out. The Anita with whom I dined at the St
Georges was quite a different person from the woman next
to whom I had sat at Mary Borden's dinner. We became
quite good friends. That experience taught me a lesson.
When I am with people who know nothing about me, who
see nothing particularly striking at a first glance in my
manner and appearance, I recognise that I must make a
special effort to prove myself amusing.

Life was enjoyable in the winter of 1941–2. Beirut was
picturesque, its streets and waterfront dotted with elegant
young women, sauntering by, with black hair falling
over their shoulders. There were entertaining night-clubs
and good restaurants. Shop windows were well stocked.
Commodities were still priced at the Vichy value of
the franc and the black market offered a good exchange
rate. There was no lack of gallantry.

In the summer it became even more picturesque. Most
days I lunched at the Bain Militaire, a narrow strip of protected water with a blue and white striped lighthouse guard-
ing it. It had a bar. One took out a picnic, or else one lunched
at the restaurant on the rocks behind it. It was patronised
by the Lebanese. Exquisite slim, black-haired nymphs
scattered themselves along the beach. Mary Borden has
described it enchantingly in *Journey Down a Blind Alley*. I
cannot pretend that I was not having 'a good war' that
early summer. I could not, however, resist a sense of guilt. I
was extremely bored by such little work as there was for me
to do. Anyone could have done it. I ought to be making a
more substantial contribution to the war effort

Relief came suddenly and unexpectedly. A new establishment was issued for the mission. That establishment did not

include the services of a staff captain and I was an intelligence corps appointment, entitled to draw staff pay.

'What happens to me now?' I asked the *chargé d'affaires*.

'If I were you,' he said, 'I should go to Cairo, report to Intelligence Corps Headquarters, and see what they can offer.'

I went down by train. Standing by the canal at El Kinatra in the early evening, I saw a young officer whose face was familiar. I looked at his identity disc. Captain Robin Maugham. I had met him once before in 1936 in his uncle's villa on Cap Ferrat. We dined together on the train. The Egyptian State Railway had still a fine cellar of wines that it was selling off at almost pre-war prices. The superb red Burgundy that we shared upon the train was the beginning of a friendship that is today one of my most valued treasures.

Next morning I went round to the Intelligence Corps Headquarters. They had there, not unnaturally, no record of my existence. But in England I had attended the War Intelligence course and the Field Security course; that was good enough. They had a vacancy for a captain. 'You can stay here till something more suitable turns up,' they said.

It was a very congenial section in which I found myself. It was run by a young and friendly major who expected his staff to work hard when a flap was on, but did not believe in unnecessary work. He remembered Wellington's complaint to Whitehall that he was too busy training his troops to fight the French, to answer trivial enquiries. If there was no work to do we could read, write letters or play chess. His G3 was young, athletic and an old Shirburnian, who was recovering from a wound received in the western desert. There was a happy atmosphere in the office. If at half-past ten or eleven one wanted to go out to Groppi's for a cup of coffee and a cake, one had only to ask permission.

I reported for duty late in July. It was a good time to arrive in Cairo. There was excitement and confidence in the air. Rommel had been checked. 'Ash Wednesday', when in fear

of evacuation top secret files were burnt and the sky was
dark with smoke, had become a memory. 'The Auk' was in
control, the troops were confident that he would again send
back Rommel 'with a bloody nose'. Soon we would be on
the attack again. Cairo had a great deal to offer.

I was staying at Shepheard's. Every morning I walked to
my office, under a warm but not yet heavy sun, along
broad, well-tended streets that were brisk with traffic. In the
afternoons I would play golf at the Gezira Club, taking a
swim there afterwards. In the evenings there was the Turf
Club, of which the members of the General Staff were
honorary members. There was the international Mohammed
Ali Club, of which quite a few of the staff were members
through their London clubs. There were excellent small
restaurants. As Evelyn had prophesied, I found innumerable old friends there. Robin Maugham was on sick leave.
We went to cinemas on my day off. We often dined. Richard
Usborne was now on duty there.

There was indeed only one drawback to Cairo and it was a
drawback with which there was no means of accommodation – a middle-aged captain with middle-aged tastes could
not live there on his pay. There were no messes at this time.
One had to take all one's meals at restaurants. For a quadragenarian, with a private annual income of five hundred
pounds, Cairo in the early 1940s was singularly pleasant,
particularly if he had served for a few months in the western
desert, and would in consequence have no sense of guilt
about living in comfort while his juniors were in danger and
discomfort. For such a one the rank of captain was ideal.
He would have no responsibility. He would not have a
great deal of work to do. No one would be trying to get his
job away from him. He would have to fulfil his minor
periodical obligations as a duty officer and conduct himself
with decorum in the presence of his seniors. But he did need
that additional five hundred pounds, and that was precisely
what I had not got. My income as a writer for the English
market had ceased and though on the journey round the

Cape, I had written three short stories, two of which had been bought in the USA, and though I had written in Cairo another short story for which Carol had found a buyer, I had arranged with her to keep in New York any monies that I might make so that when the war was over, I should find in New York a bank balance that would finance my early months there. I had in fact less spare cash than I had had for twenty years. And as an additional source of discomfort there was the fact that though in Cairo there was a challengingly large number of young and attractive females, they were outnumbered by young men in the ratio of a hundred to one.

Cairo was no place for me and when the G2 asked me if I would like to go as G3 to the new Persia and Iraq force that was just being formed, I accepted gratefully. Its headquarters were in Baghdad, and one of the complaints against Baghdad was that the climate was so fierce in the summer that no ATS personnel were allowed there. There was an occasional secretary, the wife usually of some official and a few nursing sisters. There were in fact no temptations of what is called 'that kind' at all, which suited me fine. I set off in a convoy across the desert in a buoyant mood.

I was now for the first time in an organisation that was part of the established military hierarchy. By that I mean that I was part of the automatic process of promotion, in which a G3 became a G2, and a G2 became a G1. That was how it should have worked out for me. Unfortunately I fell down on the job. When I went back to the army as a forty-one-year-old lieutenant I knew sooner or later I should find myself under the direct command of a man who could be as much anathema to me as I would be to him. He would be, I fancied, a man with a chip upon his shoulder for whom I typified everything in life that had conspired to put that chip there. The G2 I found waiting for me in Baghdad could not have been more different.

Ernest I—— was in his middle twenties – a product of

Eton and King's College, Cambridge. He was tall, elegant, handsome. He had quiet wit, he was amusing company, he was the son of a general who later in the war was to be ennobled. He had spent most of, if not the entire war on his father's staff. Perhaps the fact that he was rarely in danger and campaigned in comfort made him punctilious about working at full pressure. Perhaps security is not the best arena for a man with a highly developed conscience. Anyhow he suspected a spy at every keyhole. In Ninth Army when he was G3 it was the practice to hand over the swill from the kitchens to the civilian population. The populace was hungry and welcomed the swill. The practice was in everybody's interest but Ernest disapproved of it. A spy he said could estimate from the dimensions of the swill, the number of troops in the neighbourhood. He got the practice stopped.

He and I were quite wrong for one another. I was concerned with getting things done. He was concerned with getting things stopped. I became restless under his scrutiny. I felt that if he had been in an operational branch, he would never have allowed his troops to launch an attack on the grounds that an attack would reveal their position to the enemy and the types of weapon they possessed.

I looked him up in *Who's Who* the other day. No entry could have contained less information. It recorded his war service, the fact that he had been mentioned in despatches, and had been a lieutenant-colonel in the Rifle Brigade. He was married in 1945. It was a childless marriage. From then on the inquisitive were given no information about his career, no hobbies, no clubs, not even an address; c/o Barclays Bank, Cambridge, an entry I felt after his own security-conscious heart.

It was not surprising that we got on one another's nerves. In the end I put up a bad black. I left a highly secret document in an open file. He looked at me in dismay. 'I'm afraid I'll have to tell the Colonel about this,' he said.

For a few bleak days I pictured myself travelling back

across the desert to the pool in Cairo, 'dropping a pip' along
the way. Luck was, however, on my side. There was in
Baghdad an organisation called CICI (Combined Intelligence Centre Iraq). Before the Rashid Ali coup it had
been under the RAF. After the coup, it was absorbed into
Paiforce, under the command of a regular Indian Army
Officer in the Guides, who decided to recruit his enlarged
staff from officers who had somehow found themselves at
odds in their original postings. He and I had met once or
twice and felt in tune with one another. He had been warned
against me, so he was to tell me later. 'He's a writer, he
must be a crank,' they said. He replied 'That's the kind of
person I find that I can use – if it turns out wrong I can
always post him back to Cairo.' His chancings of his arm
never did turn out wrong, however.

His centre was to earn itself quite a reputation. Its
functions combined because of its locality the activities of
both MI5 and MI6. MI5 looked after security within
British-owned territories. MI6 worked in foreign countries.
MI6 work is therefore the more clandestine; it is cloak and
dagger work. CICI needed to combine MI5 with MI6
because Iraq was on the Turkish border, and in order to
protect Iraq we had to know what was happening across
the frontier.

When I first went to CICI, my job was to watch the clubs
that were constantly being formed – not clubs in the European sense of the word, a group of men with similar tastes
who occupy premises where they can meet, but a group of
men who pursue clandestinely political aims, generally
hostile to the government. I was soon concentrating on
spy rings. I have described one of these rings in my novel
about the Middle East – *The Mule on the Minaret*. It was
organised by the German Embassy in Ankara; it sent a
wireless set into Baghdad on which information was to be
sent back to the Germans. The wireless set had been sent
down by train. Most of the Pullman porters were double
agents. There were also letters being sent up to Ankara in

secret writing. Until 1918 Baghdad had been part of the Ottoman Empire. Turkey had been the ally of the Kaiser's Germany. Many of the older Baghdadis had been trained in the Turkish army and they had retained their old associations and affinities. We had close contact with the Turkish War Office, who kept us supplied with information. We also sent up our own agents into Turkey. This was when we trespassed into the activities of MI6. We worked very closely with the Iraqi CID, which was supervised by a British technical adviser. I have described that officer in the chapter 'My Second War' in *My Brother Evelyn and Other Portraits*. And he was the original of Whittingham in *Island in the Sun*. I learnt a lot about police procedure during my months with CICI. Later during my stay there, a group of parachutists were dropped into north Iraq. All of them were captured and I took part in their interrogation.

They were led down by an ex-Iraqi student. The Germans in Ankara often managed to recruit Iraqi students who were failing in their exams. The Germans would suggest that they cross the frontier into Bulgaria and get their degree there. Once across the frontier they were in German power. We did not immediately arrest the spies. We preferred to keep them under supervision. We could learn more about them while they were at liberty. We did not arrest them till we had ceased to get valuable information from their correspondence. I was present at the eventual arrest of several of them.

That was a valuable experience for a novelist. They took their arrests very calmly, with the exception of one man, a barber, whose shop several of the conspirators used as a *poste restante* – in the same way that Englishmen use their clubs. He was completely innocent. But this we could not tell. When we arrested the others, we had to arrest him too. He was terrified, remembering no doubt all the stories of innocent men who had been taken to prison by mistake. The others, who knew exactly what they had done, stayed calm.

CICI's headquarters were in a large rambling house on the west bank of the Tigris, facing the Alwiyah Sports Club, of which visiting officers were honorary members. It had a wide terrace on which we dined in the summer. It was very hot in the summer, so hot that the flies died off. But it was a dry heat, and it suited me. I have bronchial tendencies. We used to sleep out on our own balconies in the summer. At four in the morning a faint breeze blew off the river and we would pull a sheet over our shoulders.

Our offices were in an adjoining two-storey house built round a small garden from whose centre a palm tree rose. We each had a separate room. We looked like so many monks in their cells as we sat at our desks over our files. It was very quiet; now and again the Colonel would come out on his balcony and call for one of us by name. 'Hackforth, Alec, Pam.' I was there for two years and was never bored. I worked very hard, but it was the kind of work for which I was fitted by taste and training, co-ordinating information, assessing probabilities, arranging concise summaries so that busy senior officers could discover at a glance what was happening. I do not think I wasted their time.

The PEN Club had a branch in Baghdad, which was then very active. It had as its secretary Majid Khaddouri, the author of several books, who after the war emigrated to America and earned an important place for himself in the Johns Hopkins University. One of its chief members was Fadhil Jamali, who had been prime minister and also minister of education. He had, to my surprise, heard of me as the author of *The Loom of Youth* and invited me to attend their meetings. Once a month or so they would have a meeting in which one of the members read a paper. After the paper there would be a discussion followed by a dinner. My colonel gave me permission to attend these dinners. The members were prominent in Baghdad public life. It would be useful for the centre's work for me to know them and to be in a position to report on them. They asked me about my writing plans. They supposed I was too busy with my work at CICI to do any writing now. I shook my head. 'As a matter of fact I'm doing a book of wartime memories.'

In Christmas 1942 Robin Maugham, on a visit to Baghdad, had brought me as a present an elegant leather-bound manuscript book. I felt that I had to put this to some use. During my six months as a staff captain at Spears' mission, when I had very little to do, I had made a series of notes about my experiences since I had sailed from England. Why not, I thought, incorporate these paragraphs into a consecutive narrative starting at the very beginning in September 1939 and calling it *His Second War*. I could not bear not to make this elegant book fulfil a purpose.

Waking early as usual I put in about ninety minutes of work on it, before breakfast. By April I had covered the ground at my disposal. I included one of the stories that I had written going round the Cape, and the one that I had written at Cairo. The book totalled some 60,000 words. I thought it rather good. I had it typed and sent it back to Cassell's. Cassell's said they were pleased and proposed to print an edition of five thousand copies. I was delighted and told my friends about it. Then Cassell's changed their mind. Paper was in very short supply and Cassell's were particularly short. Publishers were rationed in terms of the amount of paper they had used in 1936. Cassell's had not reprinted their encyclopaedia in 1938 and had used less paper than usual. Macmillan on the other hand had reprinted a large edition of *Gone With the Wind*. Collins, because they printed prayer books and Bibles, also had a large ration. They decided to use a lot of their ration on novels and general books. This was very lucky for their authors, who were able to maintain if not increase their public. All books that were printed sold out within six months. The firm of Macdonald came into existence because a West Country firm of printers that had issued racing guides had a ration of paper and no guides to print, so they went into general publishing. Cassell's in their predicament decided on second thoughts that they would rather use their meagre supply of paper on other books. They had other authors to consider and they knew that I who was drawing army pay did not desperately need the money. They did not tell me this, however. They said that they did not think *His Second War* was up to my standard and its issue now would prejudice the sales of my first novel after the war.

Their change of mind was a considerable blow to me. I had never thought that a book of mine would not find an English publisher. Moreover I had told my friends in Baghdad that the book was in the press. Vanity would not make it easy for me to admit that the book had been postponed. I wrote to Peters urging him to insist that Cassell's revert to their original decision. I had been their author for thirteen years. I was under contract with them for another novel. My feelings had to be considered. Peters' power of persuasion proved effective. Cassell's reluctantly agreed to print three thousand copies.

The book came out nine months later. It had a reasonable press and within five months was out of print. I could not tell whether Cassell's was justified in thinking that *His Second War* would prejudice the sale of my next novel, because when my next novel came out in December 1948 there was still a paper shortage. Cassell's paid me an advance of £600. They printed enough copies to repay them for this advance. Another novel of mine did not come out till March 1953. By then the paper shortage was over. But my 1953 novel, *Guy Renton*, was rather good and sold quite well. So I have still no means of knowing whether or not I was justified in insisting that Cassell's publish a book against what they considered their and my best interests. At any rate I did not have to eat humble pie in Baghdad.

My book of Profiles contains a chapter, 'Arthur Waugh's Last Years'. My father died in the summer of 1943. The cable announcing his death did not come as a surprise. His handwriting had become increasingly difficult to read. He could no longer hold his pen firmly. The script trailed across the paper, often in scratches. For his sake I could not feel sad. I wished though that I had been with him during those last weeks. I wished I could have 'seen him off'.

We had been very close. When I had been in trouble at school, he had known by telepathy before he got the letter that confirmed it. More than once he had said, 'If there is an after-life, I am sure that I shall be able to get through to you.' And indeed a curious thing did happen. He had suffered from asthma and during the winter before going to bed, he had burnt a powder called 'Himrod's Asthma Cure'. It had a very peculiar and pungent smell. In early days my father's bathroom was always associated for me with that smell. One morning soon after my return from the Middle East, I walked into what had been his bedroom and my nostrils were assaulted by the familiar smell. I mentioned it to my mother. 'It is extraordinary,' I said, 'how the smell of Himrod lingers. It was very strong this morning.' 'But that's impossible,' she said. 'He never burnt Himrod after we moved into this flat. Besides I've had the room repainted.'

Until 1930 Iraq had been a British Protectorate and Baghdad still had many of the characteristics of the British Raj. When Iraq achieved independence, it retained a number of British technical advisers in commerce, in education and the law. Oil had brought many British families. In addition to the Alwiyah Country Club there was a town club of which I became a member. There was a cricket club, The Casuals, for which I played every Saturday and Sunday during the summer. Because of the heat we played from four to six. I never made many runs, but I was not unsuccessful as a bowler. I found it easier to turn the ball off matting than I had off grass and also I got a little lift. I bowled right hand slow medium, round the wicket, and I got batsmen either leg before or caught at short slip.

There was a reasonable golf club and I played most afternoons in the winter. There was also Freemasonry. I joined the lodge of Iraq and became a master there. I led an active social life. When I left Cairo I had been warned that I should find a great lack of feminine society. But this I had been prepared to welcome. For a quadragenarian gallantry and a captain's pay do not 'go together like a horse and carriage'. My life in Baghdad was completely celibate. There were no temptations.

In spite of this deprivation, I would be content to live those years again, and just at the moment when my work threatened to lose its interest – after the rout of the German army, there was no likelihood of German spy activity through Turkey – I was moved out of Intelligence into Public Relations.

The troops still stationed in Paiforce were in a disgruntled mood. They had ceased to feel that they were usefully employed. They had been here now for two years. Had they not been left here because they were second-raters? Some of them had never been in action. They had begun to feel that their folks in England did not appreciate what they were doing. Conditions in England were very difficult. V bombs were falling. Food was scarce. They pictured their folks as saying: 'While we are putting up with this, there are Bill and Bert having the time of their lives in the sun, gorging themselves on the fat of the land.' Moreover now that England was full of American troops with money to spend and gifts to bestow, every unit had its own story of broken marriages and engagements. Worst of all the men had the fear that when eventually they got home, they would not be welcomed as 'conquering heroes' but as 'astute scrimshankers' who had known how 'to get it easy'. The troops needed cheering up in fact, and it was decided to form a Public Relations branch, that would send back to local papers in Great Britain accounts of what individuals in Paiforce were doing under unusual and difficult conditions. I was put in charge of this branch with the rank of major.

It was a lively assignment. It meant that I had to travel round the command, interviewing the members of the various units. The command stretched from Basra to Tehran. I had to do a great deal of travelling. I was completely on my own. I went exactly where I wanted. I really saw the country. The forming of this PR section was the personal idea of the head of Paiforce, Lieutenant-General Sir Arthur Smith. During my first month there he 'vetted' my manuscripts himself, correcting them here and there, making suggestions and amendments, subjecting them to the kind of scrutiny to which Harold Ross used to subject the contributors to the *New Yorker*. I have in my time had my prose examined by a number of editors. I have no hesitation in asserting that the most efficient and perceptive editor I have ever had was General Sir Arthur Smith.

By the beginning of May I had visited every unit in the Command, and that was the very time when my age group was due for demobilisation. The Army was arranged in groups, in terms of their age and length of service. I was nearly forty-seven. I had been in the Army from the start. I was in the second batch to be repatriated from the Middle East. When I arrived in New York a few months later, a woman asked me if I had had 'a chic war'. 'No,' I said, 'but I had a lucky one.' At my age and with my lowly rank, I might have had a dreary one as garrison adjutant in some provincial city or I might have vegetated in London in some administrative backwater, doing work of little interest, and managing with difficulty upon a captain's pay. As it was I had a varied time. I covered a lot of ground, and in terms of my future as a novelist, I could scarcely have had a luckier war. I had, in the first place, a six-year break in mid-career. In 1939 I had been writing for twenty years and I needed 'a breather'. I was beginning to get a little stale. Without that breather, I doubt if I could have stayed the course. As it was I went back to writing, for my second innings, with a great deal of new material. I had seen the Middle East at first hand; that added a dimension to my interests. My spy experience in Baghdad gave me an insight into police methods that I could not have otherwise acquired. Of the seven novels that I have written since the war, five could not have been written unless I had had that experience in Baghdad. The war rejuvenated, refreshed, replenished me. It also, because of my low rank, set me in the company of men several years younger than myself.

Previous to the war, my friends had been mainly older than myself. The success of *The Loom of Youth* had made my opposite numbers men ten years older. Now the process was reversed. I was among men ten to fifteen years younger than myself. I saw life through younger eyes. I made four very good friends, several years younger than myself, whom I was then meeting on equal terms. Robin Maugham, Richard Usborne, Majid Khaddouri, whom I was to see regularly in Washington, and the banker Geoffrey Seligman.

I had first met Seligman in September 1940 at a security intelligence course in Matlock. I remember his high indignation when the carburettor of his car was appropriated, perhaps on security grounds during the blackout. 'Is this what we've come here to learn?' he said.

Later he was to be posted to Baghdad to take my place as G3 there. We found we had a lot in common. We also had the bond of having an Australian wife. His wife, Merrie, one of the Jonah twins, was to become a warm friend of mine; so was her twin, Gwyneth, of whom I was later to see a great deal in New York. Through Geoffrey, I was to meet in New York his cousin Eustace, whose hospitality was to add so much to my enjoyment of my life there.

Very few of my actual contemporaries are still alive, but thanks to the war, I have those four chief friends among many others, whom I can feel to be my contemporaries. I am less alone now than in 1939 I could have expected to be.

Yes, I had a lucky war, but six years is a long time. There are debit entries on the balance sheet. I never quite got back into my marriage, and I never quite became again a part of London life. I lacked the bond of shared experience. As I have said, during the early bombings, when I had to spend a night out of London I felt resentful at missing any part of London's Calvary. That bond became much stronger during the long, slow-passing years. I was surprised and touched when I went back to the Savile, to find how much the members liked each other. During those dreary slow-passing years this club had been their home, their bastion. They had come in here night after night out of the bombing, out of the blackout. They had drawn sustenance from one another. There had grown up a kinship between them.

CHAPTER 17

Return to New York

At one point during the last part of the war, some officers who were serving in exceptionally sensitive positions were interviewed by a psychoanalyst whose business it was to discover how they would respond to certain pressures; Evelyn was subjected to this treatment. After he had been interrogated for some ninety minutes he said, 'You have been asking me a great many questions. Do you mind if I now ask you one?' The psychiatrist agreed. 'Why then,' Evelyn asked, 'have you not questioned me about the most important thing in a man's life – his religion?'

I could supply a '*tu quoque*' in my own case. Among the papers found upon Evelyn's desk after his death were six or seven pages of what are believed to be the resumption of his autobiography. Of one of these pages, I am the subject. I print it here as an appendix. I am touched that he should have written about me so warmly, touched too that he should have spent some of his last hours thinking of me. At the same time I cannot but contend that he presents an incomplete picture of my life. 'His later years,' he writes, 'have been spent among the palm trees of the Mediterranean, the Pacific and the Caribbean. They have been illuminated I believe by love affairs with ladies of a great variety of age, race and appearance.' He also refers to 'the large and heterogeneous collection of cronies, drawn from the stage, from journalism and literature who have stood by him through life'. This is true enough in part, but only in part. Why is there no reference to my life in the USA, and particularly in New York, which was the axis round which my world revolved after the war? Did he not realise how all-important New York was to me?

When I returned to England in June 1945 I was resolved to begin writing as soon as possible, and I recognised that I must get back to New York. I had money in New York, the proceeds of the three magazine short stories that I had sold in 1942 and the film sale of *No Truce With Time*. There was nothing that I could do in England professionally, with the paper shortage. I had an idea that I might go to Hollywood and find employment in the studios. My old friend from *Red Book*, Voldemar Vetlugin, was with MGM. I thought he would assist me. Eighteen months earlier my publishers John Farrar and Stanley Rinehart had dissolved their partnership. John Farrar had been my first New York friend. He had been my editor when I had been a Doran author. Stanley Rinehart was a very personal friend of mine. His first marriage had broken up shortly before I arrived in New York to celebrate the publication of *Hot Countries*. We had 'played in town' in the winter of 1930–1, and in London in the summer of 1932. We had been together when he had met his bride-to-be, Fay Yeatman. I did not know what John Farrar's future plans were. At the moment he was working with the American Ministry of Information. But he would almost certainly be going back into publishing now that the war was over. I had a difficult choice ahead.

I had another move too, ahead of me. Carol Hill had been asked by MGM to act as their New York representative. The offer had come to her through her friendship with Vetlugin. She was offered fifty thousand dollars a year, the use of a chauffeur-driven car, a sumptuous office in the Paramount building and an unlimited expense account. Her insistence on being treated as a prima donna had certainly paid off. Here I had no difficulty of choice. There was no question of my going to Peters' representative. I went back to Brandt. Carl wrote to me 'this is like old home week'.

I arrived in New York in mid-September. The next four months were as good as any I have known. I do not suppose that anywhere in the world at that time was there half as much fun to be found as there was that winter in New York. The war was over. Families were soon to be reunited. There were hardly any shortages, only shoes were rationed, and that restriction was shortly to be lifted. In London clothing was still rationed and it took a year to get a suit made. Alan Rinehart introduced me to his tailor, Earl Benham, and I replenished my wardrobe. I crossed by ship, and during the trip I wrote a short story which *Red Book* bought. That gave me the encouraging belief that I should be able to slip back into my old place in the magazine market. I wrote another short story and *Red Book* bought that too. I could face the future with confidence. I was full of energy, full of ideas. It was good to be a writer again. At the moment though I was having too good a time to concentrate upon short stories. I was making up for the barren months when I had been in uniform. Back again in the Algonquin in suite number 711 – a lucky number everybody told me – I felt that I had never been away. I was charged only $9 a day. Most of my old friends were around. St Clair McKelway, who had reached the rank of Lieutenant-Colonel, was almost the only one who had seen any service action. When I arrived the Wolcott Gibbs were still at Fire Island and I spent a night with them. A hurricane was threatened, and the following morning Wolcott wrote the piece about their cat in the previous year's hurricane that appeared in his *Seasons in the Sun*. He wrote it in the course of a single morning, pulled it out of the typewriter and handed it to Elinor. It is the only time that I have seen a piece of solid merit actually being composed.

That hurricane missed Fire Island but the Gibbs accepted it as a warning and within a week they were back in New York. They gave a party for me. It was good, it was very good to see so many old friends again. James Thurber was there, John O'Hara, and Dorothy Parker. I met Charles Addams there and Roland Young, who were to become very close friends during the years ahead. One Sunday afternoon walking down Fifth Avenue, I encountered Michael Arlen walking in the opposite direction. He had joined his wife and children in New York, when he had found that there was no war work available in England. He was now living on Madison and Seventy Fifth in the Volney Hotel. I had always been fond of him. He had now ceased to write and this was the first time that we had met on equal terms. I was to see him regularly over the next ten years.

Edward Wasserman, his name changed to Waterman, was in New York. He gave a small lunch party for Somerset Maugham, at which Carl Van Vechten and I were the other guests. Many years before Maugham had asked me if I had ever read *The Tattooed Countess*. It was, he said, the best light novel he had ever read. He was to ask me the same question at Waterman's lunch. Next day I read the novel at the New York Public Library. I did not think it particularly good. It has not been re-issued. Perhaps I read it at the wrong time. One day I will try again. Maugham and Van Vechten were, I could see, close friends. At one point the party divided into two duologues, myself and Waterman, Maugham and Van Vechten. I broke off my talk to look across the table. Maugham was leaning forward talking with an absorbed concentration that I had never seen before and was not to see again. 'That's the real man,' I thought.

Carl Brandt gave me a guest card for the Century Club. I was to use it constantly. During my long stay in New York in 1930–1 he had given me a guest card to the Players' Club but I had not used it. In Prohibition days there were no obvious means of obtaining alcohol in a club. Members had their own lockers. But that would have been difficult for a guest member to arrange and I could not see myself sitting down to a masculine meal without a glass of some alcoholic refreshment at my elbow. But now the Century Club filled a need that I had felt previously in New York – the need for masculine companionship. Englishmen who go to boarding schools at the age of nine feel this need strongly. I was to use the Century a great deal. It had a supremely good cellar at a

moderate cost. For four years I had been deprived of wine.
I made the most of my opportunities at the Century. I dined
there two or three times a week. I asked Carl if it would be
hard to join.

'Is there any point,' he asked, 'unless you are going to
come here for much longer visits?'

This was the first time that I had asked myself that question. Was I going to come over for longer periods? I felt so
at home in New York. I felt so much myself here. My
future as a writer depended on my ability to maintain my
position in the New York market. Would it be possible for
me to spend two or three months at a time here as I was
doing now? The idea teased me. How I wished I could.

There were other amenities in New York. My years in
Baghdad had been completely celibate. There were no
women there at all. In Cairo there had been temptations, but
men outnumbered the women in the ratio of a hundred to
one. In New York on the other hand the balance was
reversed. Half the young men were away in Europe. There
had not been as there had in London an influx of foreign
troops. There had in fact been a man shortage. I made up
for those arid years.

At the end of January I returned to England. I needed to
get back to work and I wanted to leave in New York a
reasonable balance of dollars, so that I could make another
long trip later in the year. I suspected that I might find it
difficult to build up another balance. I did not know
exactly what currency restrictions were imposed on British
subjects. I preferred to remain in ignorance.

I travelled back by the *Queen Elizabeth*. She was still a
troopship. The cabins were fitted with barrack-style bunks.
I shared a cabin with five other passengers. Only the dining
room and the large drawing room were decorated. It was a
dry ship. I brought two bottles of whisky aboard, one of
which was stolen, along with a pair of shoes. There were no
cabin doors to lock. The passage cost £40. The food was up

to Cunard standard. I wrote a 6,000-word short story which I was to sell to *Red Book*.

Within two days of my arrival I went to Devonshire to the Easton Court Hotel.

A New York friend asked me if I found England very different. 'There are,' I answered, 'pockets of resistance.' One's clubs, one's tailors, one's wine merchants, the houses of one or two friends who had not been bombed out. Easton Court was a pocket of resistance. I found it 'just the same'. Carolyn looked no older, nor did her partner, Norman Webb, who had done strenuous war service in the Observer Corps, and had attended the D-day landings. The hotel had still no liquor licence. Guests kept their own store. And every evening I used to take my bottle of gin or whisky over to Carolyn's bedroom-office to share it with her and Norman. Spirits were not easy to get, but I had good friends in the wine trade. The countryside had the same rounded beauty. And the villagers in the pubs had the same warm friendliness. Only one thing was different – the beer. I do not see how the GIs stomached it. I stuck to cider.

It was a mild winter, but all the same I was grateful to have a bedroom next to the boiler house. The wall was warm; at night I could press my stern against it. And when I woke early for a stint of writing before breakfast, my fingers were not too cold to hold the pen. I settled down to a calm routine of walks and writing. I wrote an eighteen-thousand word novelette which Carl Brandt sold to *Cosmopolitan*. It was the first time I had been in *Cosmopolitan*. That story was to become the basis of my novel *Guy Renton*.

I invited my mother to come down for a visit. She was now in her middle seventies, but she was as active as she had ever been. She could take long walks, moving at a good pace. Her mind was still alert. She had shown a steadfast spirit during the war. The daughter of an Indian civil servant, she was born in Chittagong. She had made a religion of the Empire. England's reverses in 1940 had been a grievous grief to her. Then Joan to whom she was devoted had taken her grandchildren to Australia. She missed them sorely. Then her poodle had to be 'put down'. 'There doesn't seem any point now in going for a walk,' she wrote to me. I had arranged for a friend to bring her out a poodle puppy to take his place. But she refused. 'It's more than I can undertake,' she wrote. I thought her unenterprising at the time but eight years later I was to realise how wise she had been. By 1950 – she died in 1954 – she had not the strength to give a dog the attention that he needed. She took no long walks during the last two years of her life. In June 1943 my father died. She felt very lost without him. For so long she had been indispensable. Then the V bombs began. They got upon her nerves and she left Highgate to stay with her sisters-in-law in Somerset. Now all that was over. England had triumphed and soon her grandchildren would be coming home.

She enjoyed her stay at Chagford. 'I'm so glad to have seen it. I've often thought about it. I like to be able to picture the places where you and Evelyn are.'

'I think I'll bring the children down here, until Edrington's open again,' I said.

'When will it be open?'

'In October, they seem to think.'

In the meantime, the children had to be got into schools. They were due back in April. Andrew was to go to Fernden. He would be thirteen in July. He was down for Eton and was due to take the common entrance exam in June. I had doubts about his passing. He would have had no schooling during the long sea voyage from Melbourne. He had been since the autumn of 1940 at Geelong Junior School. I was confident that at the age of eighteen at university level he would be able to meet on equal terms a boy from an English public school. He could have taken the same exams, but I suspected that the early training would be on a different pattern. They began Latin late. He might need time to make up the difference.

My qualms were intensified when I took him to Lord's

for the Easter cricket classes. I had been confident that in Australia of all places he would have been given sound basic training. He was a natural instinctive ball games player and was to develop, in the limited opportunities that he was to have as a sailor to play the game, into a sound player, but at this point he had no idea of the technique of the left shoulder; he swung across the ball. I was shocked, so I could see was Jack Robertson in whose charge he was placed. I could only hope for the best.

Fernden went back the first week in May. I saw him off from Waterloo. It was strange seeing my own son join at the familiar platform a group of boys wearing the familiar red and green school tie. I felt a quirk of responsibility for him. Five and a half years at Geelong had made him self-confident and independent. He had learnt how to manage for himself. But would he not feel himself very lost among a group of boys who had never known anything but the restrictions of wartime England? When he arrived at Fernden, he would find awaiting him a letter that I had written him the day before wishing him luck.

I had thought that I would find it very strange to meet Joan and the children. I did not though. Joan had not altered. She was the same elegant, well-groomed person. Photographs had shown me how my seven-and-a-half-year old Peter would look and how Andrew had changed from a seven-year-old to a boy about to start his teens. But in my daughter Veronica there was no change at all. She had grown but she had not altered. She broke away from Joan and ran down the platform to me with outstretched arms. It seemed very natural to be driving out with the four of them to Highgate to my mother's flat.

In retrospect I feel that it might have been better if I had tried to find a furnished flat for them in London. But I am not sure. Housekeeping in London, with strict rationing and the consequent queues, was very difficult. It seemed easier to make a series of week-to-week arrangements. I had my flat at the White House. In September Peter would be going to Fernden, Veronica to St James's School, Malvern. In October Edrington would be ours again. I needed to have somewhere where I could work. I took Veronica down to Chagford. Joan stayed with Peter at Highgate.

The weeks that I spent with Veronica at Chagford were happy ones. She was a delightful, affectionate companion. We went for walks, we took picnics, she went riding. In the mornings she took lessons from a local schoolmaster while I wrote. I was still concentrating on the American magazine market and during this summer I made an experiment whose failure was a valuable lesson to me.

I was conscious that time was running out, that I had only twelve years of my full powers ahead of me; after sixty I could expect to turn the corner. I must not waste any time. I was ready to accept any available assistance. I began to hear talk of Benzedrine. It was a great and harmless stimulant, I was told. It dispensed energy; it inspired confidence. Ralph Straus told me that he always took a tablet before he gave a lecture. I heard that RAF pilots had been given them on raids. I heard that students took them before exams. I wondered if they might increase my output.

I consulted my doctor, Christopher Howard, a fellow Old Shirburnian. 'Yes,' he said, 'they are a very useful stimulant. If you use them prudently and only when you need them. I can give you a prescription. Don't take them in the evening. They'll stop you sleeping.'

'Are they anaphrodisiac, as Dexadrine's supposed to be?'

'On the contrary, they might give you confidence.' And he quoted Housman's 'Others I am not the first, have willed more mischief than they durst.'

'Can they be taken with alcohol?' I asked.

'It makes no difference.'

'Then it might suit me. I don't do more than six months' actual writing in a year. Suppose I were to take Benzedrine while I was actually composing and knocked off when I was travelling, doing research, just having a good time.'

'That sounds all right.'

'It isn't habit-forming?'

'Not physically; it might be mentally, you might come to rely on it too much.'

'I'll try it,' I said.

I had an idea for a story about a secretary in the office of an American magazine company that published separate issues in London. I had Hearst and Condé Nast in mind. The London representative was a New Yorker. As I have said I always had an international situation in my stories, with either the heroine or the hero an American. I forget now whether the hero was a married man or not. His problem was the bottle. He was on his own in London. He would come back later from lunch in an exhilarated mood. He would stand swaying slightly in the centre of the room, he would look at his secretary. 'Honey, it's good to come back from lunch to find you here. It's like finding a great bowl of flowers on my desk. Flowers, that's what you are. Flowers all the year round. There are some letters that must get written, but I'm in no mood to write them. I must go back to my flat and sleep, but I've got to get these letters off. I've got to explain to Harrison . . .' And he would tell her what he had to explain to Harrison and what he had to explain to Thring and Colby, and what he wanted from Jones and what he needed from Smith. 'I can trust you, can't I, to do that? You would not fail, would you, to succour a poor abandoned American lost in your fair city? See you tomorrow. I'll be making sense tomorrow.'

The story would tell how he would become increasingly dependent on her, how she would take more and more off his hands, until she was in a position to take over his work completely. The conflict would be between her ambition which was prompting her to take over more and more of his work, until she was the editor, and her growing love for him, her need to protect and strengthen him. The climax would come when the No. 1 from New York would arrive, recognise what the situation was, and be prepared to sack the hero and install the secretary in the editorial chair.

I planned to call the story 'Flowers All the Year Round'. Seventy-thousand words. A *Red Book* one-shot possibly. On the morning that I was going to start my treatment, I stood in front of my shaving mirror. I put the pill in my mouth. I wanted to watch myself take the pill. I swallowed a glass of water. 'My first Benzedrine,' I thought; 'this may be an important day for me. It may be a moment I'll remember all my life. It may mark the start of something.'

I sat down at my desk. I was excited. I was curious. How soon would the pill begin to work? It was nine o'clock. At half-past eleven I would take Veronica for a walk. I am a methodical writer. I write a fixed number of words every day. At this time I was writing 2,000 words a day. I expected to have written 1,250 words by half-past eleven. To my surprise I found that the writing came much more easily than I had expected. I had written 2,400. That afternoon I wrote another 1,600. I had written with high excitement. It is said that easy writing makes hard reading. This has not been my experience. When the writing goes well, it is all right. 'Will it be the same tomorrow?' I asked myself. It was. By the end of the week I had written 24,000 words. At this rate I could write a whole novel in six weeks.

That year an Indian cricket eleven was touring the country. I had had a box at Lord's for the 1938 and 1939 Test Matches and my application this year was accepted. The sun shone throughout the match. I had brought back from New York a number of tins of chicken and salmon that were unobtainable in London then. I brought up a crate of wine from Edrington. Wine was hard to get in London. My Beaujolais was as much appreciated as my sandwiches. Among my guests that day was R. C. Hutchinson. In 1944 he had been sent out to Baghdad to write an official history of Paiforce. Until then I had scarcely known him. An acquaintanceship developed into a friendship. He was a delightful fellow, completely without conceit in spite of his high quality as a writer. His talk was for me that day one of the most pleasant features of the occasion. We had a lot to tell each other about our writing plans. 'We must keep in touch with one another,' we agreed. But we were never to meet again. It was very easy to lose touch in post-war England. Hutchinson was a recluse. I was away so much. We did not have any common ground. I think he was one of the most significant writers of our day. He had a miraculous capacity to make real a place that he had never visited, as he showed in his picture of a French small town in *Shining Scabbard* and of Russia in *Testament*.

Andrew and Veronica were also in the box. Andrew was taking his common entrance exam during the following week, and his headmaster had given him permission to come up. It would be good to take his mind off the exam. The two of them added greatly to the liveliness of the occasion.

On the following Saturday there was the Fathers' match at Fernden. I played for the Fathers. I asked Andrew if he had any news from Eton. 'In the negative,' he said. It was a blow, but it was not unexpected. He could not be expected to adjust to a whole new system within six weeks. But his not passing created a problem. He would almost certainly pass his common entrance in the following summer. The eventual passing of it was accepted in those days as a matter of course. It was not a question of passing or not passing but of the form into which one would pass. But in the meantime he had missed his vacancy at Eton and there was unlikely to be another. His headmaster, Charles Brownrigg, the son of my own old headmaster, was not worried. 'Andrew can stay on here another year,' he said. 'He'll be fourteen next summer. That's a perfectly good age to go to a public school. Let's see how things develop during the autumn. There's no need to make a decision now.'

I assured Andrew that there was no reason to be fussed. It would have been a miracle if he had made up the lost ground so quickly. He would be certain to pass if not in the spring then in the following summer. He had, I hope, no sense of failure. That was how we left it on the evening of the Fathers' Match.

But on the following Saturday I went down to Sherborne for the Old Shirburnian golf society meeting. It was a warm week-end. Sherborne looked at its loveliest. On the Saturday evening I played a four-ball with the headmaster Canon Ross Wallace. When I had put down Andrew's name for Eton, in the spring of 1935, my own long separation from Sherborne had only just ended. I had been readmitted to the Old Boys' Society, and I had attended an Old Boys' dinner, but I had not been back to the school and had not met the headmaster. It had never occurred to me to enter Andrew for the school. Eton was the obvious choice for a father who did not want to send his son to his own old school. But not only had I been down to Sherborne in 1937 to play for the MCC but Joan had spent a two weeks' fishing holiday in Ireland in the same hotel as Ross Wallace, who was there with two Sherborne masters. They became good friends and were involved in a curious fishing incident. Joan caught a salmon but the fish sought shelter in some reeds, the line got entangled in the reeds, and the fish managed to break the line. One hour later she got another 'bite' and landed the fish. On landing it she found that she had caught the same fish again, and that her original hook was embedded in its throat, attached to the broken piece of reed. The coincidence was so extraordinary that Ross Wallace wrote a letter to *The Times*. Between fishermen that kind of thing makes a very special bond, and when Joan and I, in November 1939, motored over from Dorchester to lunch we entered Peter's name for the school. I did not want to cancel Andrew's vacancy at Eton, but I would like to have a son at Sherborne.

'Tell me about that boy of yours,' Ross Wallace asked on this 1946 occasion. But it was not about that boy that was entered for the School House in 1952 he asked, but the other one who had failed his common entrance, and as I told him, for the first time the idea came to me, 'Why shouldn't Andrew go to Sherborne, as his father and grandfather had?' I went back to London with Andrew's name upon the books. It was a snap decision, but I am confident that it was a lucky one. Andrew's time at Sherborne was as happy as it was successful.

I planned to return to New York early in October. Veronica would be at St James's, Andrew and Peter would be at Fernden. Joan would supervise Edrington's restoration. The summer holidays we spent in large part at Easton Court. I took the children to Midsomer Norton so that they could see their aunts. I had stopped work on 'Flowers All the Year Round'. Some 60,000 words were done. I could see the tape ahead. I would wait to write the last 25,000 words until I had discussed the beginning with Carl Brandt. It was not, however, all that easy to get a manuscript into presentable shape. I could not type. I had no secretary. It was very difficult to find anyone in London who could type it. At that time it was difficult to get anything done in London. The quickest way in this case was to send my manuscript to New York and have it typed there. I went over the handwritten manuscript carefully. Another two weeks of Benzedrine-inspired industry and off it went. It seemed fine to me. I awaited Carl Brandt's reception with confidence. I knocked off Benzedrine and devoted the remainder of the summer holidays to my family.

It took a month to get an answer. It was far from being the answer that I had expected.

'I am puzzled about this,' Carl said. 'I don't know what to say. You'll be over in October. Let's discuss it then.' Ten days later the typescript arrived. I was puzzled by it too. The story seemed all right, the characters seemed all right, the sequence of events dramatic. Yet somehow the narrative did not 'bite'. That is the only word that meets the case. I went on reading, but the thing fell off my mind. 'I must put it away,' I thought. 'I'm too close to it. I'll come back fresh in November. It must be all right, basically. I couldn't have written it with so much excitement, if it wasn't.'

In November I went back to the manuscript; basically it seemed all right, but the narrative still did not bite. It never has. A year later, I returned to it with the same result. 'One day,' I thought, 'I'll find the answer.' But I never did, or at least I never did in the way of producing a manuscript that an editor would want to print. But I did find the explanation. Benzedrine. It was fine for keeping fighter pilots awake during a long flight, and it was fine for giving a student confidence on the eve of and during an examination. But a writer, at least a writer on a smaller scale that Balzac, does not need a stimulant to keep awake, and I have never lacked self-confidence. What Benzedrine had done for me was to send my critical faculties to sleep. After my first long talk with Carol Hill I had decided to take longer over the writing of a short story. Ten days instead of three. Now I had been giving myself only one. I must go back to my old pattern and put those pills away. I had learnt a valuable lesson. In recent years, particularly in Tangier, I have often had preached to me the merit of marijuana and it does work well for many writers. But I have not listened to those siren voices. I remember 'Flowers All the Year Round'.

I spent ten weeks in New York. They were very good. The war was definitely over. During the previous autumn New Yorkers had been coming home. Now they were home. Carolyn Cobb had given me a letter of introduction to Zaidée Bliss, the benefactress of the Museum of Modern Art. She gave a large buffet lunch party, in her house on Long Island. The men were nearly all 'soldiers from the wars returning', thirty-five and under. Life was budding for them. It was a radiant autumn day of rich colours, the garden aflame with maples. Happiness was in the air. Not all of them were going back to their old lives. Many marriages had broken during the war. Several of the young women had spent during their summer their six statutory weeks in

Reno. Among those who had was Mrs Bliss's daughter Eliza Parkinson. I met her for the first time that afternoon. It was the start of a long deep friendship. She had been accompanied in Reno by the painter Lily Cushing, whom I had met and by whom I had been enchanted before the war. Lily's first husband had been the brother of Katzie Canfield, who was now married to John Churchill, the son of the novelist. Katzie's first husband Cass had remarried the ex-wife of Charlie Fuller, the architect, a great charmer, but a heavy drinker who if he had not broken had dislocated many tender hearts. It was curious how many of that group had married *en seconde noce*, the mates whom they had contrived to miss the first time round. Eliza Parkinson and Lily Cushing were to become the focal pivot of one side of my New York life.

Another old friend was in New York, Dorothy Speare, a Bostonian, whose novel *Prima Donna* had been made into the film *One Night of Love*. A lady of immense vitality, she was a born catalyst, who loved getting together in small parties men and women whom she thought would like and be useful to each other. No one could have been more unlike Mrs Belloc Lowndes, but they had points in common. Both were good writers, intensely interested in the trade of letters, and in the careers of their friends, always doing anything to further their careers. Through her that autumn I met Carl Van Doren, Al Capp, Jack Jessup, a *Life* editor, and his vivacious wife whose sister Eleanor Clarke was to write many good books and become the wife of Robert Penn Warren.

At this time Dorothy had a suite in the Edwardian Murray Hill Hotel. In the same building John Farrar and Roger Straus were starting to lay the foundations of their partnership. I decided to throw in my lot with them. Strong though my friendship had been with Stanley Rinehart, John Farrar had been my first New York friend. Neither on personal nor on professional grounds was I to regret my choice. There are many advantages in being with a young firm that has its way to make, and has to concentrate on such authors as it can find.

Roger when I met him first was still in naval uniform. He was young, eager and ambitious. Very often a man who is no more than ordinarily good-looking as a young man, acquires with age a deeper handsomeness. Roger was not quite like that. He was always very good to look at, but he is better looking now. He has kept his figure, and his hair. He has dash and glamour. His wife Dorothea, a dark exotic beauty, is no less glamorous.

I was as close to Elinor Gibbs as ever and through her my links with the *New Yorker* staff were widened. I had met Charles and Barbara Addams the year before but only briefly, and he was still in uniform; now we became close friends. When I left in December he gave me the original of his cover for *Addams and Evil*. It hangs in my sitting room in Tangier; one of the very few possessions that have accompanied my frequent changes of residence. What a delightful couple they were, what a team they were. They matched each other so well. He so solid with that warm, deep smile and she so unmistakably the wife in the Goon family. Everyone was charmed by them. Everyone was delighted with their success. They were so universally liked that we all felt we were a part of it, that we shared it. The *New Yorker* came out on Thursday. By lunch that day everyone would be saying 'Isn't the new Charlie Addams wonderful?' There was universal dismay when their marriage broke up in 1951. 'Oh no, not the Addams'.

Through Elinor Gibbs, indirectly, I joined the Coffee House. I am very much a clubman. I have had more happiness out of the Coffee House than any of my clubs, except the Beefsteak. It is very small. Two long narrow rooms on the first floor of 54 West 45. One room consists of a long refectory table that can seat thirty guests. At the end of it is a blackboard on which the day's menu is chalked. The other room contains a number of small tables. The walls are lined with books, pictures and photographs of past members. At one end there is a dais on which is a rectangular table beside the bar. It is here that members and their guests take their cocktails. There is no 'treating'. You order what you want then move next door to the long refectory table.

After four o'clock women are admitted. Tables are laid for dinner. Dinners must be ordered in advance. There is a choice of fish or steak. You may find three or four couples or parties dining there, or you may be alone at your candle-lit table. You do not feel uncomfortable when you are alone, as you do in an empty restaurant. You feel you are dining in your own home.

On Saturdays women can come to lunch. Today this is only on the first Saturday of the month, then it was every Saturday. The women guests, if their hosts choose, sit at the octagonal table, then move to one of the tables in the room. Members make up parties among one another. At the opposite end of the room there is an oval-shaped table that can seat eight guests. Today places are laid as well at the long refectory table.

These Saturday lunches were for me the most attractive feature of the club. It meant that I made firmer friendships with my fellow members. A women is the key to a man. You cannot know a man till you know the woman or women in his life. In London this does not happen. Max Beerbohm says in one of his essays of a building that is being subjected to demolition, 'It was more than a home, it was a home against many homes. It was a club.' In London you are unlikely to know anything of the home life of your fellow members. This is one reason why I did not make a single man friend in London after the war. I will take two examples, Nigel Balchin and Nathaniel Benchley. Nigel Balchin entered the literary world during the war. I met him at the Savile immediately after my return. I liked him instantaneously. He was very much my kind of man. He was only a few years younger than myself. He was a cricketer. We had professional links. He was to write the film script for my story 'Circle of Deception'. I was always delighted when

I found him in the Savile. He came once to a party of mine. But I never knew anything about his personal life. In the later fifties, A. D. Peters mentioned that 'Nigel Balchin's divorce has just gone through.' It meant nothing to me. I had presumed that he was married, but I did not know he was. It was altogether different with Nathaniel Benchley. He has become one of my closer friends. We cannot recall now exactly when or where it was we met. It may have been at one of Elinor Gibbs's parties, but it is more likely to have been at the Coffee House. It was certainly in that autumn of 1946, and it grew quickly into a friendship, because I was constantly meeting him in the company of his delightful wife Marjorie, round the octagonal table at the Coffee House.

That autumn Carl Brandt proposed me for the Century and in the meantime the club gave me a card of guest membership. I was to be elected in 1951, and I use it regularly, but I use it in the same way that in London I use the Athenæum. I go there in the morning to read the papers. I spend a good deal of time in the library. I dine there whenever I have an evening free. There are not many members there – a dozen at the most. Members who have guests usually sit at one of the side tables. Those who are going to dine at the long table gather for cocktails round an octagonal table. A warning bell rings, a final cocktail is ordered, then the second bell rings. The Century Club ordinary is served at seven-thirty. The dining room closes at nine o'clock. The service and the food are excellent, there is good talk. I dined there about once a week. The Century has superb premises. Few other clubs have such a warm and dignified setting. I am most grateful to Carl Brandt for having introduced me to it, but it has never been personal for me in the way that the Coffee House is and in London the Savile was and the Beefsteak has become. I have only lunched at the Athenæum and the Century when I have had a guest with me. This is largely because neither in the Century nor the Athenæum do I know a sufficient number of my fellow members. It is a bore having to find out who is sitting next to you.

CHAPTER 18

Prelude to Divorce

I have now I am afraid reached a point where I am going to lose the reader's sympathy.

My conventional civic duty was clearly to devote my energies to my family, to reforging links with them, to planning for their future, to making amends for the six years' separation. That was my civic duty. Yes, I know, I know. May I refer the reader to the first pages of this book. I had been six years away from my family, but I had also been six years away from my desk. I put the claims of my writing first. Time was running out. I had to make the most of the time still left.

In telling the story of the next four years I will follow the John Marquand pattern, beginning at the end and working backwards, showing how it came about. In October 1949 I landed at New York with an emigrant's visa and in January 1951 in Carson City, Nevada, I presented to the judge my application for a divorce as a resident alien of the United States. It was not the way I had planned things. One thing led to the next thing, the way things do in novels.

I got back from America in mid-December 1946. Edrington was itself again. The books back upon their shelves, the pictures on the walls. We had not got a real cook or any staff. We never were to have a real staff again; a succession of make-do couples each more unsatisfactory, in a different way. To begin with we had the wife of the under-gardener to cook, with a girl from the village 'helping out'. Catering was very difficult. But I sent parcels from New York. We managed well enough. We had one good meal a day, and the cellar was well stocked.

On the twentieth and twenty-first of December the children came back from their respective schools. Andrew and Veronica were thrilled to see the familiar decorations on the tree. My mother came down on the twenty-third. A not unhappy time was starting for her. She was comfortable in her flat, an efficient and loyal woman who had been there in my father's time had returned from war work to look after her. Evelyn had arranged a generous trust fund. She had now seven grandchildren and during the holidays there was usually one or other of them staying with her. 14a was an invaluable feature in the family planning. Andrew and Peter stayed there when they had their cricket classes at Lord's, Bron and Teresa stayed there when they were seeing dentists. My mother would complain that she was a useless drudge, but I do not know how we would have managed without her. The children were devoted to their granny. 'When are we going up to 14a?' they would enquire.

The clock seemed to have been put back seven years on that first Christmas, and after tea the staff came in for their presents and their glass of port; with Thatcher the gardener – what an appropriate name for a head gardener – crumbling a slice of sugared cake with his great scarred fingers that were so adroit in a potting shed, so clumsy with a cup and saucer. Yes, it was all just as it had been in 1939 except that my father was no longer there and Peter was; Peter who was later to fill the role of *copain* in my life, who was to take in a sense my father's place, as confidante and companion.

That spring I worked on and completed a novel that I had started in New York. I had intended it as a novelette for *Cosmopolitan*. One of the editors was enthusiastic, Carl Brandt thought that they would buy it, but the final verdict was against it. The uncertainty of a sale adds immeasurably to the dramatic quality of working for American magazines. There is no such thing as a commissioned piece. Nothing is final until the cheque is signed. I was disappointed when the deal fell through, but that is part of the bargain. There were some projects that did not fall through. I decided to enlarge the novelette into a novel.

In July 1945, when I prepared to resume my trade of authorship, A. D. Peters warned me that I should have to be very careful with my first novel. 'A number of new writers have come up. You'll have to be regraded.' I was on my guard. I was aware of the difficulties of starting a novel right away. I had been in exactly the same position in 1919. It is odd how often in middle life one finds oneself confronted by the same problems that perplexed one's youth. It would be as difficult for me now as it had been then to find a setting for a novel, and for precisely the same reasons. My kind of novelist whose characters are involved in and are dependent on the circumstances that condition them, has to tell his reader when the story is taking place.

The war was still too close for me to attempt a war novel. After the first war it was not till 1928 that authors had wanted to write and the public to read about it. Then, starting with *Journey's End* and *All Quiet on the Western Front*, there had been a spate of war books. The same thing might happen again. In the meantime it would be as impossible for me to open a story with 'unconditional surrender' as it had been in 1919 with the armistice. There was no space to move in, for characters and situations to develop, and it would be as unsatisfactory now to open a novel in 1935 as it had been then to open one in 1910. In both cases the reader would know that war would be breaking out in a few months and into whatever muddle the characters got themselves a ready solution was waiting in the wings. 'I'm going to concentrate on short stories,' I told A. D. Peters. But within a year I had started to feel restless. I wanted to spread myself on a wider canvas, and I soon recognised that I had now in 1946 a solution that I had not had in 1920. I could not then have turned back the clock twenty years because I had not known from personal experience how adult life had been in 1900, but I could now very easily set a story in the 1920s and where could I find a better starting point than 1926? Life was radiant with promise then. War had been outlawed by the League of Nations. The world had learnt its lesson. In England political peace had been assured by the failure of the General Strike. The auguries were bright. Wall Street was as impregnable a fortress as Gibraltar. Hitler had been scarcely heard of, Mussolini was an amiable autocrat who made trains run on time. Individuals could plan their future in the confidence that the proud ship of state was sailing on an even keel.

After the tribulations of the last few years, it would be congenial for me now in 1946–7 to describe the way of life that I had then enjoyed. I recognised, of course, that I could not just sit down and recreate a period. The reader would ask himself 'Why am I being told all this now? What bearing has this story on my life today?' I would have, that is to say, to devise a story that would not acquire its full significance for twenty years in which the characters would ask themselves in 1946 whether they had solved correctly the problems that they had been set in 1926. The result of their cogitations was a novel called *Unclouded Summer*.

As I was writing the last chapter I learnt that Andrew had passed his common entrance and would be going to Sherborne in May.

Unclouded Summer was eventually published in England twenty months later in December 1948. That is how long it took to get a book published then, and I had not expected it to appear for another three months. I was surprised to find on my return from New York a parcel of six complimentary copies. They would make a useful Christmas present, I thought, and ordered a half a dozen extra copies. But I was informed that the book was already out of print. Nobody seemed to be aware that it had come out. Publishers did not need to advertise books that they were certain they would sell. They only announced their lists to show that they were still in business. The book sections of the Sunday papers were reduced. Novels were not so much reviewed as noticed, in bunches of five or six. Such reviews as I got were friendly, but they were casual, like greetings at a crowded cocktail party. 'Hi there, good to see you. You're looking fine. We must get together some time.' Far from being regraded up or down, I had the feeling that nothing at all had happened and that I was in precisely the same position as when I rejoined the army over nine years ago.

1947 was a year of contrasts. It opened in England with a period of intense cold. The government sadly miscalculated its reserves of power. The machinery of livelihood ran down. Electricity was cut off during the day. Lifts did not work. People under the age of seventy were trusted not to turn on electric fires during the daytime. S. N. Behrman wrote a very entertaining piece for the *New Yorker* called 'It's Cold at Lady Windermere's'. Then suddenly the weather mended. 'The worst turned the best.'

It was a summer of fantastic sunshine. On the banks of the Médoc and on the golden slopes south of Dijon grapes ripened to one of the classic vintages. For cricketers, particularly for the supporters of the Middlesex County Cricket Club, it was a memorable summer with Middlesex carrying off the trophy that had so long eluded them, in the main through the fantastic batting performance of the 'terrible twins' Edrich and Compton, both of whom made over three thousand runs. Championships are very often won, particularly north of the Tweed, by dour persistence, by tight bowling and ruthless in-fielding, but Middlesex were champions through the pace at which Edrich and Compton, backed by their lieutenants Brown and Robinson, could run up totals of five hundred in a day, so that the bowlers, Young, Robbins, Sims and Price, had plenty of time to get the others out. Middlesex in 1947 was the most attractive batting side that has ever 'headed the table'.

England revelled in the weather yet the economic problem was as serious in September as it had been in January and the meagre travel allowance was again reduced. 1947

was a summer of self-discovery. The troops were back home
from Europe and the Middle East. War prisoners were back
from Germany, Italy and the Far East. It was a period of
reunions; during the war one had made new friends but
lost touch with old. One wondered to what extent one
would ever get back to the old easy life. What was happening to one's favourite playgrounds – the south of France in
particular? In June, after the children had returned to
school, Joan and I went back to Villefranche. Before we
started I wrote to the Bank of England asking for permission to take out an extra allowance of sterling. The visit
would give me material for stories for the American magazines. I should bring dollars back into the country. It was
a legitimate request. I asked for £200. I was granted £150.
'One's not going to get much co-operation here,' I thought.

At a first glance the south of France was little altered.
Below the Promenade des Anglais there still were concrete
anti-tank obstacles. The pier with its casino at the end had
vanished. The bridges that had carried the railway line
across the valleys had been blown up, and looked like the
ruins of a Roman aqueduct. The race course on the banks
of the Var had been the scene of a bloody battle. The golf
course along the railway had been abandoned. But it was
not the things that were different that one noticed. There was
so much that was the same. At Villefranche the harbour
had been mined. Evacuating Germans had blown out the
front of the Welcome Hotel. But it had been repaired.
Germaine was operating her bar. The fishing nets were still
laid along the cobbles, with the women at work on them.
As I sat on the terrace, sipping my aperitif in the evening,
the same spiritual peace descended on me. 'I'll still be coming here a lot,' I thought.

Eldred Curwen was back with Peggy Bainbridge in the
Villa Marina. They had spent several months in a prison
camp. When the Americans had landed in North Africa,
they had been evacuated into the interior. If they had been
tactful, they could probably have stayed there in obscure

seclusion right through the war. But they had run the risk
of making a trip to Antibes to see what was happening in
their villa. They might have got away with that, but they
made a foolish mistake. They had a pack of noisy and not
very companionable dachshunds, who were always rush-
ing to the gate and barking. The most objectionable and
their favourite was called, appropriately, Hullabaloo. They
brought this dog down with them from the interior. It
behaved, as they should have known it would, obstreper-
ously in the train, scampering up and down the corridor,
barking at every station with Peggy and Eldred admonish-
ing it lovingly in English. This so exasperated a French
fellow passenger – how well I could understand how she
felt – that she reported their presence to the guard, and
they were taken into custody. They were now in good
health and spirits, with Hullabaloo still the only uncordial
element in that cordial household. I spent four days there
after Joan, with her travel allowance exhausted, had returned
to Edrington.

From Antibes I went to the PEN Club conference in
Zurich; I had been a member since 1922, but I had never
attended any of its conferences. I had thought that I would
be bored; too many speeches, too much acrimony between
rival partisans, the endless passing of pious and futile resolutions on the treatment of dissident writers, and the constant
presence of fellow scribes whose company in England I was
at some pains to avoid. But now, when parties were few,
when rationing made entertaining difficult, I thought it
worthwhile finding out what a conference was really like.

To my delighted surprise, I found it was not at all as I had
feared. I had a most enjoyable week. There were admittedly
some boring speeches. But one could always slide away
from them. The conferences invariably took place in an
attractive city, very often in one that was unfamiliar. Excursions were arranged round the city itself and to neighbouring 'beauty spots'. And the best way to see any place is to
hand oneself over for a couple of days to the care of guided

tours. A good deal of entertainment was provided. There was an opening party. There was a final banquet. Members of the local PEN invited visitors to their homes. There was no lack of things to do. And every now and then there would be an interesting and even an inspiring speech. I was not at the Amsterdam conference, but I have been told of the electric effect of Charles Morgan's inaugural speech that opened with the words 'A June night and no War'. But what attracted me most about these conferences was the finding of myself unexpectedly without premeditation having a long confidential talk with a fellow writer whom I had long respected but never really got to know.

Something like this will happen. It is half-past eleven in the morning. There is a series of short addresses; you have heard two and you feel that is enough. There is a brief pause between two speeches. You stand up. Across the room you notice that a writer you half know or have lost touch with is also on his feet. You catch his eye, you exchange a signal, you make for the door, and there across from the conference hall is an outdoor café with a shaded terrace. In a way you feel like two conspirators who have dodged a duty. You feel very much in tune, as you sit there sipping your aperitif. It may well be the beginning of a friendship, or it may be an isolated and unrepeated episode. Your subsequent lives may follow divergent paths, but it is one of those facets of the universal fellowship of writers that adds over the years a dimension to oneself.

Of Zurich I cherish particularly the memory of a long talk after an evening *conversazione* in the garden of the Bar du Lac with Eric Linklater. He was an exact member of my own generation with service in France at the end of the First World War. I had met him casually over the years. We had lunched together a couple of times, but we had never had a real talk together, and we were never to have another, but after that evening at Zurich I knew we spoke with the same idiom. What a wicked wit he had, what a twinkle in his eye, what a good writer. I remember also gratefully

dining alone with a friend from early days, another exact
contemporary, Louis Golding. What a number of gaps we
filled in our knowledge of one another. We had known so
many of the same people at different times in different
places. We had often discussed each other with that fine
troubadour G. B. Stern in her villa in Diano Marina.

I remember, too, a very different occasion. We had to
catch an early 8.25 train to a conference at Basle. We had had
a late party the night before. We were considerably under
par. We were consigned to a third-class carriage, but among
the seven or so of us travelling in the same compartment
were Elmer Rice and his enchanting comedienne wife Betty
Field. The unsuitability of the hour acted as a challenge to
them. They kept us laughing all the way to Basle.

This was my first conference. But I vowed that it was not
going to be my last on the morning that the conference
broke up. I kept that promise to myself. I have attended a
dozen conferences, going as far afield as Abijan, Rio de
Janeiro, Tokyo, making new friends and turning old ac-
quaintanceships into a friendship. What good times I have
had with Henry Williamson, and I might never have met
Nina Bawden if we had not both flown over the Sahara to
the Ivory Coast. She is now one of the four or five people
that I make a point of not missing when I am in London.

That summer Ye Sette of Odde Volumes resumed its meetings. I was, and so were several of the other members,
doubtful if we should ever begin again. It had been easy to
restart the Saintsbury Club, which held only two meetings
a year, and whose cellar was intact. The membership was
limited to fifty, and there was keen competition to fill each
vacancy. But the Odde Volumes held eight meetings a year.
It demanded a membership of forty-two. It was expensive;
and there was a suspicion that its atmosphere of what Evelyn
had called 'ceremonious buffoonery' would be out of place
in an austere post-war world. We decided to discuss it over
lunch. How many would turn up to such a luncheon? It

was eight years since our last dinner; what an eight years too. How many survivors were there? In the end, considerably to the surprise of Vyvyan Holland, who was the treasurer, a dozen members appeared, and it was resolved without hesitation to make a beginning in October and I was invited to be his Oddship.

The first dinner was booked for the fourth Tuesday in October 1947 and it justified all Vyvyan's forebodings. It was held in the River Room at the Savoy. It was a foggy night and the mists from the river dimmed the lights which were still, owing to the restrictions of the spring, under-powered. Places were laid for only twenty-two. That was too small an attendance for a room that required an air of plenitude. Three of those who had promised to attend did not turn up and the empty chairs added to the gloom of the mist-filled room. I had taken a good deal of trouble over the preparation of my inaugural address and I subsequently had it printed as a booklet. How I wished I could have delivered it in October 1938. The small gathering did its best to be convivial. After all parties were scarce in that the third autumn of the peace, and champagne had not lost its power. But the auguries were not good. I made a vow, 'the Odde Volumes with its long history is not going to go out like this, under my aegis'. We had planned to hold only four meetings during the year. The next dinner would have to be a real occasion. We would sit down forty, even if it meant my bringing twenty guests myself. And if new members were not enrolled as a result of it, then we would close the Club. At any rate we would go out in style.

I kept my promise to myself. We sat down forty-five at the next dinner, twenty of them at my invitation, and there seemed enough general enthusiasm to justify another year's existence, with that distinguished Egyptologist Stephen Glanville taking the chair. Today, as I said earlier, the Odde Volumes is one of London's more prominent dining clubs, celebrating its centenary.

* * *

That spring the publishing house of Evans started a series of travel books, called *Windows of the World*. They were to be short, 50,000 words, illustrated, elegant. They asked me if I would contribute a book on the South Seas. I suggested that I should instead write a book on the West Indies. I had not published in book form any of the material I had collected on my 1938 tour to the Windward Islands. I did not think I should have difficulty in assembling 50,000 words, by adding to the historical section a couple of short stories. 50,000 words was too short a book for the US market, but I was planning to go to New York in January. I could fly down from there to the West Indies, and spend five weeks collecting new material so that I could eventually deliver a 70,000-word book to Farrar Straus. This project of Evans was to be for me the start of a new concentration on the West Indies.

I began my trip with a visit to Trinidad, to stay with my old friends the Louis Whartons. Trinidad was a good starting point and the Whartons could put me in the picture as to what had happened during the war and what was likely to happen in the immediate future. From Trinidad I would go north to Grenada, thence to St Lucia and Antigua.

I went at a good time. During the war very little had happened in the Caribbean. The islands had been cut off from the main current of events, but submarines were active. One of the Lady boats was sunk in the harbour of St Lucia. It was difficult and dangerous to get from one island to another. By the Roosevelt–Churchill pact the USA was ceded bases in Trinidad and Antigua in return for fifty destroyers, but the existence of those bases, with the consequent presence of American troops, did not greatly affect the life of the islands. The Americans kept very much to themselves, largely because they kept different hours; eating early in the evenings. The islanders led isolated, self-sufficient lives. Now all that was changing. The bigger islands were now linked by aircraft. Tourism had reappeared. Americans could get there for quick visits. They wanted information about the islands. There was a demand for travel articles. I felt the same urge that I had in the thirties to present and interpret the life of these romantic islands. And now through the Pan American network it would be easy to fly down there frequently. Only a night's flight from New York. I could come down every year.

Before I left New York, Roland Young had asked me whether I would like to write a life of Thomas Lipton. 'Why?' I asked him.

'Doubleday wants an Englishman who knows America to do it. Does the idea appeal to you?'

'Of course,' I said. It has always been my practice to agree to any project that is put up to me, hear what is suggested, then think it out at leisure. At a first glance it seemed a promising idea, but I did not take it very seriously. I returned from the West Indies, however, to find that it was a concrete proposition. Lipton's Tea was launching a new publicity campaign. They thought this would be helped by a biography sufficiently ambitious to be reviewed in the news section of the press. It would have to be written by a reasonably well-established Englishman. Doubleday had been asked to find such a writer. There were in point of fact not so many competitors for the job. English writers had not yet fallen back into the habit of dividing their year between London and New York. The campaign was being handled by Benjamin Sonnenberg. I had met him in 1930 when my travel book *Hot Countries* was a Literary Guild choice. Ben had handled the publicity for the Chatham Hotel and he had arranged for me to be the Chatham's guest for the first five days of my visit. We had not seen a great deal of one another, but we had liked each other. 'Waugh's a man I can work with,' he told Doubleday.

It was a great piece of good luck for me. Sonnenberg is one of the more fantastic characters in a city that abounds in fantastic characters. He started from scratch as a Polish immigrant. In the early fifties Geoffrey Hellman wrote a profile of him in the *New Yorker*. In a recent 'Talk of the

'Town' paragraph, he was referred to as 'the squire of Gramercy Park'. He was already established in 1948 in a large corner house there that is elaborately furnished with pictures, brass ware, books; there are four main living rooms, a dining room with red tapestried walls, a comfortable study, a reception room on the stairs where guests meet for cocktails before dinner; and a very large room at the top of the house where he holds big parties and shows films after dinner. Those are 'lived-in' rooms, but in addition to them there is a succession of bedrooms that have the air of state apartments, and that are thrown open for inspection on big occasions.

The house is a perfect background for Ben Sonnenberg. He was born at the turn of the century. He is short, with a straggling moustache. He wears eccentric but quiet clothes, dark suits – high-buttoned, single-breasted, with wide dark ties. The shirt cuffs are tight, project from under the sleeves and carry heavy links. He wears a rounded bowler hat with a narrow brim. There is nothing flash about his appearance. He is an amusing talker, but he never talks about himself. He concentrates upon his guests, or his hosts when he is a guest. He is always in the centre of the stage. But as the showman not as the actor.

That summer he was motoring from London to Southampton to catch the *Queen Elizabeth*. I asked him to pause for lunch at Edrington. I wondered what the children would make of him. They had never seen anything like him before. He took his place on Joan's right hand and looked round the table. 'Well,' he said to her, 'you've a fine quiverful here. It must be a problem to keep the balance between the three of them; there's this handsome son. You must feel very proud of him. He'll carry on the name and the traditions. Then there's your daughter. It must be exciting for a very attractive woman to see a daughter coming along to take her place in the world, repeating her own experiences, and then there's this little fellow over there; they always say that the youngest is the favourite, the one you feel the most

protective for. You've certainly a job with their rival claims;
it's a miracle how you've made such a contented family. As
I can see you have.'

It reads like a caricature of the tactless foreigner; you
could imagine the children shrivelling with embarrassment,
but it went down like a dinner. 'When's that man coming
again?' they would ask. He had an unfailing sense of audience. I never heard him say the wrong thing or saw him
embarrass anyone.

The Lipton book was a profitable deal for me. It kept me
for two years, and I was on Ben's expense account. There
were many perquisites, seats for *South Pacific* for example.
Once my arrival in New York was welcomed by a supreme
bottle of Cognac. 'Ben,' I said, 'that was really a fine bottle.'

'I'd always give you the best,' he said, 'even if I had to pay
for it myself.'

In October he gave a large evening party for me at his
house. 'As a preliminary launching,' he explained. I do not
know how many guests there were. The great feature of his
parties at that time was hot roast beef sandwiches. Baron
after baron was wheeled up to a white-coated chef who
carved slice after slice of glistening medium-rare beef.

When the book was published in January 1950 he gave,
or rather saw that Lipton's gave, a second party; this time
in the New York Yacht Club. It was so sumptuous – the
hall hung with Dutch lilac and the tables piled with caviar
and goblets sparkling with champagne – that Doubleday's
were embarrassed. The invitations had gone out in their
name. 'Our other authors will complain, that we don't do a
quarter as much for them,' they told me.

There was a trip too to the Far East. 'Don't you think,'
I said to Ben, 'that I ought to go out to Ceylon and Calcutta
and see his tea gardens?'

'Of course, of course we'll get that fixed.'

When I came over for publication, my bill at the Algonquin went straight to Lipton's. And the most warming

feature of it all was that I did not cease to be a protégé of Ben, when the book was launched; no hard black line was drawn across the ledger. If you are once a friend of Ben's, you are a friend for life. November 1975 found me at his table for Thanksgiving.

There is a snag to everything, however, and the drama of those months with Ben led directly to my decision to become a resident alien of the USA. Not on grounds of income tax. My income was not large enough for me to worry unduly about that. My problem was the currency regulations. I was spending in New York money that I earned there, leaving the balance behind in the Brandt office. And this I came to suspect was against the law. British and American citizens did not pay double tax and when I got back to England, I declared my US earnings and paid British taxes on them, but I wondered if this was good enough. Had I the right to spend in the US the money that I had earned there, and I had the right to leave in the US the balance of the money that I had earned so that I should be able to finance my next trip to the USA? I needed access to dollars.

In 1926 when I was in Penang I had received an invitation to go up to Siam and spend a couple of months in the teak forests. That trip had been of the greatest value to me as a writer. I had got the material for two of my best short stories. If such an invitation were to reach me now, I should not be able to accept it unless I had dollars on the spot. I could not operate unless I had a banking account in New York. And I could not open one without the permission of the Bank of England.

I wrote through my own bank to the Bank of England asking for permission to open one. The permission was denied me. 'Major Waugh,' my bank was informed, 'must bring back and sell to the Bank of England any dollars that he may earn in the US and he can then ask the Bank of England's permission to export them.' The word 'must' was underlined in red ink. Clearly, I could not operate on this basis. In that problematic situation of needing dollars in Penang to go north to Siam to pass from a sterling into a dollar area, I could not wait for a reply from England. Nor could I be certain that the Bank would give me the permission. When I had asked for £200 to spend in the south of France I had been given only £150. I could not work under that handicap. The Bank of England's reply was in my opinion typical of that pettifogging meticulous mentality that in Baghdad had exasperated me in the person of my G.2 Ernest I——. In Baghdad I had no remedy. I was under military authority, but I was not going to have a junior bank clerk underlining his instructions in red ink. Major Waugh *must*, indeed. I was no longer Major Waugh in that connection. 'OK,' I thought, 'if that's how they react, I'll work it the other way round. I'll emigrate to New York, pay income tax to the US on my English earnings, and spend my dollars the way I want.'

I made a snap decision. During the spring and summer of 1949 I followed the procedure that was required to emigrate to the US. The procedure was complicated. I had had the idea that an expatriate could spend six months less a day in England. I had been mistaken in thinking that. I was limited to ninety-one days. I could not maintain a residence in England, or have a residence maintained for me. This meant that I should have to make over to Joan all my English possessions so that when I came to Edrington it would be as a guest. My expenditure in England would be closely watched. I could pay only into my account monies that came to me from my agent. I could only pay out money to approved recipients: tailors, hotels, wine merchants, typists. I could not make out a cheque to a friend.

I could see the point of these regulations. Without it, I could have paid dollars to a friend in the south of France and been repaid in pounds in England. This was one of the chief leakages of sterling. I was warned that my goings and comings to England would be scrutinised, that I must not follow a fixed pattern of arrivals and departures; each individual case would be judged on its own merits.

I had many moments of misgiving during that long hot summer when Middlesex shared the championship with Yorkshire. 'What was I doing?' I asked myself as I sat out in a deck-chair in the garden at Edrington. Was I disinheriting myself? Was I surrendering my heritage? Was this not an act of incredible folly? Writing was the least certain of employments. I should no longer have Joan's Australian dividends as a bulwark if things went wrong. I had many moments of self-doubt. But I am an obstinate person. As in the case of Wyndham Lewis I do not abandon a course of action which I have once accepted. The important thing was that I should give myself the best opportunity to write the best work of which I was capable. I should not be able to do that if I was going to be the lackey of the Bank of England, with the word 'must' underlined in red.

In November 1950 I went to Nevada to present my petition for a divorce on the grounds of incompatibility. I could write 15,000 words cataloguing the complicated series of causes that sent me there. But I do not think they would serve any purpose. I had no wish to marry again. I did not believe I should ever want to marry again. I was a born bachelor. I needed to be alone to write. I could never be a satisfactory husband. In the last analysis I went to Reno because I wanted to clear my decks, to stand on my own feet as an emigrant alien of the United States though still a loyal subject of the British crown.

My divorce was attended by no publicity. I had learnt in Baghdad how one kept track of the movements of suspect characters. One checked lines of communication. One spread a net with the meshes as tightly drawn as possible. Sooner or later the suspect would strike a strand. 'Watch lines of communication.' That was what I had to do.

No one in New York knew that I was going to Reno. Lucia, whom I had visited in 1938 in Pasadena, remarried now, had made a home in Albuquerque. I flew out to see her. She was shortly going to Pasadena with her children. I motored with her to Las Vegas. Next morning she went on to Pasadena, I caught a bus to Reno. From the Reno bus station I took a taxi to a hotel. I checked in for a night. No notice was taken of me. Six-week residents do not make one-night stands.

Next morning I called on my lawyer who in the afternoon motored me out to a motel in Carson City. I told the Brandt office that I was staying in Pasadena, whither all my mail was sent, and whence it was forwarded to Carson City. This involved a four-day delay. But nothing urgent transpired during the next two months. My friends in New York thought I was in California.

A year earlier Walter Winchell had reported in his column that 'the Alec Waughs have atomiced'. That was the only press reference, an indirect one to my divorce. A year later the British tax authorities raised some doubts as to whether I really was divorced. I presented Walter Winchell's column as evidence. The evidence was accepted. It amused me that Walter Winchell should be accepted as a witness in a British court.

A few years ago Eliza Parkinson was to say to me, 'You really never were divorced, you know: you were married to Joan all the time.' And indeed I was. It is unusual for a married man to spend only three months a year at home. But any marriage that survives thirty years adapts itself to its own pattern. Joan and I were very good friends. We were partners in the upbringing of our children. Most summers we went away together for a two-weeks holiday. We never quarrelled. Our children never had to witness family disputes. They did not have to take sides. When Joan died in 1969, I missed her very much.

CHAPTER 19

I Become a Wine Writer

One of the dividends that *The Lipton Story* paid me was the commission from the House of Gilbey to write the history of their firm. Anthony Grinling, one of the partners, was an old friend of Joan's and a good one of mine. He was a frequent week-end visitor at Edrington. One of his visits coincided with the presence there of the proofs of *The Lipton Story*.

'Can I look at them?' he asked.

'Of course.'

He took them up to bed. Next morning he said, 'I've an idea; Gilbey's are celebrating their centenary in a few years' time. Why don't you write our story?'

I leapt at the idea. The result of it a few years later was a book called *Merchants of Wine*. It was not a very ambitious project. There was not a great deal of material available. The book was reviewed mainly in the trade papers. It was not news in the way that *The Lipton Story* had been. It did not sell many copies. Its circulation was in the form of salesmen's complimentary copies. But it was a pleasant assignment. I was paid in wine, a form of remuneration on which it was difficult to assess tax. I started off cellars for my two sons with three dozen bottles apiece of Croft's 1945 vintage port. Croft is a subsidiary of Gilbey. I also made a substantial contribution to the supply of champagne at my daughter's coming-out dance in 1952 – a very hot night at which the guests were very thirsty.

The research on the book was pleasant, and for four years I was on Gilbey's expense account. I went on all the expeditions that Gilbey's arranged for the press. In 1952 I went to Portugal for the *vendange*. We were offered a sumptuous dinner at the factory house in Oporto. A white Graves prepared the way for a Pontet-Canet 1929, cheese straws cleaned our palates for a tawny port. At that point, so the menu informed us, we were to be graced with two vintage ports, a 1917 and a 1927. The chairman rose to his feet. The bouquet of vintage port could not, he told us, be properly appreciated in an atmosphere that was tainted with the fumes of food; would we move into the adjoining room, bringing our napkins with us.

There a second table awaited us, set with forty places. It was a lovely sight, a gleaming stretch of mahogany under a cluster of chandeliers, bowls of red roses, high piled fruit, a Doulton dessert service, cut-glass decanters, a cherry-coloured wine to match the china; a delight to the eye, an even greater delight to the sense of smell. It is always difficult if not impossible to describe a physical sensation; it is enough to say that coming into that cool fresh room, its air scented with fruit and flowers, I had the sense of being transported to another planet; a moment later I was thinking 'I'm living in another century.'

Next day our party was taken to the Quinta da Roeda, Croft's estate, a five-hour journey along the steep hills that flank the Douro, past a succession of tiny hamlets as charming as they are lovely, with smoke curling through the tiled roofs of the cottages, scenting the air with the brushwood that burns under many an old iron pot. At the Quinta da Roeda I watched the grapes being trodden by the harvesters.

Gilbey's own a château on the Gironde, Château Loudenne. I accompanied thither a press party of some twenty members to celebrate the launching of a 'white gravotte' that was put on the market in the early fifties at a price of six shillings and sixpence a bottle. Château Loudenne is typical of the countryside. It is not impressive and historic like one of the châteaux of the Loire. Chateau does not mean castle in the English sense. Loudenne is a comfortable country house in which a family of gentlefolk could live and supervise their property. It has charm, dignity and intimacy. It is long and low, of faded rose-coloured stone, slate-roofed with a rounded tower at each end. From its long stone-flagged terrace that is in shade after the early morning, you look across a quarter of a mile of lawns and vineyards to the broad brown river and the boats, large and small, that ply between Bordeaux and the Atlantic. The wine it produces is classified as *bourgeois*, which does not mean that it is poor but that it cannot stand comparison with the *grands crus* of Panillac Margeux; André Simon classed its wines with those of Listrac, as being distinctly superior to its neighbours because of the greater care that has been given to its production.

In addition to joining their press excursions, I also had the good luck to be included in the party that Gilbey's gave for the Coronation in 1953. Gilbey's also arranged for me to visit the other big-wine-producing areas. I went to the Côte d'Or, which was a particular treat for me, and I was invited by Louis Latour to visit the annual sale of wines at the Hospices de Beaune. For five hundred years the upkeep of these almshouses has been maintained by the sale of the wines that have been bequeathed to it. These vineyards are scattered over the whole stretch of the Côte d'Or from Aloxe to Mersault and the wines are sold from the names of twenty-nine different *crus*. The occasion is a mixture of charity and publicity. The prices offered at the sale by experts are taken as a guide to the quality of a certain year. It is a big week-end for Beaune. The tapestry-decked cloisters are bright with chrysanthemums. Each taster brings his own silver '*tastevin*'. It was impressive to see the long rows of casks, each with its famous name above it. By each cask stood a man, by one or two a woman, who drew the wine out of the cask with a glass funnel and released it into the silver goblet. I watched the experts roll the wine round their cup, judging its colour and texture, raising it to their lips, rinsing their mouths, then spitting it on the floor.

The week-end is known as the *Trois glorieuses*. On the Saturday night, under the auspices of the Confrérie des Chevaliers de Tastevin, there is the '*diner aux Chandelles*' in the cellars of the Beaune fortifications, and on the Monday there is the '*Paulée de Mersault*'. At the diner *aux Chandelles*', I sat opposite Christine Latour, Louis Latour's niece. On her recommendation I was admitted into the Confrérie des Chevaliers that December and in the following June I went to Dijon to be installed. I was to attend four banquets at the Clos de Vougeat during the next few years.

I also under Gilbey's auspices went to Epernay, and stayed at Möet and Chandon's Château Saran, the first of many visits, and I have familiarised myself with the technique and customs of the champagne trade. I spent three days as the guest of the Gonzales at Jerez de la Frontera and learnt about sherry. There are close family links between the Gilbeys and the Gonzales. I spent a week on the island of Madeira. I spent three days in Cognac as the guest of Maurice Hennessy. I acquired, that is to say, a general if superficial familiarity with the domains of the wine trade. The only area I did not visit was that of the Rhine and the Moselle. The appropriate opportunity did not arrive. I did not make up this deficiency until fifteen years later.

The writing of the Gilbey book brought me a great deal of fun. But it did much more than that. It added a new armoury to my equipment as a writer. *Merchants of Wine* concentrated on the Gilbey family and its operations. It had no general interest, particularly in America. But one of the editors of an American publishing house, William Sloane, on reading it had the idea that I should write a full-length book on wine, giving the history of wine and a full description of the various kinds of wine and spirits. The idea had not occurred to me, but I saw the possibilities of it immediately. The result of it was my book *In Praise of Wine and other noble spirits*. It is one of my very favourite books, and on both sides of the Atlantic had a good press and sold reasonably well, particularly in the US where it was graded as a kind of textbook. Since the end of the war America had become increasingly a wine-drinking country, particularly when the qualities of Californian wine were recognised. I began to receive and to invite commissions to write articles on wine. When Time-Life issued their series *Foods of the World* I was asked to contribute their book on *Wines and Spirits*. The series as a whole was a great success. It contained as one would expect from Time-Life a number of first-class photographs; its editors contributed a number of appendices and recipes, with instructions on the care and handling of wines. Sam Aaron, one of the directors of the wine merchants Lehman, supervised this side of the production. My book was one of the more successful books in the series, and it is still in active demand, Time-Life having kept it up to date. I was now classed as a writer about wine; a very useful addition to my professional equipment.

CHAPTER 20

A Rootless Person

My decision to become a resident alien of the United States involved me in a number of problems that I had not anticipated. I was now for nine months of the year a rootless person without a home or base, living in hotels. It was a role that I had invited, but it was expensive, and complicated. I considered the idea of taking a flat in the south of France but I did not feel ready to undertake the responsibility of a new establishment. That would be another tie, and I wanted to be without ties; it was easier to leave the suitcases in the Algonquin, the Hôtel Escurial in Nice, later at the Hôtel Velasquez in Tangier with my files and the nucleus of my wardrobe still in Edrington.

This rootless existence gave me complete freedom to travel. I went to the Caribbean every spring, deepening and widening my knowledge of it. I took a trip to the Seychelles, then one of the most out-of-the-way of the civilised sections of the globe; you had to go there by ship either from Mombasa or Bombay; there was only one boat plying between India and West Africa, and only one of its sailings stopped there. You could not stay for less than six weeks; it was more remote than Tahiti, which in some way it resembled. I went there because I had been told that the Seychelloises were, after the Tahitians, the most attractive and accessible women in the world. I had been correctly informed. The Seychelles also resembled 'the West Indies', and I was to make use in *Island in the Sun* of some of the material that I acquired there. They had been French originally. They were taken over by the British during the Napoleonic Wars, they were largely French-speaking still; they were predominantly Roman Catholic. They had no original inhabitants; they were populated by imported African immigrants who had been accorded grants of land, and various adventurers.

The Seychelles are now associated with the curious double coconut that grows in a valley on the island of Praslin and nowhere else and which when stripped resembles the intimate section of a woman. When these coconuts were washed up on the west coast of India, the Indians, who did not know whence they came, thought from their appearance that they must have aphrodisiacal properties and compounded their soft inner flesh with ingredients of their own. Perhaps because of those ingredients the brew was efficacious. They were called *coco de mer*. I retain one in Tangier as a souvenir.

In the middle of the nineteenth century General Gordon was sent to the Seychelles on a military mission to see how the islands could be worked into the general pattern of colonial defence. The General was a very religious man and he convinced himself that the valley in Praslin was the garden of Eden, and that the *coco de mer* was produced by the original tree of good and evil. He wrote a lengthy treatise to prove his case.

I financed my trip on the proceeds of *The Lipton Story*, but those proceeds were soon exhausted, and I began to wonder how I would be able to finance my new way of life. I had not realised how expensive it would prove, and it was just when I was wondering this that I struck a lean patch. An ambitious novel about London life, *Guy Renton*, though it did well in England where paper was now available, 'flopped' in America. Farrar-Straus indeed suggested that I should show it to another publisher who might have more confidence in it. I would have liked to accept their suggestion; there is no point in being on the list of a publisher who does not believe in one, but I had a contract for this novel and I could not afford to relinquish the advance – $2,500 – a reasonable sum in those days. Three years later Farrar-Straus were as relieved as I was that I had been unaccommodating.

In the meantime, however, my stock stood low on the New York literary bourse, for as an additional source of disquiet, my short stories had ceased to sell. The writing of magazine short stories is a knack. For fifteen years short stories at a thousand dollars a time, five or six a year, had been my main source of support. But I suddenly unaccountably lost the knack. I was never to recover it. 'Where do I go from here?' I asked myself. I could not picture myself abandoning my immigrant status in the USA and returning to Edrington with 'my tail between my legs'. I could not subject myself to that humiliation nor, if I did, should I have been a very satisfactory person about the house, either as a husband or a father. I should no longer be able to take a pride in myself; and when a man cannot do that he is better somewhere else. I began to wonder whether I should not be forced to have recourse to the packet of barbiturates that I had hoarded as an insurance policy, providing myself on each trip abroad with a prescription for a dozen luminal tablets. I could take them on some remote West Indian island, where local police demanded a speedy burial and there could be no post mortem, and consequently no scandal. Fate, however, was generous, and in February 1954, the very last short story I ever wrote, 'Circle of Deception', was bought by Twentieth Century-Fox. I have been very lucky, professionally, the right thing happening at the right time, even in this final case at the eleventh hour. 'Circle of Deception' took care of my finances for thirty months and by the time the funds from it were exhausted, the proceeds from *Island in the Sun* had started to roll in.

The next sixteen years were the best years of my life. Cyril Connolly told an interviewer that his idea of happiness was 'to be at table at a dinner party of six people, to be writing a tolerably good book, and to be travelling south with someone whom one's conscience permitted one to love', and that is pretty well how it was for me during those sixteen years.

For nine months of the year I was an unattached male,

free to move where I liked when I liked, with a comfortably dimensioned income, an essential requisite for the middle-aged man who has not abandoned the claims of gallantry.

When I was in London and New York I led a busy social life, I was guest or host at a series of gourmet lunches and dinners; and I produced a succession of solid books, four novels, three of them 200,000 words in length, two auto-biographies, two books on wine, a history of the West Indies, and a biography of Bangkok. In the chapter 'Nearing Sixty' in *My Brother Evelyn and Other Portraits*, I described the pattern that I followed during those years. I was alone when I did my writing. I travelled a great deal. I went to the West Indies. I once went to Hong Kong. I once went round the world. I worked in ships and in hotels in the places that I visited. I wrote half a novel during my second and ten weeks' long visit to Bangkok. But most of my writing I did in the Hôtel Escurial at Nice, and at the Macdowell colony at Peterboro, New Hampshire.

I paid seven visits of two months each to the Macdowell colony. My debt to it is very great. I have described it in *My Brother Evelyn*. The men live in two separate guest houses; the women have a larger house to themselves. There is a central hall where the colonists meet for breakfast and for dinner. Each colonist has a studio in the woods to which he goes after breakfast. He has complete privacy. No one may visit him without his invitation. His lunch is brought to him in a basket and left outside his door. The routine of day-to-day eventlessness allows one's ideas to put down roots. More than once I have found that I had never guessed how much there was in an idea of mine until I took it to Macdowell.

It was founded in 1906. Edward Macdowell, the composer, had a farmhouse there and built a chalet in the woods where he could work. He found the freedom from pressure there so satisfactory that he built a second studio for Edward Arlington Robinson. When he died, his widow in tribute to his memory enlarged the accommodation, building new studios, raising funds. When I went there first it was only open in the summer; now the studios have been heated and it is open in the winter. The roll-call of past and present colonists shows how valuable it has been to writers, painters and composers. In early days Willa Cather, Thornton Wilder, Stephen Vincent Benet and Aaron Copland went there. In recent years there have been John Brooks, James Baldwin, James Ramsay Ullman, Virginia Sorensen, Nancy Hale, Leonard Bernstein, Milton Avery, Ned Rorem, St Clair McKelway, Mæve Brennan, David Del Tredici, Marya Mannes and Alfred Kazin. I went there for the last time in 1975 and I found the atmosphere unchanged.

In Nice I stayed first in the Hôtel Escurial, later in the Hôtel Windsor, two small bed and breakfast hotels, between the Avenue Victor Hugo and the Promenade des Anglais. I went there in the late autumn and early spring before the rush of summer charabancs had started; I lived very quietly, waking early, going out to breakfast at the Brasserie de Lyons, reading the *Nice-Matin* over my roll and coffee, writing through the morning, going out for a walk along the promenade, buying my lunch at a delicatessen, lunching in my bedroom with a bottle of red wine at my elbow, drinking two-thirds of it, slowly, reflectively, thinking out my story, letting my characters talk to one another. I wrote 2,000 words a day, exactly, stopping as often as not in the middle of a sentence. If I had not finished my daily quota by lunchtime I would write the remaining three or four hundred words in the early afternoon, before taking a siesta. When I woke, the London papers would be on the bookstalls. I would buy *The Times*, take another stroll along the Promenade des Anglais, then sit in the Café Monnot, where there was an orchestra, and read my paper over a cup of chocolate.

By then the Avenue de la Victoire would be crowded with pedestrians, and bicyclists going home from work. The temptation was great to sit in the Brasserie de Lyons with a glass of beer and watch the world pass by. But I knew that if I did, I should order a second beer, perhaps a third. Then it would be half-past seven and the temptation to go to one of Nice's excellent small restaurants would be irresistible. I should drink a half-bottle of wine with it. I should probably follow that half-bottle with a liqueur, which was my normal ration for myself when I was on holiday, but if I followed that usual practice I should not wake quite fresh next morning. It would take me forty minutes to get adjusted to the day. I resisted the temptation. Instead I went to a cinema. When I came out, the Avenue was relatively quiet. There would be no danger now in sitting in the Brasserie de Lyons, drinking a single beer, watching a diminishing world go by. I was back at the Escurial by nine o'clock to finish the bottle of wine and whatever was left over from my lunch. By ten I would be asleep.

I led a very quiet life socially. Eldred Curwen died in 1955. An Australian painter, Sam Atyeo, had a villa in Vence and on Sunday we would watch Nice play football, lunching first at the Chinese restaurant on the Avenue Georges Clemenceau. Cecile, my friend from Villefranche who had had a bar in the Rue de Poilu, was living in Cimie and once or twice I would take a trolley up the hill for an hour or so's chat with her, walking back in the early evening. Somerset Maugham was usually in residence at the Villa Mauresque. We would exchange lunches with one another. He and Alan Searle coming into Nice, I going out to his villa. It was always just the three of us. I got to know him well and I became very fond of him. I never found him difficult; on the contrary I found myself tempted to be confidential. Prudently, I think, I resisted the temptation. It is best to know all except a very few of one's friends, superficially. Maugham added greatly to the enjoyment of my stays in Nice.

CHAPTER 21

Virginia Sorensen

A chapter in *My Brother Evelyn* tells how I got the idea for *Island in the Sun* in March 1953, when I was returning to England by the *Ile de France*.

It was the first time that the Caribbean had given me more than an idea for a slight sketch or two and I mentioned this to Maugham.

'That's curious,' he said. 'Kipling told me that the West Indies were full of stories, but that they were my stories not his. I went there but got nothing.'

He was to use the penal settlement on Devil's Island in 'A Christmas Holiday' and in two full-length short stories, but these are not West Indian stories.

Perhaps the history of the Islands is so long, so crowded and complicated that it needs treatment on a broad canvas. At any rate it was on a broad canvas that I visualised *Island in the Sun* – 200,000 words. I went down to Nice to work on the first chapters.

In *My Brother Evelyn* I have described my year and a half of working on it, at Nice through 1953, and after another visit to the West Indies, to the Macdowell colony in the following summer, but I did not tell of my meeting there with Virginia Sorensen.

I went to the Colony in the middle of May 1954. Work on my novel proceeded smoothly. I would have it finished by the end of my second month. On July the first, a new group of colonists arrived. That evening as I was walking to Colony Hall, a car went by, driven by the manager, George Kendall. Beside him was sitting what looked like a youngish woman. I could not see her face, only the back of her neck. It sent a shiver along my nerves.

That evening I went to the library. I was standing by one of the shelves, when she came in, and paused beside me. I felt an imperious impulse to put my arms about her; so imperious an impulse that I put my arms behind my back and clasped my left wrist in my right hand.

The colony provides the perfect setting for a love affair. There is seclusion, the privacy and comfort of a studio, there is an inevitable affinity between fellow artists. They have the same problems professionally, also probably in their personal lives. Otherwise they would not be there. At that time studios were out of bounds after dinner. That gave evening visits the lure of the forbidden; you had to screen your candles and the firelight. This was my sixth monthly term there, and my five previous visits had been strictly celibate. I had come up here to work. The others, too, had come to work; I was not going to disturb them.

Virginia and I talked together for a minute or two. Her face wore a radiant expression. She was so happy to be here, to have these two months to concentrate upon her writing. From what private problems she was escaping I did not know, as yet. But as she walked back to Colony Hall, she seemed to be floating down the path. 'Steady,' I warned myself. 'Steady. These two months are all important for her. A chance such as she has never had to produce the best work of which she is capable. You must not spoil it for her. Do you hear, you mustn't.'

I submitted to that virtuous resolve for sixteen days.

Virginia Sorensen was then forty-two years old. She was of medium height, with a trim figure. Her hair was dark and came down into a point above her forehead. She had been born in Utah, and raised there as a Mormon; though her mother was not one, and her father was a Jack Mormon. He never rose above the rank of 'Deacon' and he smoked a pipe. They were a family of six. They drank coffee with their meals. But Virginia herself went regularly to church. Her best friend was the daughter of a bishop. She married at the age of twenty-one a college professor, tall, handsome, with a fine singing voice. He was four years older than herself. They were married in the temple. His mother was a strict Mormon, and was horrified when she saw on the washing line her daughter-in-law's short underclothes.

She inflicted her presence on the young couple, living in their house, and is largely to blame for everything that subsequently went wrong between them. At the start it was a happy marriage. There were two children, a daughter Beth born in 1934, and a son Frederick born in 1936. They had congenial holidays, without the grandmother, in a cabin in the mountains, playing a guitar and singing round the fire. But I do not want to tell the story of her marriage; that is her story which maybe she will herself tell some day. I think the main trouble, apart from the mother-in-law, was that her husband wanted to write and could not, though he wrote some quite graceful verses. He was exasperated by the fact that his wife wrote novels that were published and praised.

Her first novel was a Mormon saga *A Little Lower than the Angels*. She finished it in 1941. She wrote to Farrar, Rinehart and to Knopf asking them if they would like to see it. Knopf replied first, so she sent him the manuscript.

The betting is, I suppose, a million to one against a young woman, who had not only never lived in literary circles but had been brought up in such an exceptional and limiting atmosphere as that of Utah. But this was the millionth chance. Knopf was enthusiastic, accepted it and put his personal imprimatur on the jacket. It was very well reviewed, and sold as well as could be expected of a book dealing with a very special subject, with America just involved in a world war. After the war she wrote four other novels, and she was granted a Guggenheim to visit Sonora, where she obtained material for a novel about the Yaqui Indians, *The Proper Gods*. Otherwise she always used Mormon subjects, usually placing the action in the past. She was limited in her range by the fact that she could not, as the wife of a college professor, describe the life that she was leading; such novels might prejudice his position with his colleagues. She had also written a book for children called *Curious Missie* about a girl who had the idea of starting a book mobile. She had now come up to the colony to write a second book about children.

Far from being disturbed by my failure to keep to my pious resolutions, Virginia entered upon a period of intense creativity. She not only finished the book that she had come up to write, but she produced another one as well; not only *Miracles on Maple Hill*, but *Plain Girl* too; her two best children's books. That is a fact that in retrospect astonishes us both. To write two such books within two months; and it is not unromantic to reflect that during those three months at Macdowell, with one month of which our stays coincided, we produced the books on which professionally and personally we have lived ever since.

I stayed on at Macdowell for an extra week. It was a halcyon period. Life had kept for me its best wine till last. And my last days were reassured by the news that Virginia had been granted a second Guggenheim. She would be going to Denmark in December to get the material for a book on the first Danish Mormons – her family had a Danish background.

'I'll come and join you there,' I said. When we parted early in August, it was comforting to know that we would be meeting in four months' time with the prospect of some five months together.

On my last day at the colony Virginia and I motored through Boston, to Worcester—where we lunched off a succulent Maine lobster tying a napkin round our necks—to see Virginia's daughter Beth, who was one of the supervisors of a holiday camp for diabetics. Beth, who was a diabetic herself, was that afternoon teaching a group to swim. A couple of her pupils were brought up and introduced to us; when they heard my voice, one of them cried out excitedly,

'An Englishman! He can help us with our accents.' They were rehearsing a play that contained an English character.

Beth was then twenty. She was tall, slim and blonde. She was both beautiful and pretty. She had a soft voice and a friendly manner. I was enchanted by her. I have remained enchanted. We took her for tea to a Howard Johnson. It was the first time I had been to a Howard Johnson. Whenever I pass one now, I think of her. She told us about her current boyfriend, Bob. She complained that he visited her at the end of the day, and kept her up when she needed sleep.

'Why don't you tell him that you can't see him?' Virginia said.

'But I want to see him, Mama.' She had a tender heart. I could guess that she would need Virginia over the next few years. I had no doubt by now that Virginia's marriage was on the rocks. But Beth must have the first claim on her for a little while. Virginia and I would have to see each other as often as we could manage. In the meantime there was Copenhagen in the winter.

Virginia was due to reach Copenhagen by ship on December 19th. I decided to leave England on November 30th; my ration of ninety-one days a year was running out and I liked to keep a week or so in hand in case of an emergency. Moreover I wanted to make myself at home before Virginia arrived, so that I could show her things, introduce her to things. I wanted to be the leader.

On my last afternoon in London, I went out to Highgate to have tea with my mother. She was very feeble now. She had not been out of the house for two years. But she was anything but senile. She had many friends, there were the visits from her grandchildren, but she was very tired. When she was called with her morning cup of tea, she would say, 'Still here, Mrs Yaxley.'

We were on confidential terms. Usually I told her about whatever it was I had upon my mind, and at that moment I had a good deal upon my mind. I had had a very discouraging report about *Island in the Sun* from my agent, Peters. He had not a good word to say for it. I had bitten off more than I could chew, he thought. It was much too long. It was not a question of pruning but a major operation. The murder should be taken out.

I was dismayed. The murder was the entire book. He asked me to come round and discuss it with him. I declined. I would re-read the book. I would ask Virginia's view of it. I did not want my re-reading prejudiced by his objections; but I was very worried. I wrote to Virginia, 'If this man is right, I don't know where I go from here.'

Normally I would have told my mother about this. As a publisher's wife she understood and was sympathetic to a writer's problems. But I refrained. Why worry her? Better to let her think that her sons had no professional problems, that they could deal with unhampered minds with her grandchildren's problems. We sat and talked of this and that, of friends, of distant days. It was a contented afternoon.

I was glad on the following Monday evening that I had refrained; a telegram announced that she had died.

More than once when a friend had lost a mother I had written, 'I can guess how you must be feeling, from guessing how I shall feel when I lose my mother.' But that is not true. In ways that one cannot enumerate or explain, the world is a different place when one has lost one's mother.

I got back in time for the funeral. Next day Evelyn and I went over the flat appraising what was left. There was very little to discuss. I had arranged with my mother that Evelyn should inherit the estate, apart from a few personal bequests to Joan and to my children. Evelyn had provided my mother with a generous allowance over the last eight years; moreover he had six children who would be glad of the furniture one day. My mother had not liked this arrangement, but I had insisted. It was just, and I had been anxious to avoid any unpleasantness over 'the dividing of the spoil'.

I do not think that Evelyn and I would have quarrelled over an issue such as that, but it was as well to make quite certain. I spent one night alone at the flat. It had been my base for over twenty years. The pictures, the bookcases, the furniture had been the background to all my holidays. I walked from room to room looking back, remembering. 'Never again,' I thought, 'never again'.

I returned to Copenhagen, four days before Virginia's arrival.

For the next five months I was in Copenhagen, on and off, all the time. I had made the practice whenever I visited a foreign city for any length of time of writing to the British Council, offering my services in terms of unremunerated lectures. By this I have established contact with the British community, been put up for the British club, if there was one, and had trips about the country arranged for me. It also ensured that I should start being a part of the community right away, instead of having 'to feel my way'; a process in the course of which one may make contacts of which one may be glad later to be rid.

The head of the British Council at this time was Stephen Clissold, who had served in Yugoslavia in 1944 with Evelyn and Randolph Churchill and who was later to contribute an article about the mission to David Pryce-Jones's *The World of Evelyn Waugh*. He invited me to dinner on my first Monday there. Another great piece of luck for me was the presence there as British Ambassador of Sir Eric Berthoud. Berthoud had the gracious custom of inviting to lunch at the Embassy as soon as possible, any relatively well-known Englishman who signed his book. I was invited on my second day there.

Berthoud was a man who had been just too young for the first war; he had gone up to Oxford, to Magdalen in 1920. He had started his career in oil; in that capacity he had held a succession of important posts in Anglo-Persia. During the war he had moved to the Diplomatic Service, making a very successful visit to Russia – the Russians had liked him because, though seeing their point of view, he had talked back straight at them. He and I had two considerable bonds, a love of cricket and a love of wine. He was very generous and hospitable to me in Copenhagen, and he has become the one real English friend that I have made since the war. Whenever possible we watch the first day of the Lord's Test Match together, sitting on the top gallery of the pavilion, directly behind the bowler's arm and bringing our own wine. He brings a hock or a Moselle, I a Beaujolais and a tawny port. We are joined by Sir Keith Falkner, Eric Gillett, who was at Oxford with him and played hockey with him in the University XI, and in his lifetime by A. D. Peters. In terms of wine, I introduced Berthoud to the Saintsbury Club, to which as a member he has brought a succession of distinguished guests. We have made trips together, to Dijon where we attended a banquet of Les Chevaliers de Tastevin, and to Coblenz where he has family connections, as a base for a trip along the banks of the Rhine and to Moselle.

He had, not surprisingly, a sympathetic staff working under him: James Curry, now Sir James Curry, whom I was later to meet at the PEN Club in Rio de Janeiro as Consul-General, while the Consul was Grace Thornton, with whom Virginia became a special friend and who later was honoured in the service.

We stayed at the Codan, a hotel looking on the sound from which we could see the midnight boat sail to Aarhus, and the red lights of the DFDS shone onto our ceilings. We organised a working routine. Virginia went after breakfast to the Royal Danish Library where she did research on the Danes who had emigrated to Utah in the 1850s. I worked on *Merchants of Wine* for Gilbey's and my autobiography, *The Early Years of Alec Waugh*. I had now re-read *Island in the Sun* and felt it was as good as I could make it. Virginia also approved, so I instructed Peters to send it over to Brandt and Brandt. Carl Brandt was enthusiastic and Roger Straus, who had been losing money on me for seven years, wrote, 'This is the book we have been waiting for. We will print a first edition of ten thousand copies.'

I had nothing to worry about on that score.

'Our little marriage' as Virginia called it was a time for which I could have wished nothing different. Winter is not the tourist season for Copenhagen. Tivoli, the great tourist attraction, is closed, but for the Danes themselves it is 'the season'. They shut up their summer cottages and return to their town houses, for the opera, for dances and for dinner parties. The Danes are a delightful people, so friendly, so light-hearted. Ordinarily I find that every three days or so something happens to put me out of humour; somebody pushes past me in the street, somebody blows cigarette smoke in my face. But in Denmark after a month I found I had not lost my temper once; not because I was myself in a more harmonious state of mind, but because the Danes are themselves so even-tempered. Copenhagen is full of appetising restaurants. Sometimes Virginia took sandwiches to the library. More often we lunched out, on one occasion at Krog's, the great fish restaurant. We were having such a good time, toasting each other in Cherry Heering, that we caught the eye of two Danes at the next table. One of them was Peter Heering himself. That was the start of quite a friendship.

The days are short in Copenhagen in the winter. If one lingers over a lunch table, the sky is darkening when one comes out into the street. Usually we supped at the Codan. We kept a bottle of Aquavit on the ledge between the double windows and ordered up beer and open sandwiches. Then we read poetry to one another.

The British Council arranged one or two lectures for me in the country. Virginia had cousins at Veddum with whom she spent a week. We spent five days at Hvidsten Kro in the inn that during the German occupation was the centre of the resistance.

At the end of March Virginia went to visit with her cousins. I went back to London for ten days. We met again in Paris and took a bus south to Nice.

It was exciting to show Virginia Paris and the south of

France. Eliza Parkinson was at Antibes with her daughter Zaidee; so was Lily Cushing. We made a number of excursions; then followed two fantastic weeks when there happened to me all the things that writers dream of having happen to themselves. I have written a description of it in *My Brother Evelyn*.

One afternoon I returned to Nice to find a message that New York wanted me on the telephone. It was Carl Brandt. *Ladies' Home Journal* had bought the serial rights of *Island in the Sun*. Three days later I learnt that it was the Literary Guild choice for January. Another couple of days and a cable announced the sale to the *Reader's Digest* Condensed Book Club. On April 27th Virginia was due to visit a cousin who was in the American Embassy at Brussels. I was to return to London. Virginia and I were to meet again at the end of the following week in Copenhagen. We parted company at Geneva. On our last morning at the Escurial, just as we were about to catch a bus, the night porter told me that New York had been trying to reach me on the telephone. I had been in Virginia's room and had not got the message. This could only mean one thing – a film. We wanted to get the news of this when we were together. So I cabled to Carl Brandt telling him the name of my hotel in Geneva and when I expected to arrive. Sure enough that evening the New York telephone call came through. Twentieth Century-Fox, a hundred and forty thousand dollars.

Within ten days we were back in Copenhagen. This time we were staying at the King of Denmark. Spring was on its way. The days had lengthened. Tivoli was open. We hired a small car and motored across the country. At Ribe the storks were nesting on the chimney stacks. The PEN Club were holding a conference in Vienna in early June. I had hoped to persuade Virginia to come there with me but she was beginning to feel restless to get home. She had problems to be settled there. Her children needed her. We had always known that 'our little marriage' would have to end in the early summer. Better to leave a fortnight too early rather than a day too late. She booked a passage on the *Maine* – a cargo-type ship that sailed straight to New York. It sailed on May the 25th. We had been together for five months.

CHAPTER 22

Best Sellerdom

I was fortunate to have my lucky break at the age of fifty-seven. If I had had it at the age of thirty it would have presented me with a whole new group of problems. It would have made accessible for me a whole new way of life, a way of life to which I might have found it difficult to adjust myself. I had reached the age of settled tastes. I liked the way of life that I was leading. I had no wish to alter it, though I welcomed the opportunity to lead it on a more ample scale. Had I had this sudden addition of funds at the age of thirty, I should have been perplexed with problems of tax, of forming trusts, of watching the stock market. A source of perpetual harassment. As I saw it, I needed now to get stacked away a collection of blue chips that would serve as a bastion to my old age, but I saw no point in building up a block of capital on which the interest would be taxed and such legacies as I made would be exposed to death duties. My children had been well taken care of by their grandfather's will. They would eventually inherit quite a little from their mother. I did not need to worry about them. I decided to have fun with my 'unexpected wealth'. I had not ahead of me after all so very many years.

Though I was paying heavy taxes, eighty per cent on the last hundreds, I could run a large expense account; all of my trips, much of my entertaining; about half of my living costs in fact. My income was considerable and the Internal Revenue Service regarded these expenses as legitimate. Once I was subjected to a two years' audit and the IRS made no complaints.

* * *

I had a more or less regular programme. I would spend my
ninety-one days' allowance in England, the half of it at
Edrington. I spent about three or four months in the USA,
two of them in New York. I did my writing at the Macdowell
colony and at Nice, moving in the 1960s to the Windsor,
a rather more comfortable hotel, in the same area as the
Escurial which I passed every morning on my way to
breakfast at the Brasserie de Lyons – now promoted to
calling itself the Grand Café de Lyons. I made one major
trip a year to the West Indies, to the Seychelles, or to the
Far East. I travelled mostly by air – except on crossings to
New York, by the *De Grasse*, the *Ile de France* and finally the
France.

I went to the PEN Club congress in Tokyo and Rio de
Janeiro. In November 1956 I went round the world. I took
with me the first 75,000 words of a novel *Fuel for the Flame*
that was set in an imaginary island, an independent kingdom,
in the Malay Archipelago. It is over 200,000 words in
length. I finished it during nine weeks in Bangkok at the
Oriental Hotel, three weeks in Fiji and three weeks in
Hawaii. During the 1960s I did some magazine articles.
Reader's Digest sent me to the Virgin Islands and to Malta,
Venture sent me to the Windward and the Virgin Islands,
Holiday sent me to Buenos Aires, *Sports Illustrated* sent me
to the European spas.

In 1957 I met Peggy Mann, the author of *A Room in Paris*
and *The Last Escape*, the story of Jewish refugees to Palestine
in 1939, and a number of children's books. Married to an
Englishman, William Houlton, she was working at Doubleday's in publicity for the Dollar Book Club which handled
Island in the Sun. We became great friends and I am the
godfather of her elder daughter Jenny Houlton, who had
made a debut as a TV juvenile in 'The Doctors'. Peggy
Mann was always invaluable to my trips for these magazine
articles. She always knew the right person to make them
easy. She introduced me to Pan American's key man – a most
useful contact – and to Maurice Hennessy, who arranged my

visit to Cognac for my wine book. She introduced me to
Michael Pobers, who ran the publicity for Vichy. He 'fixed
me up' in most of the French spas. I do not know how I
should have got the material for my *Sports Illustrated*
article without him. In fact I wonder how I would have
managed quite a few of those articles without Peggy Mann.

I organised my visits to London carefully. In New York
I would let one or two people know that I was on my way.
Then I would sit by my telephone in the Algonquin and the
wheels would start revolving. You cannot do that in London.
Londoners plan their diaries three weeks ahead. If you
start telephoning on your arrival, you find that you cannot
arrange anything till the week after next. So three weeks
before I returned to England, I would send out invitations
for a lunch and dinner party during my first three days so that
I could 'get back into things' right away. I kept up with
most of my old friends.

Most years Joan and I went for a two weeks' holiday in
Italy. Capri was our favourite place. In 1955 Veronica
married Christopher Keeling – the son of the late Sir Edward
Keeling. Christopher had a seat in Lloyd's. I liked him very
much. He was a member of MCC, played for the Eton
Ramblers. In *The Early Years of Alec Waugh* I said that the
second question I should ask any suppliant for my daughter's
hand would be 'Are you a cricketer?' Cyril Connolly,
reviewing it, asked, 'What would be the first?' I am glad I
was not asked that question in a TV interview. What *would*
have been the first question?

At first Christopher and Veronica had a house in London
and they came down to Edrington every other week-end.
Later they took a house at Axford, an hour or so's drive
away, and they often came over for lunch on Sundays and
to stay the night. Veronica has a daughter and two sons.
When I was a boy I had a small wheelbarrow in which
I delighted. My parents gave it to Andrew; he too delighted
in it and wheeled it round the garden. It somehow continued
to remain among the litter in the loggia. I was very touched

to see Veronica's elder son Simon, when the car drew up, jump out into the drive and scamper to the barrow.

In 1951 Andrew passed into the Royal Navy. It was very obviously the career for him, and he is now, married and with two sons, a captain. I think it was a piece of luck for him that he failed his entrance to Eton. If he had succeeded he might not have passsd into the Navy. Even today, there must be many young Etonians who do not need to exert themselves to make their way in life as strenuously as their contemporaries at Marlborough, Cheltenham and Tonbridge. At a school like Sherborne everyone knows that he has to work hard if he is to get himself out of the rut. At Eton Andrew might have made friends among boys who did not need to be strenuously ambitious. I cannot tell; I am very glad that things turned out the way they did.

After he passed into the Navy, Andrew was often out of the country. He served in the Korean War, but leading my rootless existence I had several opportunities of seeing him abroad. In 1952 his training ship took him to the West Indies. In 1955 I was in Hong Kong at the same time that he was. We have met on several occasions in Singapore. Now I am in Tangier and Gibraltar is one of his ports of call. I am very proud when I see him in uniform on duty. He is so obviously the right man in the right place.

My younger son Peter also went to Sherborne. He had quite a successful time there. He was in the sixth. Because of his eyes, he gave up cricket, at which he had made a promising start after taking nets at Lord's, and as a footballer played in a winning Three Cock which neither his brother nor myself had done. Readers of *The Loom of Youth* will know what I mean by a winning Three Cock. It is the match that the School House plays against the best two of the outhouses. Peter had always at the start, being five and four years younger than Andrew and Veronica who were very much a team, thought of himself as the odd man out. He was now still a schoolboy while his brother and sister were launched in life. He was alone at Edrington. In consequence

I was to see very much more of him than I had of the other two. He came on holidays with me to Villefranche and Tangier. We motored through the Côte d'Or staying at the Hôtel de la Poste. He came to a Chevaliers de Tastevin dinner at the Clos de Vougeat. We spent two days in Paris, and he came with me to a superb lunch that the Sven Neilsens, my publishers at the Presses de la Cité, gave for me. Once when I was doing a cure in Zurich at the Bircher-Benner Clinic, he met me on my release and motored me across France to Perpignon, where I had arranged for him to spend three weeks with a French family.

He is a delightful companion. One of his greatest charms is the interest he takes in other people. I have never found it easy to talk to people about my writing. It is so very personal for me, but I can talk about it to Peter. He became a real *copain*, in the same way that Eldred Curwen had been. Indeed in some ways he took Eldred's place.

He describes himself as an individualist, by which I take it he means doing things in his own way. He got into the sixth form at Sherborne. By then a pattern of 'O' and 'A' levels had been established which I have never quite understood. I gathered he did not do too well, but I managed to enter him for Oxford, for Lincoln College. Perhaps the authorities hoped that the nephew of Evelyn Waugh and the son of Alec Waugh would be an 'individualist' in some special way. Military service was still obligatory and he earned a commission in the 7th Hussars. At the end of his service, he insisted on having a year on his own in France and Germany. I think that this was a mistake. I think that he should have got back into the educational machine as soon as possible. But if he had not had his own way, he would have failed in his 'prelims' and retorted, 'Well, I told you, didn't I?' He had his year in Paris and Heidelberg and it was then that we motored from Zurich to Perpignon. I had hoped that these three weeks would put the final polish on his French, but he fell in love with one of the daughters of the house and conducted his courtship of her in English.

'I couldn't get my exact meaning across to her in French,' he said.

He went up to Oxford after his *wanderjahre*; I think he missed meeting his fellow undergraduates on equal terms. He was the wrong age for them and never seemed to enter into the life of the college. I went up to see him after he had been up a month; I asked him to show me the JCR and he did not know where it was. Most week-ends he came back to Edrington. He had fallen in love with the 'girl next door'.

On that issue Joan and I were soon reassured. In these days it is impossible for parents not to worry about whether their son is going 'to turn out gay'. When Peter was in the Army, one morning Joan had gone to the kitchen to brew herself an early cup of tea. She came up with her eyes bright. 'There's the sound of a girl's voice in Peter's room.' Nothing queer about Carruthers.

Peter made no friends at Oxford, though he took part in the Pentathlon. He was, at this time, most at his ease with people considerably older or considerably younger than himself. He failed his 'prelims'. He was allowed a year in which to prepare himself for a second try. He failed again. In my absences he used my study and spent a lot of time writing poetry. I would not trust my opinion on modern poetry. I asked him to show me some of his college essays but students do not apparently write essays nowadays. At any rate he had nothing to show me from which I could judge whether he had 'a sense of words'. I wrote to the college authorities and asked if they had seen in his work any signs of literary talent. No, they said, they had not detected any.

'The Individualist' was now in a predicament. Where did he go from here? It was too late for any of 'the professions'. Neither Joan nor myself knew any of 'the right people' in business. I suggested wine. I had many contacts in the wine trade and we had as a neighbour a very good friend, R. H. Cobbold, the former Eton cricket captain and Cambridge 'blue' who was one of the partners in Justerini and Brooks. His firm was recruiting for a three-year training course with the prospect of a job in Justerini's at the end of it. Cobbold agreed to take him on. He was impressed by Peter's enthusiasm. 'Why do you want to go into wine?' he asked him.

'I was brought up in an atmosphere of wine,' he said. 'As a boy I was taken down into the cellar and watched my father decant his port. I was always given a sip of wine at table. I think wine is one of the things that make life worth living.'

Peter was given a sound grounding in the wine trade and was sent on a number of trips abroad, to Jerez, to Bordeaux, to the Rhine. At the end of his three-year course, he was offered a job in the London offices. But he did not like an office routine. At that time a process of general amalgamation was at work, Justerini's along with Gilbey's became part of a large combine. Peter told me that he did not have the right temperament to make his way in a big organisation in which he had no family links.

He wanted to become a photographer. Anthony Armstrong Jones, now Lord Snowdon, had been a friend of Veronica's. She had worked in his firm and he had been a guest at Edrington. Why should he not follow his example? He would take a course at the Polytechnic. He would be able to draw a government grant while he was taking it. Myself, I wondered. There were so many people taking photographs. The life of a photographer was surely as much a rat race as that of a journalist. There were resemblances between the two; but his heart was set on it and he got his way. He drew the government grant. He arranged with his mother for an allowance, in anticipation of his eventual inheritance. He took a flat in London. He came down to Edrington for week-ends, bringing a lot of dirty clothing for the laundry, returning with the clean laundry from the previous week, the back of his car laden with vegetables from the garden and groceries from the larder.

*   *   *

I have not seen nearly as much of my children as I would have liked. I have been a casual father. But their company has immeasurably enriched my life. I hope I have not been a nuisance to them.

CHAPTER 23

Virginia on her own

It was in May 1955 that Virginia had returned to the US in the *Maine*. I was only to see her three times in the next four years. Her husband was a professor at Edinborough, Pennsylvania. In February 1956 Virginia was invited to a book fair in Cleveland. I joined her there for three days at the Statler. We had one curious experience. The Rowfant Club has close links with the Sette of Odde Volumes. Three years earlier, seventy members of the club with their wives had flown over to London for a joint banquet with the brethren. It had been a great occasion and when the Rowfant learnt that I was in Cleveland they insisted on entertaining me. I was delighted but I did not want to desert Virginia. 'Of course,' I said, 'provided I could bring my friend Virginia Sorensen.' This created a problem. Women were not admitted. But I was very much in the news. *Island in the Sun* had just come out and I felt I could lay down conditions. They continued to demur but they felt in the end that an exception must be made for a member of the Odde Volumes; so it was arranged that the wife of the President should act as hostess. She was delighted. It was the first time until then that she or any other woman had been inside the sacred portals. That rule has now been modified.

The Rowfant Club provides impressive premises for its members. It has one unusual rule; that each member should have his own candlestick, engraved with his own name, which is set before him every time he dines. When he dies it is put upon a special shelf.

* * *

We had only three days together in Cleveland. But we had a whole week together in October. Virginia had been appointed as writer in residence in the University of Seattle. A two weeks' assignment. I arrived in New York early in October and we arranged tentatively that I should come out to Seattle. Virginia had two weeks free at the end of her course to visit first old friends in Tucson, then her brother, an Air Force officer and doctor in San Antonio. Due to a breakdown in communications, I never got the letter detailing our arrangements. At that time two other men whose names began with W were regular visitors at the Algonquin – Alec Wilder and Thornton Wilder. Our mails often got confused. At one time Thornton Wilder was travelling round the Mediterranean in Alec Wilder's shirts. This time Alec Wilder got my mail. I had planned after Virginia had gone on to San Antonio, that I should visit a very old friend, Colin Kinby's daughter, now married to William Banning in Duarte. As I had not received Virginia's letter, I went straight to Duarte and made contact with Virginia from there. Janet suggested that we should go to the Arizona Inn in Tucson. It had a very discreet block of suites, each with a separate front door, round a corner but inside the building, the suites interconnecting through the bathroom.

We met at the airport and went together to the Arizona Inn. In later years, Virginia and I were to pay several visits to Duarte. The Bannings nicknamed her 'Seattle'.

The Arizona Inn was practically empty, but the weather was warm. We had an idyllic time, in the mornings drinking mint juleps by the swimming pool.

There was to be only one meeting after that. In October 1957 she went to New York for the presentation of the Newbery medal. Harcourt Brace, her publishers, provided her with a flat for her three-day visit. I contrived to get seats for *My Fair Lady*.

Professionally those were exciting years for Virginia. *Plain Girl* was published in the autumn of 1956 and was given the annual award by the Child Study Association of America. The citation read 'The tender and sympathetic story of a young Amish girl who in reaching out for the different ways of her school mates still holds dear the love and respect for her family and the traditions of her people.'

The following year, *Miracles on Maple Hill* was awarded the Newbery medal for the year's most distinguished contribution to American literature for children. Both books were very great successes. The other day on Harcourt Brace's spring catalogue both *Miracles on Maple Hill* and *Plain Girl* were listed as best-sellers among the paperback best-sellers and *Miracles* was a hard cover best-seller as well. After twenty years that is something. But in spite of her professional success, personally her home life was becoming more and more difficult. Her daughter Beth was now married to a young school teacher who was reading for his doctorate, her son Frederick was doing his military service and was away from home. Virginia was alone with her husband, and the strain was growing more than she could stand. I was not surprised to receive a letter in October 1958, telling me that she had finally and definitely left him and was going to the Macdowell colony. I welcomed this news wholeheartedly. I was about to start on a trip round the world, during which I hoped to finish my novel *Fuel for the Flame*.

I wrote to her, 'I expect to arrive in Boston the first week in March. You get your novel finished in Macdowell. I'll get mine finished during my trip, then we'll work out a plan. My first idea is that you should come with me to Tangier.'

It was not difficult to dovetail our plans. She had her life to lead and so had I. I needed at least four months a year alone to do my writing. She had her family in America. We thought we would spend five months or so a year together, partly in Tangier where I had made several visits during the last few years, partly in the USA, partly on trips together. 'As long as I have a ticket in my pocket,' Virginia said, 'I'll be all right.'

Virginia's brother Paul had now moved to Washington; she took a flat first in Georgetown, then in Alexandria, Virginia. It was a happy arrangement. Three times we went to the West Indies. We went on a tour of the European spas. We went to the PEN club conferences in Menton, Dublin and the Ivory Coast. I had been commissioned to write a book on Bangkok and we spent a month in the Far East, going to Singapore, Cambodia, Angkor Wat.

Tangier we found increasingly congenial. We stayed at the Velasquez Hotel. It has a rounded turret-style addition facing the sea, like the prow of a ship that contains on each floor a three-room flat, with a hall separating the two bedrooms. The extra bedroom was self-contained. I had a sufficient feeling of privacy to be able to work there.

Tangier itself had acquired a somewhat sultry reputation up until 1956. It was an international zone, and was the base for dubious traffickers in ill-gotten goods. Now incorporated in Morocco, Tangier is as law-abiding as a port can hope to be. It has a friendly atmosphere. There is not only a British colony of the type that in the 1920s you would find on the French and Italian Rivieras, but an American one as well. There are the remains of an American base a few miles away; there is a Voice of America broadcasting station. There is also an American school, financed by Washington partly for the children of American officials but mainly for Moroccans. The staff of the school brings into the community a youthful and healthy atmosphere.

This succession of departures and reunions maintained the spirit of romance between Virginia and myself. Though I have been married most of my life, I know really nothing about marriage; I mean by that the developing of an early romance into – Galsworthy's words – 'Vintage full and sweet with sunset colour on the grapes.' I know perfectly well that there are many couples who fall in love, marry, and without actually continuing to be in love, retain a sexual awareness of each other. I know that there are such marriages. Perhaps there are very many such marriages, but they lie outside my experience. For me the magic of love-making dies with propinquity, with use and wont.

Apart from the slightly devious pair in my erotic comedy *A Spy in the Family* I have never put a happily married couple in a novel. I do not know what life is like for a couple, married for ten years who are still alert to one another. Virginia and I were lucky in not being subjected to the corroding wear and tear of habit.

I never expected 'our affair' to last. When I had learnt that her marriage had broken down, my first thought had been 'I must get her back onto her feet.' That was the role I pictured for myself. Over the years, the pattern that Donita had set in 1936 had been followed by more than one successor. Most of my loves had been American. I had met someone; there had been a mutual attraction. There had been an equivalent for Miami. I had returned to England; there had been the period of writing on a novel, preparing the means for a reunion; there had been an equivalent for the Atlantic Beach club. Then she had come to recognise that there was no satisfactory future in this for her. There would be a separation, then a 'dear John' letter. That was what I expected to happen this time. It was what I wanted for her; the right kind of marriage with a solid fellow American.

It was not though what I wanted for myself. Life, as I have already said, had kept its best wine for me to the last. I prayed that it would last as long as possible. I did my best to make it last. I did my best to ensure that those 'tickets in her pocket' would be each of them a gateway to a fresh adventure. Only in Tangier, in the Velasquez Hotel, was there a similarity of setting. Even my visits to America were different.

Virginia had two sisters and three brothers. In Washington her brother Paul introduced me to a group of wine enthusiasts; one of them, a wine merchant, organised a series of tastings, where we sampled some superb red wines, accompanied by cheese; the session being brought to a close with a rich cream cake that required a sweet wine – a sauternes or a big hock. Paul was a keen fisherman, and when we were both in Springville, Utah, where his father lived, we went trout fishing in the mountain streams.

I became good friends with Virginia's sisters, Helen the elder who had been brought up almost as a twin, lived in San Francisco, and Geraldine–Gerry–the kid sister who had felt herself as a girl the 'odd one out', lived in Salt Lake City. Her husband was a school teacher and Gerry, too, taught in school. Both had happy marriages.

Helen's was a second marriage. She had worked in a bank. One day a customer presented his cheque, and beside it a folded note on which was written, 'Will you dine with me tonight?' She took a steady look at him, then nodded her head. They have no children. Very often a childless marriage, disappointing though it may be at the beginning, if it manages to survive at all, provides a more intimate relationship. Each needs the other; each depends exclusively upon the other. Helen and her Fred had the great bond of music. She plays and he sings together in concerts.

Gerry's marriage was very different. It was a boy and girl romance that indeed developed into 'vintage full and sweet with sunset colour on the grapes'. Her Jim was a school teacher, tall and strong, who in later years because of Gerry's excellent cooking became very fat. Neither of them has ever looked at anybody else. When I invited them to a party, Gerry would always say, 'Please let me sit next to Jim, I never see him.' They had three sons and one daughter, Sue, the youngest of the family.

Between Sue and myself there was – and it still exists – a relationship unique in my experience. One can scarcely say that a girl of ten and a man of sixty-four can fall in love with one another, but I do not know what else one is to call it. On a summer evening on our first meeting we were sitting on a swing chair in the garden, and found ourselves talking together with complete ease and openness as though we had known each other all our lives. That summer I was in

Utah for six weeks and we saw each other constantly. We continued to chatter away together, as equals and contemporaries. Once the family were dining in an outdoor restaurant where there was music and a dance floor.

'Let's dance,' I said.

'I can't,' she said.

'That doesn't matter. It's quite easy, follow me.'

She was fascinated by the speed at which I talk. She once came up to me with one of her school friends. 'Talk fast,' she commanded. She was like a gangster holding up a victim. We have kept in touch over the years.

I never met Virginia's mother. She died at just about the time that Virginia and I were starting our life together, but I spent two months in Springville in the summer of 1962 and became good friends with her father. He was not so very much older than myself. He was tall, slim, handsome, with a teasing Danish wit. We watched TV and washed dishes together after meals. He was lively company. He seemed in good health, but he had an aneurism and was likely to die at any moment. Virginia spent as much of her time with him as she could. She spent most of the autumn of 1962 in Utah and prepared for publication her collection of stories about her childhood and early girlhood *Where Nothing is Long Ago* which is my favourite of her books. Her father died in the following spring.

Utah added a dimension to my life. It is like no other state in the Union. The US as a whole was populated by Europeans who were out of tune with the way of living in the country of their birth. They were in search of a new country; as were the Mormons in their long trek across the continent in 1847; but they were not in flight from Europe but from the United States itself. When Brigham Young looked down from the hills and said 'This is the place,' he was not looking down upon a future territory, but on a part of Mexico.

I never quite feel that I am in the US when I am in Utah. But that does not mean that I do not like being there very much. I have no sense of kinship with the teaching of the Latter Day Saints. Meals without wine are a penance for me, but the general atmosphere of Salt Lake City is most congenial. It is very beautiful looked down on from the hills. It is clean, well ordered, and well run. There is a basic rectitude about it all. It is one of the few places where I should be content to make a permanent home.

Every couple of years Virginia and I went to Salt Lake City. In 1966 we went there for a writers' congress organised by that excellent poet, Brewster Gheslin, the author of *The Creative Process*, an educational classic. It lasted for two weeks and it was immeasurably enlivened by the presence of James Dickey. What a man he is, so full of warmth, so full of fun. He has read more contemporary English writing than any American writer whom I know. There is no need to describe James Dickey. He appeared as the sheriff in the film that was made from his novel, *Deliverance*. It was a good film, made from a very good novel, but in retrospect all that I can remember is the acting of James Dickey – large, powerful, good-humoured. He is at his happiest with a guitar across his knees. He has a full rich voice. As a corollary to the friendship that started at the Salt Lake City congress, we entertained and were entertained by each other on the next two Thanksgiving dinners.

Carl Brandt died in the autumn of 1957. He had been ill for quite a while, and a year earlier Carol, whose association with MGM had been terminated by a Palace Revolution, and who had been waiting for a few years on the touch line, came into the firm. I was very sad at losing Carl, but I was happy to be again with Carol, and I soon became good friends with young Carl. I particularly recall warmly the visit he and I paid to Pleasantville to discuss with *Reader's Digest* an article on the US Virgin Islands. On the way there Carl said, 'You can never tell what kind of a reception you will get here. It may be coffee and eggs in a cafeteria or a slap-up luncheon in their suite.' Fortunately it was a slap-up luncheon with Jack Daniels on the rocks and a noble burgundy. Appropriately, the deal went through.

In 1962 in England, and in 1963 in the USA, I published the first instalment of an autobiography, *The Early Years of Alec Waugh*. It had a good press on both sides, but it did not sell very many copies. It is one of the rules of authorship, never to make a novelist the hero of a novel. His problems never seem quite real to readers. The novelist's problems are so different from their own. Nor are they dramatic ones. They are solved not in the hurly-burly of life, in dangerous expeditions, in boardroom battles. They are sorted out by a man or woman sitting at a desk. The novelist appears to lead a very easy life. And an autobiography is a novel told in the first person. There is no reader identification and the minor characters in a novelist's autobiography are often writers too. I had been warned that this would be the case; but I had hoped that my book would be 'somehow different'. It was not though. The reviewers were laudatory and extensive as I might have known they would be. It is very easy to review an autobiography. The reviewer knows the plot already, he has only to turn the pages swiftly to get at the key passages. One hour at the most. He is grateful to the novelist for giving him an easy job. I have never had a better press but on neither side did it sell more than 3,000 copies.

I sent the manuscript to Evelyn. There was not a great deal about him in it. I felt I could not enter imaginatively into the life of a man to whom religion was the thing that mattered most. But I thought there might be something in it that he would like said differently or not said at all. His reply surprised me. He was complimentary about the book, as a whole; but he had one major reservation.

'You say,' he commented, 'that you have been more of an uncle than a brother to me. May a nephew offer his uncle this advice. You will cause great offence to many Anglicans by stating that you take communion regularly. It is very clear that you do not accept the doctrine or moral teaching of your Church.' Every time I took communion, he insisted, I was committing an act of blasphemy. If this is so, in view of the general moral permissiveness of Tangier's social life, what a saga of blasphemy has been committed before the altar of St Andrew's!

In the autumn of 1963 I went on a coast-to-coast lecture tour. In Oklahoma, Clifton Warren, a professor at the Central State College, Edmond, asked if I would care to come there as writer in residence. I said I would. I usually accept offers, putting the fulfilment of that promise a certain way into the future, suspecting that something will happen to interfere with my fulfilment of it. In this case I put the date forward to September 1966. Surely something would turn up to stop me going. Nothing did, however, and as the months passed I became more and more apprehensive.

As it happened, it was to prove an enlivening experience. I had to give only two seminars a week, of an hour each, on the Monday and the Wednesday. I was given a two-room apartment inside the college. I was given the run of the cafeteria. No alcohol was served in the cafeteria, so I used to fill a bag with the basic material for a meal and take it back to my flat where I had a bottle waiting. I had about twenty students in my class. Two-thirds of them were middle-aged. I do not believe that 'creative writing', as it is called, can be taught, but it can be encouraged and two of my students did get their work published in hard-back editions – Georgia Solaska, who wrote a series of classical novels about Homer's characters, and Moselle Richardson, who is building up a genuine reputation as an author of gothic novels. I received the other day the latest of them, *Daughter of the Sacred Mountain*, inscribed to Alec Waugh 'who started the whole damn thing'. I became genuinely fond of my class. It was my first experience of the teacher–pupil relationship. I could understand its attraction. After my Monday seminar, I would invite three or four of my students back to my apartment for a glass of wine and sandwiches. I made a number of friends among the residents of Oklahoma. And there was one couple, the Winants, who used to invite me over for week-ends. I became very fond of Oklahoma itself and of its way of life. It was my first experience of life in a state capital.

Virginia paid me two long visits and, as she always does, made herself very popular. Frank Finney, the head of the English department, asked her if she would be writer in residence in the following year. This continued my association with Edmond for another year. I came to feel myself very much at home there and my sojourn was enriched by the manager of the Cellar Club in the Hightower Building, John Bennett. Oklahoma had been a dry state until only a very few years earlier and wine and spirits were only served publicly in clubs, though you could lay in bottles for your own home, from liquor stores, as is the case in several states – Utah for example.

Bennett and I became good friends. His restaurant had a superb cellar, and during Virginia's last week he gave a remarkable party for us. He hired a private train in which some thirty of us were driven out to the neighbouring town of Ardmore. A champagne breakfast was served upon the train. In Ardmore station there was an ample luncheon in which ducks and a sucking pig were accompanied by Moselle and Hock. After a tour of the town, a very attractive one, we returned by train, on which sausages were served with Beaujolais.

I did a good deal of writing during my year at Edmond. The 1960s were my most productive period. Two novels, two autobiographies, a collection of short stories, a book on wine, a history of Bangkok, several magazine articles. I was still prominently in the public eye but I felt that I must make as much profit as I could out of my presence there. Subconsciously I realised that I was living on borrowed time. *Island in the Sun's* successor, *Fuel for the Flame* – a novel set in an oil community in the Far East – which was published in 1960, was nine weeks in the best-seller list. *Ladies Home Journal* bought the serial rights. There was a good paperback sale and MGM paid a pleasantly dimensioned fee for an option that it did not take up. But its successor, *The Mule on the Minaret* had a very different reception. A substantial book, about the Middle East in wartime, I preferred it to *Fuel*. Carol was enthusiastic, so was John Farrar, and Roger Straus took their word for it. It came out in October 1965. It did not sell serially; there was no paperback sale, no film option; it failed by a whole wad of currency to earn its advance. Roger Straus did not hold it against me. He had made a lot of money out of *Island in the Sun*, but there it was. I had moved, as a novelist, into a different category. It was what I had expected to happen sooner or later, but it had come just that little sooner than I had hoped. At the same time I had not much to worry over and I did not worry. Everything was going well enough.

While I was at Oklahoma, I had received the offer to contribute the book on *Wines and Spirits* to the Time-Life *Foods of the World Series*. This commission came to me through Peggy Mann's husband William Houlton, who was handling the publicity for Californian wines. He was himself practically a teetotaller, confining himself to an occasional tankard of beer, but he threw himself into the promotion of Californian wines as if he had been like my children, sipping vintage port as a schoolboy. This was another example of my indebtedness to Peggy Mann.

I enjoyed the writing of this book and the general production and launching of it as much as any of my books. The general editor of the series was Richard I. Williams, who is now an editor for the *Smithsonian* magazine. He came down to Tangier to discuss the book with me. He brought with him his pretty and lively wife, the author of an entertaining book called *Marriage for Beginners*. I did not meet him at the airport; not knowing each other we might easily have missed. The airport is very crowded and confused and planes run late during the tourist season. I left a message for him in the Velasquez where he was planning to stay too, that I should be dining round the corner at the Grenouille. 'I have', I wrote, 'a charming travelling companion.' Because of Tangier's sultry reputation, he presumed that this companion was a man. He and Mary were delighted and relieved to find me with a female, youngish, attractive and a compatriot. Their relief started off our relations on a happy basis.

I have over the years been very lucky in my editors. I was never luckier than in Dick Williams. He was then in his late forties. He had warmth and charm and knew exactly what he required. 'We want to bring out this book within fifteen months. Your share of the letter press will be forty-five thousand words. How long will that take you?'

Forty-five thousand words. The book would need no research. I had done all the research already for *In Praise of Wine*. It was only a question of bringing it up to date with a few reference books.

'Five weeks,' I said.

Dick looked surprised.

'You really mean that?'

'You wait and see,' I said.

Within five weeks to a day the book was finished.

It was the easiest piece of writing that I have ever done. My agreement with Time-Life stipulated that I should spend three weeks in New York. They would pay my passage and make me an allowance of thirty dollars a day while I was there. In 1967 a man could perhaps have managed on thirty dollars a day but not in a suite at the Algonquin. But I had wanted to go over to New York then anyhow, so I did not repine and I persuaded Dick to transport me there not in a plane, tourist, but in the *France*, first-class.

In New York a pleasant surprise awaited me. Dick had found me as my consultant-editress, Barbara Leach, a most attractive and efficient person. We liked each other instantly and the research we did together was not a matter of consulting dusty volumes in a library but of attending wine tastings. Wine merchants were very accommodating in this respect. The technical editor was Sam Aaron, one of the chiefs at Lehmann Brothers. He was most helpful and organised a lavish party when the book came out. Barbara and I have stayed in touch. We always meet when I am in New York and once she and her husband, the painter Wayne Ensrud, spent five days in Tangier.

While I was in Tangier, after the Williams had gone and Virginia had left to take up her duties as writer in residence in Oklahoma, I received a telegram from my son, Andrew, announcing his engagement to Vivienne Gorges. His ship, he told me, would be in the Mediterranean shortly and he would fly over from Gibraltar to tell me all about it. I had not met Vivienne, but had heard about her.

Andrew had met her when he was ADC to the Governor of Rhodesia. It had been a considerable romance and she had been down to Edrington more than once, but they had drifted apart. Recently Andrew had met the former governor, Sir Peveril William-Powlett.

'Do you see anything of Vivienne nowadays?' Sir Peveril asked him.

'I'm afraid I don't, sir.'

'Do you know her address?'

'I'm afraid not, sir.'

'Then I can give it to you.'

Andrew wrote to her. He was, at that time, at the Admiralty. She was employed by a firm of decorators. They had not time for a real lunch. Only a champagne cocktail and a sandwich at the Ritz Bar. A bare forty minutes, but it was enough – 'The old love came back to the vacant dwelling'.

They were planning to be married in November. It was very good news for me. Andrew was now thirty-four and Joan and I had begun to worry about him 'in that way'. He was too old for debutantes and he might very well find himself involved with some young married woman with a couple of children, which would have been the very worst thing for his career. Vivienne, who was then twenty-eight and had spent a lot of time out of England, sounded 'just the thing'. I was back in England for a few days before returning to New York under my Time-Life contract. She came down to Edrington for a week-end. They looked very right together.

They were married in the Old Church, Chelsea, where Joan and I had been married. It had been heavily bombed during the blitz, but it had been restored to its old dignity. Brother officers with drawn swords stood as a guard of honour; the reception was at the Hyde Park Hotel. My wedding present was a trip to the West Indies.

For the last ten years I had made a practice of going every eighteen months or so to the Bircher-Benner clinic in Zurich for a check-up and to adjust my weight. I had a booking there for late October in 1968. Virginia was to join me and we were booked to take a Kuoni tour to the Far East, so that I could get the final material for my book on Bangkok.

It was a two-week tour, but as Andrew was stationed in Singapore we made it a four-week tour so that we could go south and see him. We included in our itinerary a side trip to Angkor Wat. We had five days in Singapore. It was very good to see Andrew in the atmosphere of his job; to see Vivienne in her role as a sailor's wife. It was very clear that she got on well with Andrew's brother officers. They liked her very much, as she did them. She told us that she was in the second month of her pregnancy. As sure as one can be of anything I am of the future of that marriage.

Our side trip to Angkor Wat involved us in a very long coach ride over a bumpy road. It was more than worth it. I had not seen Angkor Wat before and I had long wanted to. Even more than the sight of the temple, we enjoyed the glimpses we got of the Cambodian way of life, with the fishermen propelling their river craft among the reeds. They looked so at peace. Where are those fishermen today?

In Bangkok, staying as before at the Oriental Hotel, I saw most of my old friends, spending a day at Prince Chula's palace, as the guest of the Princess. We finished with a placid five days by the swimming pool at Patiala, where I converted my notes into a narrative.

CHAPTER 24

An End and a Beginning

Virginia and I returned to Alexandria a few days before Christmas. We found a large mail awaiting us. Among my letters was one marked 'express' from Peter. It told me that Joan had inoperable cancer. She had not very long to live. Veronica had insisted that she not be told. Joan was now back at Edrington and every week she was driven to Oxford for radio treatment. Peter told me that I must not return to Edrington. If I did his mother would learn the truth. I must not in my letters give her the least suggestion that there was anything permanently wrong. I must write as though I were to return as I had planned at Easter.

I think this was a wise decision of Veronica's. Joan was planning to fly out to Australia in the autumn, pausing with Andrew at Singapore. The chauffeur who drove her to Oxford told me that on her drives she talked all the time about her visit to Australia and Singapore. She had the pleasure of looking forward to that visit. She was not in any pain, so Peter said, and she would not be in any pain, but she was very weak. She spent most of the day in bed, going down in the evening to watch the news and the serial of *Peyton Place*.

Nothing could have surprised me more. Joan had been always in sound health. She had had some minor illnesses – appendicitis and a gall stone. Last summer she had had trouble with her throat, but the operation that she had to have, had been, her doctor assured me, a minor one. It had been satisfactorily cleared up. When I had been over in October, she had been in perfect health. On my last day we had driven over to Newbury where my nephew Auberon had a house, to lunch with him. It had been a happy day.

If I were recounting this as a novel, I should here have a Marquand switchback, with the 'I' of the narrative looking over his marriage, moralising over it, wondering where it had gone wrong, if it had gone wrong; whether the compromise that we had achieved was as satisfactory as the compromise that so many marriages become. It had lasted for thirty-six years. We were very good friends, as I said on an earlier page. We had had all along good times together. We had never quarrelled. We had been a team in the organising of our children's lives. Our children had not had to take sides in periods of domestic conflict. What better can a couple do that have ceased to be electric about one another; when that does happen, neither is to blame.

That is how I should have dealt in a novel with the days that lay immediately ahead, but in fact that was not the way it was. I did not subject myself to a process of self-questioning. I was concerned with the immediacy of the moment. Something had happened, something was happening, something was to happen.

At that time Virginia had a small, pleasant if tumbledown house in Wolfe Street, Alexandria. For the last two years her son Frederick had shared it with her. His marriage had broken up, his health had broken down, and he had come home to be nursed back to health. Completely recovered, he was now employed as an orderly in the local hospital. It was not work that very many young men would want to undertake, but it was important and necessary work and he had a feeling of fulfilment in performing it. He knew that he was needed. He is a very independent person. He enjoys writing poetry. I think it is good poetry, but he has no ambition for it. He does not seem to care if anybody except his mother reads it. He is very musical. He plays records, he strums on his guitar. For seven or eight years he had not seen his mother. He had been in the army, during the time that his parents' marriage had been breaking up. Then there had been his own marriage. And his wife Anne had not liked and had been jealous of Virginia. But since they had come to Alexandria, he and Virginia had found that they had a great deal in common. It was the first time that they had been alone together; there had always been Beth before and Beth's relationship with her mother was very special. But now he and Virginia found that they enjoyed doing things together. They bicycled along the river, and they strummed the guitar and sang in the evenings before the fire. Virginia does not like being alone. She never has been alone. I was very glad that he was with her when I was away.

I myself lived in a carriage house that Virginia fixed up as a garconière. It had a single big studio room with a shower and a kitchenette. It was a good place to write; its only drawback being that it had no air-conditioning and the heat that summer of 1968 was overpoweringly oppressive.

Through January I worked steadily on my Bangkok book. A couple of days a week I went into Washington to the Library of Congress. St Clair McKelway had been the correspondent of the *Bangkok Mail* in 1931 at the time of the revolution that had turned Siam into a democracy with a hereditary and constitutional monarch, and I found his despatches invaluable. It was on my return from Washington on Wednesday, February 5th, that I learnt from Virginia that Christopher Keeling had been on the telephone from London and that I was urgently needed back at Edrington.

'I've booked you on the seven o'clock from Dulles,' she said. 'I'll be round in twenty minutes.'

A Diner's Club card makes it possible to move nowadays at a moment's notice. Twenty years ago with banks closed, I could not have left that night.

I was at Reading Station by ten o'clock next morning. I rang up Christopher Keeling at his office. He had been talking to Virginia at ten o'clock London time. He believed that I was calling him from Washington. He could not believe that I could have crossed the Atlantic in so short a time.

'Is she in hospital?' I asked.

'No, she's at Edrington. Veronica's with her. I'll be coming down tonight. Andrew will be getting home tomorrow. I haven't been able to locate Peter yet.'

How typical that was, that Peter, the one who lived in London, had been the one that it had been difficult to find. I rang up Edrington. Joan answered the telephone, 'So you're just in time,' she said. Her voice was firm.

'I'll be out in an hour and a quarter,' I said.

'An hour and a half.'

'My bus leaves at half-past,' I said.

'Too mean to take a taxi, I suppose.'

'Exactly.'

It was just the slightly snide remark that she was inclined to make. 'That's the last time I'll hear her voice over the telephone,' I thought.

I was surprised that her voice should have been so firm. An hour and a half later I was surprised that she should be so unchanged. She was extremely thin. She held up her arm and it was very wasted. But the curves of her cheeks were rounded still. I had been afraid that she would wear a shrivelled look. Her spirits seemed high. She talked with animation. She rang up friends. Friends rang her up. There was no sign of senility. Her memory was accurate. She had a bottle of pills beside her. She was in no pain. 'And she won't be in any pain,' the doctor said.

Her only minor trouble was her shoulder. She had fainted the day before when she was moving to her dressing table and she had bruised it. It was this fainting fit that had warned her that there was something seriously wrong.

'How long will it be?' I asked.

'A week, ten days, one can't tell exactly.'

Peter had, by now, been located. He would be down in time for lunch. I spent a good deal of that day with Joan. It was difficult to believe that in two weeks' time she would not be here. She was so unchanged. 'What are you going to do now? What are your plans?' she asked.

'I'm going down to Nice. I've a novel to get finished.'

It was not the answer she had expected. She was curious to know how I should rearrange my life. But that was a question that I was not ready to answer yet. I did not want to think about what I would be doing when she was no longer here. In the meantime I had my papers to get organised.

After Evelyn's death I had sold the letters he had written me to the University of Texas. A few weeks earlier I had been in New York, and I had seen there the man who acted as agent for the university.

'I shall have a lot of papers, manuscripts, letters and things to sell in a few months,' I told him.

He gave me the address of the shipping office that would take care of that. I asked Andrew when he arrived whether he intended to keep on Edrington. He shook his head. 'I couldn't afford it,' he said, 'and it's much too big.'

He loved his home. He had always pictured himself as living there, though he had realised in recent years that after death duties had been paid, he could not afford to keep it up.

When I became a resident alien of the United States, Joan had altered her will, leaving Edrington to Andrew and, apart from certain special bequests to Peter and Veronica, all its furniture. I was convinced that I would never want to make a home for myself in England and, leading the scattered life I was, what use could I make of pictures and ancestral silver. There was only the library to be considered. And that was a problem. I had never counted up the number of books I had. There must have been several thousand. There were bookshelves in every room with my father's library as well as my own. I had once thought of bequeathing to the Sherborne School Library the basis of a special Arthur/Alec Waugh section, of inscribed and association volumes. But the last time I was at Sherborne I had realised that that was not a practical project. There was no room for it; and indeed there was no real library at Sherborne. There was no college or institution to which such a collection would be an appropriate bequest. I could not imagine any of my children wanting it. There was only one thing to do.

'Peter,' I said, 'will you sell this library on a twenty per cent commission?'

I looked round the shelves nostalgically. Each book had its separate meaning. I had built it up book by book. I had spent many happy hours, taking down book after book. I thought of all the poems that I should never read again; poems that had appeared in books that were now out of print, and that had not been rescued in anthologies. The minor Victorian poetry that had been sent to my father for review. Only the other day I was wanting to read Stephen Philipps' 'Marpessa'. Where could I find it now?

There were a great many presentation copies, signed by brother and sister writers. I did not like the idea of their appearing in secondhand booksellers' catalogues to be seen by their donors who would think – 'Is that all they meant to him?' I asked my nephew Auberon if I should write a letter to the authors explaining my predicament. He shook his head. 'That wouldn't do any good. They'll think, he must have taken some books away with him, why couldn't he have taken mine?'

I looked at my cricket books, my row of Wisden's, dated back to 1904, the volume that contains the matches for 1903 when Middlesex first won the championship. I should feel bereft without them. Then there was my complete set of Evelyn's books, inscribed. I gave that to Peter. I knew that he would value it. I had to decide what books I should take with me. I did not take very many. I did not even take a complete set of my own; an omission I have regretted since, when some of my novels from the 1920s and 1930s have been reprinted and I have had difficulty in finding copies.

I possessed a wooden zinc-lined box that my uncle

Bassett Raban had used for his uniform when he was in the Indian army and that is covered with labels to Karachi. I filled this with books and a few minor possessions, photographs and some of my clothes. 'I'll let you know later where I'd like this sent,' I said to Peter.

It did not seem a very substantial gathering from a seventy years' lifetime. It bulked considerably less than the collections of manuscripts and papers that I was proposing to take to the University of Texas' shipping agent before I went back to the USA.

There was a strange quality about those last dinners at Edrington. We should never be again together as a family and that last-time feeling made us talk intimately, or at least for the children to talk intimately in a way they never had before; there was quite a lot of laughter.

Each day Joan grew weaker. She had no appetite. Chris on the Friday night had brought back some oysters. It was the one time that there was a look of pleasure on her face as she swallowed them. On the Saturday we tried to get some more but there were none in Reading. But though she was growing weaker, her mind was as alert as ever. We did not make any pattern of turns to keep her company. Usually one or other of us was in the room with her. 'I'm glad,' she said, 'to have my kiddies round me.'

I cannot remember what we talked about. A second time she asked me, 'What are *you* going to do now?'

For a second time I answered, 'I'm going down to Nice to get a novel finished.'

I could not yet think about my plans. I could not look ahead. I wanted to live within the moment, within these last moments. I do not think that there was anything very special about what we discussed, but I knew that there was something that had to be said between us. 'On the Tuesday,' I thought, 'that will be the time.' But on the Monday evening suddenly, unexpectedly, the things that had to be said poured out. I made my peace with her. It was the most emotional moment in our thirty-six years together.

It was the last time I talked to her. On the following morning Peter came into my room and said, 'Ma wants to see you.' But before she could say anything, the woman from the village who was looking after her had brought in her bread and milk. Then the doctor came. Later downstairs he said to me, 'I've given her heavy medication, she's in a coma now.'

She remained in the coma till the following morning. She lay on her back breathing heavily. We took it in turns to watch with her through the night.

After breakfast Peter came into my room.

'She's ceased to breathe,' he said.

The funeral was fixed for the Saturday. Most of the next three days I spent in my study. I had letters to write, a few final files to be tidied up. I wanted to be alone, to think. I sat at my desk, looking down the drive. Soon it would be bright with daffodils, as it had been three years back when I had returned from France for Evelyn's funeral. I should never see those daffodils again.

This was the end of many things for me – of my marriage, of my home, of my life in England. In a way too of my fatherhood. I should lose day-to-day touch with my children. Joan was a wonderful correspondent – she had written to me every five days or so and had told me what they were doing week by week in a way that their occasional letters in the future could never do. I remembered how when my mother had died I had lost touch with a whole group of family friends of whom she had written to me. The same thing would happen now with Andrew, Peter and Veronica. They would be on their own. They had come into their inheritance. I had no place any longer in the direction of their lives. I did not suppose that I should come to England so very often; a Londoner needs a base in London. As a foreign resident, I could not build myself a base there. Fewer and fewer of my London friends were left. I should come over for Saintsbury dinners, for the Test Match, but I should cease to be a part of London's life. I should be an expatriate.

The funeral was on the Saturday. The church was crowded. Joan was well loved in the village. The lesson was read by my son-in-law. He read it very well and looked very handsome standing at the lectern. I was very fond of him. His warmth, his friendliness, his consideration were a bastion of strength for me during the last ten days. The last thing I expected was that within three years he and Veronica would have dissolved their marriage.

On the Sunday Peter drove me over to Oxford to see my grandson Simon at the Dragon's school. On the Monday morning he drove me to London and I delivered my files and papers to the agent for the Texas University Librarian. The next day I returned to the US. I knew now the answer to Joan's question 'What are *you* going to do?' I went straight to Alexandria. Virginia was sitting by her fire. I sat beside her.

'I hope,' I said, 'that you'll agree that after a proper and appropriate interval we should get married.'

Appendix

Page 7 from Evelyn Waugh's unfinished
autobiography to have been called 'A Little Hope'

... the extraordinary indulgence which my brother, Alec,
showed us then and later. He has left his own account of
those years. He had a far sharper memory than I. But the
picture he presents of his London life is far different from
what I remember. He writes of himself as straitened in
means and humdrum in experience. To me and to my
friends he was flush of money, generous and socially pro-
miscuous. He had now, in circumstances which he has
delicately itemised, annulled his marriage with Barbara,
whom I never saw again (though my mother corresponded
with her until her death). After a second false start
she married an American and has been, I believe, deser-
vedly happy. Alec was now on his own living in an
agreeable flat between Kensington High Street and Ed-
wardes Square. He had not repeated the great success of
his first novel, *The Loom of Youth*, but was quietly settled
in the profession of letters. It may be encouraging to other
aspirants to reflect that he wrote one best-seller at the age of
17, toiled on for forty years, continuously writing, earning a
fair subsistence but not in general very highly regarded
until at the age of 57 he wrote another and still more successful work.

His later years have been spent among the palm trees of
the Mediterranean, the Pacific and the Caribbean. They have
been illuminated, I believe, by love affairs with ladies of a
great variety of age, race and appearance. It may well be
that in contrast the early 1920s seem to him drab. He em-
phasises Saturday afternoon winter journeys by tube to the

outer suburbs for games of football; summer afternoons on
the cricket field with forgotten writers. I saw little of that
part of his life. To me he was someone who owned Havelock
Ellis's *Studies in the Psychology of Sex* in which I lubricously
browsed, as a host who introduced me to the best restaurants
of London, on whom I sponged, bringing my friends to
his flat and, when short of money, sleeping on his floor until
the tubes opened when I would at dawn sway home to
Hampstead in crumpled evening dress among the navvies
setting out for their day's work. My brother had his books
bound by Riviere, his shirts made at Hawes and Curtis. He
was not an ostentatious dandy – indeed neither he nor I was
built on the right model for that – but he was judicious in
his expenditure and was already accumulating the large and
heterogeneous collection of cronies, drawn from the stage,
from journalism and literature, who have stood by him
through life. I have seldom shared his taste either in friends
or in women. My heart sinks when a new acquaintance intro-
duces himself as a friend of Alec's. But in the years of my
poverty and obscurity I was constantly at his table. Once I
even played cricket for a side of his and to the manifest dis-
approval of our fellows knocked up a few runs in unor-
thodox costume and entire absence of style.

Index

311